THE
ENCYCLOPEDIA
OF
ANIMALS

MAURICE BURTON
& ROBERT BURTON

SILVERDALE BOOKS

Contents

This edition published in 2002 by
SILVERDALE BOOKS
An imprint of Bookmart Ltd
Desford Road, Enderby
Leicester LE19 4AD

This book is adapted from *Encyclopedia of the Animal Kingdom*
and *The Little Brown Encyclopedia of Animals*
ISBN 1-85605-707-0

Production by Omnipress, Eastbourne
Printed in Singapore

Little, Brown
An imprint of Time Warner Books UK
Brettenham House, Lancaster Place
London WC2E 7EN

Introduction

The word 'animal' is often equated with mammals in every day usage, but the term includes a wide range of organisms from the single-celled protozoans to humans. This being so, it is worth restating the characteristics that distinguish animals from plants: animals cannot manufacture their own food, they have a sensitivity that is usually operative through special sense organs, are capable of locomotion, and have no cellulose cell walls.

It is usually stated that there are a million species of animals. More correctly, this should be at least a million known species. By 'known' is meant species that have been given a specific name and of which a description has been published in a recognised scientific journal. It is important to make this distinction because the truth is that there are not enough zoologists classifying animals to keep pace with the collection of new forms. In addition, there must be large numbers of species yet to be discovered, and estimates of the true number of animal species living today vary between three and ten million.

The great majority of the million usually referred to are insects, of which there are at least 750,000. If we ever reach the point where all the species of insects have been described and named the total will probably be nearer three million.

There must be few, if any, large animals yet to be discovered. Among mammals, small species are occasionally discovered, especially mice, shrews and bats.

Most of the species yet to be discovered, apart from insects, must comprise those of microscopic size, particularly Protozoa, as well as the parasitic species, such as the various kinds of so-called worms, like the threadworms and flatworms. There must also be a very large number of mites yet to be identified and described. Thus we have the anomaly that most of the most familiar animals, including those of large bulk and those upon which the human economy is based because they represent food, beasts of burden or sources of supply of raw materials, represent only a small minority in terms of numbers of species and populations.

The present day classification of animals emerged after a series of tentative attempts on the part of a number of authors to arrange the animals in orderly groups, but the real breakthrough came with the acceptance of Darwin's theory of natural selection and involved a long arrangement along evolutionary lines. The theory of evolution itself had been mooted long before Darwin's days, but his theory of how species arose gave the maximum publicity to an idea that had previously only been studied by a select few scholars.

Arrangement on an evolutionary basis meant that the classification was based mainly on the study of comparative anatomy. In practice, this meant putting the simplest, least organised animals at the top. The rest were arranged intermediately according to the degree of organisation of their bodily structures.

The most that can be done to represent the millions of species, and this is the purpose of this volume, is to give a skeletal representation in pictorial and textual form of the living members of this vast assemblage of organisms we refer to when we speak of the animal world.

In the following pages, a selection of animals known to be in existence today are detailed, representing the vertebrates and comprising of four sections: fishes, amphibians and reptiles, birds and mammals. With a few exceptions, most of the phyla are illustrated and the effect is to provide within two covers a brief outline of the scope of the animal world, its components arranged in their evolutionary sequence, so far as we know it.

Fishes: The First Vertebrates

It is an accepted convention to visualize the classification of the animal kingdom as starting with the Protozoa, the single-celled animals typified by the amoeba and ending with the mammals, which includes the human species. This resulted in a catch-phrase, less used today than formerly 'from amoeba to man'. When set down on paper in tabular form, such a classification gives the impression of a steady and continuous progression from the Protozoa, through the lower invertebrates and the higher invertebrates to the vertebrates. It must be nearer the truth to suppose that somewhere among the more organized echelons of the lower invertebrates there came a parting of the ways. One path led to the higher invertebrates, the other to the vertebrates. This bifurcation may have occurred at the level of the phylum Echinodermata (starfishes, sea-urchins and others). There is, however, a distinct gap here in our knowledge that can be bridged only by speculation based on fragmentary information, and it is not our purpose here to discuss these questions.

It is sufficient to note that the first true vertebrates were jawless fishes and that there is living today a form of pre-vertebrate, the lancelet, which embodies all that could be expected in the ancestral vertebrate. How it was evolved from an invertebrate stock is, however, still shrouded in mystery. That a form like the lancelet must have preceded the fishes seems reasonable.

The earliest fossils of fishes have been taken from rocks of the Ordovician period, 450 million years old. They are recognizable as being fishes, though they lacked jaws. Relatively few species of these jawless fishes have been discovered and fewer still have survived. From this ancestral stock, however, sprang two main lines of descent: the cartilaginous fishes typified by the sharks, skates and rays, which were almost entirely marine, and the bony fishes, represented by the more familiar fishes in our present-day rivers and lakes as well as many others in the sea. The bony fishes outnumber the cartilaginous fishes by more than thirty to one. The latter have, however, the distinction of having produced one of the largest of all animals, the whale shark, reportedly having a maximum length of 60 ft and a weight of 20 tons or more. This leviathan is outmatched only by the larger whales, particularly the blue whale. On the other hand, the bony fishes include the smallest of all vertebrates, a goby from the freshwaters of the Philippines which, fully grown, is under $\frac{1}{2}$ inch long.

The first primitive jawless fishes of the Ordovician period found an environment inhabited by invertebrates, in which the only animals rivalling them in size and agility were the cephalopod molluscs, represented by the ammonites and belemnites, the ancestors of modern squids, octopuses and cuttlefishes. It was near to being an empty ecological niche and they took full advantage of it to diversify. By the middle of the Devonian period, a little over 50 million years later, they had evolved many species and spread widely through both salt and fresh waters of the world, so much so that the Devonian period has become known as the Age of Fishes. The jawless fishes, which appeared first, soon began to decline in numbers, and are represented today only by the lampreys and hagfishes. The cartilaginous fishes fared better but in numbers of species are poorer today than in those distant times. It was the bony fishes, the last of the three groups to appear, that finally became dominant, as they still are.

It is worth noting, within the context of what has been said previously about evolutionary trends, the courses followed by the three groups. The jawless fishes threw off relatively few species and there were no startling variations in form. So far as we know their colours were mainly unobtrusive, if not positively drab. Much the same can be said of the cartilaginous fishes. They did achieve a change in shape so that they are basically of two forms, the typical fusiform shark and the flattened rays and skates. Apart from this, in these two groups, the one free-swimming, the other bottom-living, there is no great diversity in behaviour, exploitation of environment or colour. The bony fishes, especially those of today, combine a remarkable range of size, a great diversity of colour and bodily adornment and an exploitation of almost every kind of aquatic habitat.

The major groups of fishes are as follows:

Class Agnatha (lampreys and hagfishes)	45 species
Class Chondrichthyes (cartilaginous fishes, sharks and rays)	600 species
Class Osteichthyes (or Pisces) (bony fishes)	20,000 species

Maneater shark

A single species of heavy-bodied shark bears the ominous name of maneater, or great white shark. It grows to 20 ft long or more and is bluish-grey to slate grey above, shading to white below, with fins growing darker towards their edges. It also has a conspicuous black spot just behind where the pectoral fin joins the body. Its snout is pointed and overhangs an awesome, crescent-shaped mouth which is armed with a frightful array of triangular saw-edged teeth. In large individuals the largest teeth may be 3 in. high. The pectoral fins are large. The pelvic fins, and the second dorsal and the anal fins, which lie opposite each other, are small. The tail fin is nearly symmetrical instead of having the upper lobe larger as in most sharks. There is a large keel along the side of the tail in front of the tail fin.

The maneater belongs to the family of mackerel sharks, which includes the porbeagles and mako shark. These are similar to the maneater but smaller, 12 ft long being about the limit. They feed on fishes such as mackerel, herring, cod, whiting, hake and dogfish. They also provide sport for sea anglers because of the fight they put up when hooked. Most mackerel sharks are dangerous to man.

The maneater is found in all warm seas and occasionally strays into temperate seas. It lives in the open sea, coming inshore only when the shallow seas are near deep water. One maneater was caught at a depth of 4 200 ft off Cuba and other evidence also suggests the shark is a deepwater fish.

Not as big as was believed

Maneaters may be much maligned monsters. They are neither as big as is generally said nor as voracious. Very little is known about the habits of the maneater except what can be deduced from its shape and the contents of the stomachs of individuals caught and dissected. Its shape suggests it can swim rapidly, but from those hooked and landed with angling tackle it is fairly certain the maneater is not as swift as the smaller mako. Since young have been found in a female's body the species is presumed to bear its young alive. The maneater is said to be of uncertain temper, yet skin divers report it to be wary and even easily scared. It is probably less dangerous than the mako which is known to attack small boats as well as swimmers. The maneater's bad reputation probably rests on its large size and fearsome teeth, coupled with occasional attacks that look deliberate. On the first of these two points it is hard to speak with certainty. The largest maneater of which we have reliable information measured 36½ ft long, and this one was caught a century ago, off Port Fairey, Australia. Most of the others are between 20 and 25 ft. One that was 21 ft long weighed 7 100 lb; another 17 ft long weighed 2 800 lb. Maneaters have been said by authoritative writers to grow to over 40 ft but there is no solid evidence.

Nothing refused

Several books have been published in the last 10 years which give details of shark attacks. Two are devoted solely to the subject. They are: *Shark Attack* by V M Coppleson, an Australian doctor who has collected the case histories of injuries from sharks, and *Danger Shark!* by Jean Campbell Butler, whose narrative is based on the New Orleans Shark Conference of 1958, at which shark researchers pooled their findings. Putting the information from these and other sources together, there is the general impression that sharks, the maneater in particular, will try to eat anything that looks like food. As a result they snap at living animals, including bathers or people who have accidentally fallen into the sea, as well as corpses and carrion, even inanimate objects such as tin cans. The attacks on boats, as in the attack on the 14ft cod boat off Nova Scotia in 1953, by a maneater, which left some of its teeth in the timbers, are probably due to mistake rather than malice. Several times whole human corpses have been taken from sharks' stomachs but they proved to be of people who had been drowned.

Maneater or corpse swallower?

There are several instances of maneaters found to contain the intact bodies of other animals. These include a 100lb sea-lion, a 50lb seal, and sharks 6–7 ft long. While human beings have been badly bitten, usually producing frightful wounds, some of which have proved fatal, there is little evidence of limbs being severed, and less of a person being swallowed whole. Two things have also emerged from the studies so far made. The first is that sharks digest food very slowly and animal remains swallowed take days, even weeks, to be digested. The other, which seems linked with this but is learned more from sharks in captivity, is that sharks seem to eat little.

Extenuating circumstances

When one speaks of malice in relation to shark attack one is only reflecting the attitude of mariners to these beasts. As a class they are hated. There are many stories of captured sharks being treated with savagery, being disembowelled and then thrown back live into the sea. Yet in the economy of the sea they are scavengers rather than evil predators. Moreover, in areas where shark attack is heavy there is reason to suppose man has not been blameless. For example, in the region around Sydney Harbour, Australia, and again at Florida, blood from abattoirs seeps into the sea, and sharks are drawn by the smell of blood. In the Bay of Bengal, where human corpses are floated down the Ganges from the burning ghats, shark attack is again high.

None of these things lessens one's sympathy for victims of shark attack, nor lessens one's own fear of the sharks themselves, but they put the subject in perspective zoologically. One of the first scientific conclusions we are led to is that while sharks may be ferocious they seem not to be voracious, as they are so often described. In fact, because they will engulf almost anything they come across, sharks have at times aided the course of human justice.

Silent witness

The classic example of this concerned the United States brig *Nancy* which was captured on July 3, 1799 by HM Cutter *Sparrow* and taken to Port Royal, Jamaica, Britain and the United States then being at war, to be condemned as a prize. The captain of the *Nancy* produced papers at the trial which were, in fact, false and he was about to be discharged when another British warship put in at the port with papers found in a shark caught on August 30. They proved to be the ship's papers thrown overboard by the captain of the *Nancy*, when capture seemed inevitable. They led to the condemnation of the brig and her cargo.

class	**Selachii**
order	**Pleurotremata**
family	**Isuridae**
genus & species	***Carcharodon carcharias***

Malaigned monster: the maneater shark's bad reputation stems from its large size and supposed voraciousness. Most maneaters measure between 20 and 25 ft and not 40 ft as often quoted. They seem to eat anything that looks like food which results in bathers, corpses, carrion and rubbish being taken.

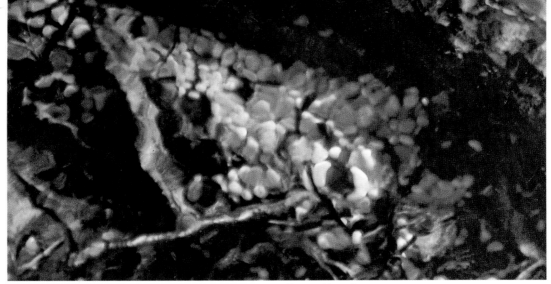

△ *Suffering from exposure: waste eggs trapped in stream debris. Eggs are usually covered by sand.*

Pacific salmon

There are six species of salmon in the North Pacific, by contrast with the North Atlantic where there is only one species, called the Atlantic salmon. Except for the Japanese species, the masu, these range from about Kamchatka in Siberia to the American west coast as far south as California. Of these the chinook, also known as the tyee, quinnat, king, spring, Sacramento or Columbia River salmon, weighs 10−50 lb, with a maximum of 108 lb. The sockeye, red or blueback salmon weighs 5−7 lb, but may weigh up to 15½ lb; the silver salmon or coho weighs 6−12 lb, going up to 26½ lb; the chum, keta or dog salmon weighs 8−18 lb; but is sometimes as much as 30 lb, and the humpback or pink salmon which is 3−5 lb, may weigh up to 10 lb.

Drastic changes for spawning

Pacific salmon return to spawn in the same river in which they hatched, and when they do so they become brilliant red, and their heads turn pea green. The males grow long hooked snouts and their mouths become filled with sharp teeth. The females do not grow the hooked snout. Most of the returning salmon are 4−5 years old. The humpback matures the earliest at 2 years, the silver salmon at 3, but some of the sockeye and chinook may be as much as 8 years old.

The salmon return in early summer, even in late spring, or in autumn in the case of the chum. They stop feeding as their digestive organs deteriorate and head for the coast from their feeding grounds out in the Pacific. On reaching the mouth of a river they head upstream, except the chum which usually spawns near tidal waters. The silver salmon moves only a short distance upstream. The chinook, on the other hand, has been known to travel as much as 2 250 miles up rivers. One exception to this is a subspecies of the sockeye which is non-migratory. In contrast with the Atlantic salmon, however, Pacific salmon never survive the spawning run.

Mating ends in death

By the time the salmon near the spawning grounds, they are mere bags of bones housing the eggs or the sperms. The males often look the worse for wear as they fight with each other. The females look for a place in the sandy or gravelly shallows where the water is clear with plenty of oxygen. Then they start digging troughs (redds) in the river beds with their tails; each one lying on her side and flapping with her tail. When her trough is deep enough, she lies in it to spawn, her mate swimming over to her to shed his milt to fertilise the eggs. Each female lays several batches of eggs, to a total of 3−5 thousand, in different troughs, by the end of which time she is completely exhausted. With her tail fins worn to stubs, her skin blackening and with blotches of grey fungus attacking it, she dies. The males share the same fate, and the carcases of both drift downstream or are stranded at the edge.

Down to the sea as infants

Each batch of eggs becomes buried under sand as fresh redds are dug and the loosened sand is wafted over them. Thus protected, the orange-pink eggs hatch 8 weeks later. The alevins or young salmon remain under the gravel feeding on their yolk sacs for some weeks before wriggling to the surface as fry. They feed heavily on water fleas and other small animals and in the following spring are carried downstream by the current. The humpback and chum go to the sea as fry but the sockeye may go as fry or as 1−3 year fish, and the quinnat and coho go when 1−2 years old.

Finding their way home

There has always been a great interest in how salmon find their way back to the streams where they were hatched. The full story has not yet been pieced together but sufficient is now known to sketch in many of the details. There is evidence, for example, to show that the thyroid gland plays a part in the salmon's changing preference for water of varying salinity. When the coho was injected with a certain hormone it sought sea water. When the injections were stopped it sought fresh water. The opposite effect was found in the humpback. Probably other glands are involved, as well as the length of day and possibly the diet. The sense of smell may play a part, as it does in finding food. Temperatures also influence the fish, certainly once they have entered fresh water. When these are too low or too high the fish make no effort to surmount obstacles. There is some evidence also that celestial navigation, using the sun by day and the stars by night, as in migrating birds, keeps the salmon on their compass runs along the coast to the mouths of the rivers they came from.

Expert water-tasters

Of the different ways that salmon find their way back, one of the easier to test is the odour, or the taste of the water from which the fishes originated. Laboratory experiments have shown beyond doubt that fishes, including salmon, can recognize waters of only slightly different tastes; smell and taste are closely linked. This is not so very surprising since water-tasters dealing with the purification of drinking water are able to tell by tasting, in an almost uncanny way, where a particular glass of water came

△ *The remains. Reduced to blackened bags of bones after spawning, dead sockeye salmon are washed up at the river's edge.*

△ *On home ground. A pair of sockeye salmon, having swum from the Pacific Ocean up to the head waters of the river in which they hatched 4 or 5 years before, are now ready to spawn themselves — then die, starved and exhausted by their marathon journey on which they do not feed at all.*

from. These same tests show that the memory of a particular type of water persists for a long time in a fish, and that the younger the fish the longer the memory will probably be.

Controlled fishing

Many people living a long way from the Pacific are familiar with the Pacific salmon —in canned form. The salmon fishery is commercially highly valuable, with 2–10 million sockeye alone being caught and canned. The salmon are taken in gill nets, reef nets and purse seines on their way to the Fraser River in British Columbia. Unrestricted fishing could kill the industry,

so by an agreement between Canada and the United States, 20% of each race of fish are allowed through to continue their journey to the spawning grounds. This is taken care of by a joint International Pacific Salmon Fisheries Commission, which also arranges for the catch to be divided equally between the two countries. There is co-operation also in providing concrete and steel fishways to assist the salmon up the rivers. The Pacific salmon fishery is therefore as near as it has so far been possible to an actual husbandry of a wild resource. Moreover, research is being carried out to produce strains of salmon that can tolerate less favourable rivers than they

use at present, and to transplant fry which, when mature, will return to spawn in waters earmarked for cultivation.

class	**Pisces**
order	**Salmoniformes**
family	**Salmonidae**
genus & species	***Oncorhynchus gorbuscha*** *humpback*
	O. keta *chum*
	O. kisutch *silver salmon*
	O. masou *masu*
	O. nerka *sockeye*
	O. tshawytscha *chinook*

Trout

The European trout, of very variable colour, is known by three names. The brown trout is small, dark and non-migratory. It can weigh up to 17 lb 12 oz and lives in the smaller rivers and pools. The lake trout is larger and paler. It lives in larger rivers and lakes and it may be migratory. The sea trout, large, silvery up to 4½ ft long and weighing up to 30 lb, is distinctly migratory. All three belong to the same species.

The European brown trout and lake trout are greenish brown, the flanks being lighter than the back, and the belly yellowish. They are covered with many red and black spots, the latter surrounded by pale rings. There are spots even on the gill covers. These two and the sea trout resemble the salmon in shape and appearance except that the angle of the jaw reaches to well behind the eye and the adipose fin is tinged with orange.

The North American species are similar. The cut-throat trout has two red marks across the throat. The Dolly Varden is named for its conspicuous red spots, coloured like the cherry ribbons worn by the Dickens character. In the brook trout the pattern is more mottled but it also has red spots on the flanks. The rainbow trout has a reddish band along the flanks. The lake or mackinau trout lives in deep water, down to 400 ft. The golden trout lives in water 8 000 ft or more above sea level.

▷ Like some figment of an angler's daydream, a big New Zealand rainbow trout jumps from its shoal for a flying titbit.

▽ Mixed bunch, with rainbow trout in front of brown. Because of aquarium glass, the red line on the rainbows' sides cannot be seen.

Temperature important

Trout grow best in clear, aerated waters and although they are sometimes found in turbid waters it is only when the surface layers are well supplied with oxygen. They are readily affected by silt; it may spoil their spawning sites, reduce their food supply or act directly on the fishes themselves. Laboratory experiments have shown that particles in suspension in the water, at a level as low as 270 parts per million, abrade the gills or cause them to thicken. The rate of growth of trout varies in other ways as well, often to a remarkable extent, with the conditions of their surroundings. Temperature, for instance, is highly important, and an example can be seen at the time when they resume feeding after the winter fast. Normally, trout stop feeding in autumn and resume in spring, in about March when the water reaches a temperature of $2°C/36°F$ or more. In a mild winter they may begin feeding in December and continue until the first cold snap of the following autumn.

The rate of growth also varies from one river to another, or from river to sea. Trout living in small streams grow more slowly than those in large rivers, and those in large bodies of fresh water grow more slowly than those living in the sea. A trout in a small river will grow $2\frac{1}{2}$, 5 and 8 in. in its first, second and third years respectively. Corresponding figures for a sea trout will be $3-5$, $4-5$ and $10-11$ in.

Diet changes

The diet of trout varies with their age. Fry eat mainly aquatic larvae of insects, rarely the adults. Later they eat large numbers of winged insects, as well as water fleas and freshwater shrimps. When adult they eat mainly small fishes as well as shrimps, insect larvae and adults, especially the winged insects. Sea trout feed on sprats, young herring and sand eels and also on a large percentage of small crustaceans, including shrimps and prawns.

Correct place to spawn

Male trout begin to breed at two years, females at three, returning to do so to the place where they themselves were hatched. This homing has been verified experimentally, by transporting marked trout to other parts of a river system, then finding them later, back on their 'home ground'. Breeding usually takes place from October to February, the time varying from one locality to another. Spawning is normally in running water, trout living in lakes going into the feeder streams.

For spawning the female makes a 'redd' in gravelly shallows, digging a depression with flicks of her tail. As she lays her eggs, the male, in attendance on her, fertilises them, stationing himself beside her but slightly to the rear. It has been found that a successful redd is one with a current flowing downwards through the gravel. The eggs hatch in about 40 days. The fry are $\frac{1}{2}-1$ in. long at hatching, and the yolk sac is absorbed in $4-6$ weeks.

Surrounded by enemies

WE Frost and ME Brown, in their book *The Trout*, state that 94% of fry are lost during the first $3-4$ months of their lives. After this the mortality drops to 20%. Eels are often said to kill trout and especially to ravage the spawning grounds, but there is no evidence of this. The chief enemies of trout are water shrew, mink, the common rat, and to some extent otters and herons. Another enemy of trout is larger trout. Well grown ones have sometimes been found to have another trout, $5-6$ in. long, in their stomachs. The record for the brown trout comes from New Zealand, where the fish were introduced. In 1967 a 20lb trout had a foot-long trout in its stomach. In their cannibalism, therefore, trout vie with pike, always regarded as a traditional enemy, which, with few exceptions, take only medium to large sized trout.

There are two other contributors to trout

Many species

The wide variation in size and colour of the European trout is brought out by the history of its species. In 1758 Linnaeus named three species: the Swedish river trout, the sea trout and the lake trout. Dr Albert Gunther, leading authority on fishes, wrote in 1880: 'We know of no other group of fishes which offers so many difficulties . . . to the distinction of species'. He recognized 10 species in the British Isles alone—the sea trout, sewin, phinnock, Galway sea trout, Orkney sea trout, river trout, great lake trout, gillaroo, Welsh blackfinned trout and Loch Leven trout. Thirty years later, C Tate Regan, Günther's successor, put forward strong arguments for treating these and all species and races in continental Europe as one very variable species.

depletion—apart from man. Numbers of other animals compete with it for food, and of these, which include several water birds, the eel is probably one of the worst, more so in rivers than in lakes. The other natural 'enemy' is lack of oxygen, especially during the winter. When the pools and lakes are frozen over, trout must rely on oxygen trapped under ice. This is replenished by oxygen given out by water plants. When, however, the ice is blanketed by snow, light does not penetrate, plants cannot 'work', and trout are asphyxiated.

class	**Pisces**
order	**Salmoniformes**
family	**Salmonidae**
genera & species	***Salmo aguabonita*** golden ***S. clarki*** cutthroat ***S. gairdneri*** rainbow ***S. trutta*** brown ***Salvelinus fontinalis*** brook ***S. malma*** Dolly Varden ***S. namaycush*** lake, others

Young brown trout, easily identified by the red spots on the side of its body, swims in clear river water; the clearer the water, the faster it grows.

Butterfly fish

It is virtually impossible to speak about butterfly fishes without confusion since the name is commonly used for different kinds of unrelated fishes. The same can be said of angelfishes. Attention is drawn to this on page 30, where butterfly fishes are described, together with their very close relatives, the marine angelfishes. Here we discuss this subject in order to deal with a freshwater fish that has been called a butterfly fish. At the same time this gives us the opportunity to contrast and compare it with the marine fishes, inhabitants of coral reefs especially, which are also called butterfly fishes. For our

description of the habits of marine butterfly fishes we must refer to page 30. But here on the following pages we portray these fishes, belonging to the family Chaetodontidae, in a series of fascinating and beautiful photographs.

The one species of freshwater butterfly fish is sufficiently extraordinary to merit close attention on its own. Never more than 4 in. long, it lives in the rivers of tropical West Africa. Its head and body are boat-shaped, flattened above, bluntly rounded below. It is coloured grey-green to brownish-silver, marked with spots and streaks. The large mouth is directed upwards, and the nostrils are tubular. Another remarkable feature is its fins. The pectoral fins are large and wing-like.

Each pelvic fin has four very long filamentous rays not connected to each other, and the unpaired fins are large, transparent and supported by long rays.

For a long time the relationships of this fish, first discovered in 1876, have been in doubt, but it is now placed in a family on its own near that of the large South American fish, the arapaima. It has no relationship with the marine butterfly fishes of the family Chaetodontidae.

▽ The freshwater butterfly fish is not related to marine butterfly fishes of the tropical seas.

▽▽ Four-eyed butterfly fish, so-called because of the false 'eye' markings at its tail end.

▽ Vividly-striped marine butterfly fishes are deep-bodied and flattened from side to side

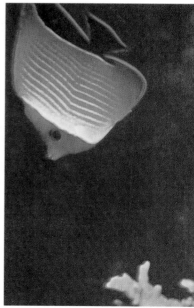

A fish that flies

This remarkable fish is reckoned to fly over the water, flapping its wings like a bat or a bird. The freshwater butterfly fish spends most of its time just below the surface of still or stagnant waters in the Congo and Niger basins, in the weedy backwaters and standing pools. But it is most renowned for its ability to leap out of water for distances up to 6 ft, its large pectoral fins being used, as are those of the true flying fishes, in gliding flight. It has also been credited with flapping these fins in true powered flight, as in bats and birds. By 1960, however, it had been generally agreed that this was not so.

Then came a remarkable sequel. PH Greenwood and KS Thomson investigated the anatomy of this fish. They found it had a most unusual shoulder girdle, the arrangement of bones to which the pectoral fins are attached. In fact, these two authors described it as unique among fishes. The bones were so thin that they had to be very careful not to damage them while dissecting them out. The whole of the shoulder girdle is broad and flattened to give support to a highly developed system of muscles, comparable with the large pectoral muscles that work the wings of birds. The two scientists also found that the fins could not be folded against the body, as is usual in fishes, but could be moved up and down. In brief, they concluded that, while it was still unproven whether or not the butterfly fish could make a powered flight, its shoulder girdle and muscles were such that it ought to be able to fly. The best that can be said is that the fish has been seen to beat its fins up and down when held in the hand. It has, however, been suggested that this is only used to give the butterfly fish a push-off from the water to become airborne.

Insect feeder

The food consists almost entirely of the small insects, such as flies, that fall on to the surface of the water.

Life history

Relatively little is known about the breeding, and such details as we have are from the few butterfly fishes that have bred in captivity. Numerous false matings have been seen, with the male riding on the back of the female, sometimes for hours at a time, holding her firmly with the long rays of the pelvic fins. Mating finally is effected by the two twisting their bodies together to bring the vents opposite each other. Fertilisation seems, however, not to be internal. As soon

▽ ▽ *Marine butterfly fishes* **Chaetodon** *live around coral reefs in shallow tropical seas.*

▽ *The butterfly fish* **Heniochus acuminatus** *lives in the warm seas around the Philippine Islands. It has a very deep body, most of the depth being due to a highly arched back.*

*The freshwater butterfly fish **Pantodon buchholzi** found in the waters of western Africa is one of the strangest of the so-called flying fishes. It spends most of its time swimming just under the surface and is capable of leaping out of the water for a distance of 6 or more feet.*

as they are laid the eggs float to the surface, and in 3 days these hatch. The fry remain at the surface feeding on the tiniest of the insects, such as springtails and aphides, which fall on them.

Flying or gliding
The ability to make either gliding or powered flights through the air is rare among fishes, although to be able to leap from the water is common enough. For years, scientists have argued among themselves whether or not the flying fishes of the oceans beat their wings when airborne. At present, evidence suggests that they do not. Similarly, it may be some years before we can be sure whether the West African butterfly fishes beat their wings or not. There is, however, one group of freshwater fishes that do beat their fins to achieve true

flight through the air. These are the hatchet fishes of northern South America, found from the River Plate to Panama.

As so often happens, another confusion of names arises. We already have it over butterfly fishes, as we have seen. There are also two kinds of hatchet fishes. One is marine hatchet fish and the other is freshwater. Both are named for their shape, the body being flattened from side to side, so that it looks like the blade of a hatchet.

The freshwater hatchet fishes beat their pectoral fins rapidly when making a take-off run over the surface before becoming airborne, and they continue to beat their fins when airborne.

To make the confusion even more confounded, it may be mentioned that freshwater hatchet fishes do a butterfly-like dance

during their courtship. Fortunately we can note the scientific names and there can be no doubt as to the animal referred to. Each animal has a binomial name of genus and species, rather like the surname and christian name used to identify humans.

class	**Pisces**
order	**Osteoglossiformes**
family	**Pantodontidae**
genus	***Pantodon buchholzi***
& species	*freshwater butterfly fish*

Piranha

Few accounts of travel in South and Central America fail to contain some references to the piranha or piraya, the small but allegedly very ferocious fish that inhabits the rivers of this region. In some places it abounds in such vast numbers as to be a serious pest, making the infested streams either very hazardous or quite impossible for fording or bathing.

The name piranha applies loosely to about 18 species, of which only 4 seem to be dangerous to humans. All are members of the genus **Serrasalmus**, having a general similarity of appearance and habits. Some scientists, however, classify them differently. Most of the species average 8 in. in length but **Serrasalmus piraya,** of the River São Francisco in eastern Brazil, one of the most dangerous, may reach 2 ft. Most of them are olive-green or blue-black above and silvery or dark grey on flanks and belly. Some species have reddish or yellowish tinted fins. The colours seem to vary considerably from place to place and with age. For example, old specimens of the white piranha **Serrasalmus rhombeus,** found in the Amazon system and north-eastern South America, are often dark enough to be called black piranhas.

The body of the piranha is deep, short and rather compressed from side to side. A large bony crest on top of the skull supports a keel on the back, and a similar keel on the belly is strengthened by a firm

Red piranha (Serrasalmus nattereri); close-up of fish lurking among weeds.

row of enlarged scales bearing sharp, backwardly-directed points, so the deep and heavy forepart of the fish is provided with a cut-water above and below. There is a fleshy adipose fin on the back between the dorsal and tail fins. The tail is slender and muscular and together with the broad, tough, blade-like tail fin helps to drive the body through the water with great force. As in all really swift fish the scales are very small. The most striking feature is the mouth. The massive lower jaw has relatively huge muscles operating it. The teeth are large, flat and triangular with very sharp points. These points merely pierce the skin, the rest is done by the

usual erratic spawning behaviour of most of the other members of its family. The male guards the eggs as well as the fry, when they hatch. These became free-swimming about 5 days after hatching.

Ferocity exaggerated?

The ferocity of the piranha has become almost legendary. Stories are told of a cow or a pig, falling into a river, being stripped to a skeleton in a few minutes. One of the most famous stories is that of a man, fording a stream on horseback, who was brought down and killed by a swarm of piranha. Later the bones of horse and rider were found, picked perfectly clean, the man's clothes undamaged. It is probable that a lot of the stories have been exaggerated. Some travellers now say that they have waded in or swam in rivers infested with piranha shoals and have never been attacked. Yet others say they have come on villages where hardly a native had not suffered the loss of a toe or finger. It is difficult to know what to believe but there must be some truth in the danger from these fish.

It is possible that the ferocity of the piranha may vary with the species and from place to place, and it may be that they are much more aggressive at the beginning of the rainy season when the males are guarding the eggs. This could also explain why it is that they will attack bathers at certain places in a river, where perhaps they have laid eggs, leaving others unmolested not far away. Nevertheless, those aquarists who keep these fishes admit to treating them with respect and taking extra care in feeding them, or when netting them to transfer them from one aquarium to another.

edges, which are literally razor-sharp. The teeth of the upper jaw are similar but much smaller and fit exactly into the spaces between the points of the lower ones when the mouth is closed. The jaws are so strong and the teeth so sharp that they can chop out a piece of flesh as neatly as a razor. The fact that there is a reliable record of a 100lb capybara reduced to a skeleton in less than a minute shows the efficiency of the teeth.

A few of the smaller species are kept in aquaria, the most popular seen in tropical fish stores and public aquaria being **Serrasalmus nattereri,** *the red or common piranha, up to 1 ft long and coloured red on the underside and fins.*

Some piranhas are found only in certain river systems, such as the Rio São Francisco, Rio Paraguay or Rio Orinoco, while others range over a wide area.

Water alive with fish

Piranha hunt in shoals, sometimes of several thousands, so in places the water seems to be alive with them. Smaller fishes form their staple diet, but any animal entering or falling into the water accidentally may be attacked. They often attack each other. It is said that they will instantly be attracted by blood in the water but apparently anything out of the ordinary will attract them.

Waterplant hatcheries

It is thought that piranha breed when the rainy season sets in about January or February. The female deposits her eggs on water plants or roots. On hatching, the fry stay attached to the vegetation in clusters until they have absorbed most of the yolk sac, and then become free-swimming. *Serrasalmus spilopleura* is one of the few species which has been seen breeding in an aquarium. The female deposited her eggs carefully on aquatic plants, which is unlike the

class	**Pisces**
order	**Cypriniformes**
family	Serrasalmidae
genus & species	***Serrasalmus nattereri*** red or Natterer's piranha **S. piraya** *piraya* **S. rhombeus** white or spotted piranha **S. spilopleura** common piranha others

The electric eel, unrelated to the true eels, emits high-voltage discharges which stun or kill fishes or frogs, those dying near the eel being eaten.

Electric eel

The South American electric eel, which can kill a horse with an electric shock, is not even related to eels. It has less than 50 relatives, which include the gymnotid eels, and knife-fishes, all tropical American and probably generating electricity to a greater or lesser extent; but the most spectacular and notorious is the electric eel itself, which can discharge up to 550 volts when fully grown.

The electric eel has a cylindrical body, a uniform olive-brown, up to 6 ft long — the largest recorded 9½ ft — running to a pointed tail. It has no fins on the back, only very small paired fins behind the gills, and a long conspicuous anal fin running from the tip of the tail almost to the throat. Its eyes are very small. About ⅞ths of the body is tail, with the internal organs crowded into a small space behind the head. The tail contains the electric organs, made up of 5–6 thousand electroplates (elements) arranged like the cells in a dry battery. Moreover, there are three parts to the electric organ, two small batteries and the main battery. The electric eel is positive towards the head end, negative at the tail end, the reverse order to that of the electric catfish.

Poor gills, no lungs

The electric eel lives in waters poor in oxygen. It comes to the surface from time to time to gulp air. In its mouth are patches of superficial blood vessels which take up oxygen from the air gulped at the surface, so acting as auxiliary breathing organs.

It swims by undulating the long anal fin and is said to be able to swim forwards or backwards, up or down, with equal ease. So long as it is still its main electric organ at least is not working, but the small battery in the tail is working continuously. As soon as the eel starts to move it gives out electric impulses at the rate of 20–30 a second which later increases to 50 a second. These are used for direction-finding, it is now known, although they do not form an electric field, as in the Nile fish.

High-voltage jolts

It has been said that the second of the small batteries probably fires the larger battery, which gives out a series of 3–6 waves at intervals of 5/1000 of a second, each wave lasting 2/1000 of a second. These are the high-voltage discharges which stun or kill fishes or frogs, those dying near the eel being eaten. Larger animals coming into contact with a large electric eel are stunned. A stunned horse falls and is liable to be drowned. A man can stand the shock, but not repeatedly.

Unknown breeding places

Little is known of the breeding; there is no obvious difference between the sexes and the breeding places are unknown. The eels disappear from their usual haunts in the breeding season. When they return young eels 4–6 in. long come back with them, still guarded by the parents. Young eels are light brown with bands. Later they become marbled and finally olive-brown with the throat brilliant orange.

Millions of years ahead

Even more remarkable than the electric eel is the story of the first man to study its electrical discharge. From the beginning of the 16th century Spain had refused all non-Spaniards permission to visit her American colonies. In 1800, when rapid strides were being made in the study of electricity, the German naturalist, Baron Friedrich von Humboldt, applied for and was granted permission to visit South America. With a companion he arrived at the upper reaches of the Orinoco River and Calabozo, a town of exiles.

Von Humboldt took with him a large amount of scientific apparatus. Oxygen had only recently been recognized and von Humboldt took the latest apparatus in order to analyse the gases in the swimbladders of fishes. He also took the latest electrical apparatus, only to find that Carlos del Pozo, resident in the town of exiles, had begun making similar apparatus thousands of miles from the centres of learning in Europe — a remarkable coincidence. And there also von Humboldt found large fishes that had developed their own electrical apparatus, but millions of years in advance of del Pozo and the European scientists.

This gifted German gave the world the first scientific accounts of the behaviour of the electric eel. He stood on one of these fishes and experienced a painful numbness. He also found that for the rest of the day he was afflicted with a violent pain in the knees and in the rest of his joints. Having studied the eel he made a remarkable prophecy: 'The discoveries that will be made on the electromotive apparatus of these fishes will extend to all the phenomena of muscular motion subject to volition. It will perhaps be found that in most animals every contraction of muscle fibre is preceded by a discharge from the nerve into the muscle.' He also predicted that electricity is the source of life and movement in all living things.

class	Pisces
order	Cypriniformes
family	Gymnotidae
genus & species	*Electrophorus electricus*

The South American electric eel lives in waters poor in oxygen. It comes to the surface from time to time to gulp air. In its mouth are patches of superficial blood vessels which take up oxygen from the air gulped at the surface, so helping with breathing.

Electric eel *(Electrophorus electricus)*

Trunkfish

The trunkfishes are the nearest we have to fishes masquerading as turtles. They are also known as boxfishes and cofferfishes because their bodies are enclosed within bony boxes made up of 6-sided bony plates fitting closely into one another, leaving only the tail unarmoured. Inside, the backbone is short with only 14 vertebrae between the skull and the beginning of the tail, all joined in a compact manner.

A typical trunkfish has a more or less conical head, the face sloping down at a steep angle to the small mouth, which is armed with strong crushing teeth. The eyes are large and there is only a small opening from the gill chamber. The length of a trunkfish seldom exceeds 1 ft. The single dorsal fin and the anal fin are fairly large, as are the pectoral fins, but there are no pelvic fins. The fleshy, naked tail ending in a large fanlike tail fin projects backwards from the bony box and, except for the other fins, is the only part capable of movement. The box enclosing the body is flat on the undersurface and it may be 3-, 4- or 5-sided in cross section, and one or more of its edges may be armed with strong spines.

Trunkfishes live at or near the bottom of warm waters, especially in tropical seas, all round the world.

Geometrical fishes: a comparison between the fishes above and overleaf will show the 3- and 4-faced arrangements of trunkfish armour. These arrangements vary according to species and serve as a rough means of classification.

△ Its transparent, fan-shaped fins beating rapidly, the cumbersome body of a smooth trunkfish moves slowly forwards. Unlike most fish, trunkfishes swim almost entirely by just a rapid beating of their fins.
◁ Passing beauty: **Ostracion meleagris** in the Hawaii reef. Like other trunkfishes, it can adopt a variety of colour schemes. The sexes and young of the same species are often quite differently patterned and coloured.

17

Slow moving

Like tortoises on land, trunkfishes are slow moving, and for much the same reasons. The normal fish swims by strong side to side movements of the whole body and, more especially, by the muscular tail. A trunkfish can move its tail only to a small extent. Its swimming is like a small boat being propelled by a single oar sculling from the stern. The only difference is that the hydrodynamic principles are more complex in the fish because the tail is flexible. The main swimming force is produced by side to side movements of the dorsal and anal fins, aided by the pectoral fins. A trunkfish is the very opposite of being streamlined – in fact the flat faces must create considerable resistance to progress – and when swimming it moves its fins very rapidly, giving the impression of a great expenditure of energy with only a little gain in forward movement.

Confusion of colours

Rapid movement is not necessary for so heavily armoured a fish, which can also rely on its colour and colour changes for security, and on its ability to poison other fishes. A common trunkfish found in the seas on both sides of the tropical Atlantic is the cowfish, so named because it has two sharp, forward-pointing spines on the forehead, rather like the horns of a cow. It is pale green in colour, marked with blue spots and lines, but it can change this to yellow with blue spots or brown with a network of light blue markings, or even to pure white. The colours also differ between the sexes. The 4-sided blue trunkfish of the Indo-Pacific is an example. The females and the young fish are purplish blue with numerous small white spots scattered thickly and evenly over the whole body. The male is very different, being purplish blue with a pale blue network except for the flat upper surface, which is a brownish purple with small white dots with a brick-red border. Even the eyes differ: in the females and young fish they are blue, in the males they have a red border.

Emit poison

It has been suggested that the gaudy colours act as warning colours, advertising to possible enemies that trunkfishes do not depend entirely on their armour but have other undesirable qualities. We do not know yet exactly how it is used, but we do know that trunkfishes can give out a poison. When one of them is placed in an aquarium it is not long before the other fishes begin to show signs of distress, coming to the surface to gulp air, and dying soon afterwards. The only fishes not affected are tough characters such as moray eels, the large groupers, and other trunkfishes. The poison persists even after the trunkfish have been removed.

Search for food in corals

Trunkfishes live among the corals, which they search for food, biting off pieces of coral to digest the polyps. At the same time, in biting pieces from the coral, they expose worms and other small invertebrates sheltering in it. Some trunkfishes use their spout-like snouts to blow jets of water at the sandy bottom to uncover and dislodge worms, molluscs and small crustaceans, which they immediately snap up.

Dingleberries

The breeding habits of the cowfish of tropical American waters are probably typical of the whole family. It lays buoyant eggs, $\frac{1}{12}$ in. diameter, which hatch in 2–3 days. The larvae begin to develop the hard cover in about a week and they become somewhat rounded in shape, and it is only as the young fishes mature that the box-like edges to the body become sharply defined. During the early stages of life young trunkfishes shelter under clumps of floating seaweed. Their rounded shape has earned them, in the United States, the name of dingleberries. At this stage they seem to have rather cherubic faces, with their large eyes, small mouths and what look like puffed cheeks.

Regarded as delicacy

The heaviest mortality among trunkfishes is in the early stages, when eggs, larvae and young fishes are often eaten. Once they reach maturity their protective boxes, and in some species the poison they give out, deter predators. Also, being so slow, they lack the large muscles that make the flesh of other fishes attractive. Yet trunkfishes are eaten, even by human beings, and in some places are regarded as a delicacy. They are cooked in their own boxes, and some people of the South Pacific are said to 'roast them like chestnuts'. There are, nevertheless, other opinions, one of which is that what little flesh there is cannot be praised for its flavour, although the liver is proportionately quite large and oily.

class	**Pisces**
order	**Tetraodontiformes**
family	**Ostraciontidae**
genera & species	**Lactophrys bicaudalis** *large spotted trunkfish* **L. quadricornis** *cowfish* **Ostracion lentiginosus** *blue trunkfish* *others*

◁ *Always in shape, the complete covering of interlocking hexagonal plates of* **O. cornutus** *forms a rigid protective shield over the whole of the body except the flexible tail.*

19

Carp

*Of the extensive carp family (Cyprinidae),
this is the most widely distributed. Native
of Japan, China and Central Asia, from
Turkestan to the Black Sea and the
Danube basin, it has been introduced into
many European countries as well as
the United States. It differs from other
members of the family in its unusually long
dorsal fin, with 17—22 branched rays,
the strongly serrated third spine of the
dorsal and anal fins, and in its four barbels, two at each corner of the slightly
protrusible mouth. There are no teeth in
the mouth, but there are throat-teeth. The
colour of the wild form is olive to
yellow-green on the back, greenish-yellow
to bronze-yellow on the flanks, and underparts yellowish. The fins are grey-green to
brown, sometimes slightly reddish.*

Wild carp at home

Carp prefer shallow sunny waters with a
muddy bottom and abundant water plants.
They avoid clear, swift-flowing or cold
waters. Wild carp are found in large rivers
and, more commonly, in ponds. Their food
is insect larvae, freshwater shrimps and other
crustaceans, worms and snails, as well as
some plant matter. The barbels, organs of
touch, and the protrusible mouth are used
for grubbing in the mud, much of which is
swallowed and later ejected when the
edible parts have been digested. In winter

feeding ceases and the fish enter a resting
period, a form of hibernation. In May to
June carp move into shallow water to spawn,
the eggs laid on the leaves of water plants.
Each lays over 60 000 eggs/lb of her body-
weight. The larvae hatch out in 2—3 days,
the adults return to deeper water, while the
young fishes remain in shallow water, near
the bank. They become sexually mature in
3—4 years. Small carp will be eaten by almost
any fish significantly larger than themselves, including larger carp.

Domesticated varieties

As with many other domesticated animals,
carp are found in a number of varieties, of
two main types: leather carp and mirror
carp. The first is scaleless, the second has
large scales in two rows on each side of the
body. Both can throw back to the original
carp form. The shape of the body varies,
from relatively slender to deep-bodied with
a humpback. Some fish culturists claim these
vary with the food, sparse feeding producing the slender forms, abundant feeding
giving rise to humpbacks.

How old is a carp

Carp have probably been domesticated for
many centuries, and have been carried all
over the world for ornamental ponds, or for
food. Surprisingly, therefore, in view of
the familiarity that should have resulted
from this, there is a conflict of opinion on
important points—for instance, their longevity and maximum weights. Above all,
there are serious discrepancies about when
carp were introduced into Europe.

△ *Cyprinid fishes, for instance roach, tench and
some carp, often show red forms which breed
true to type. Aquarists take advantage, with
results like these Japanese **Hi-goi**, golden carps.*

Gesner, the 16th-century Swiss naturalist,
mentioned a carp 150 years old. Carp in the
lakes of Fontainebleau, France, have been
credited with ages of up to 400 years. Bingley,
writing in 1805, records a carp in the pond in
the garden of Emmanuel College, Cam-
bridge, England, that had been an inhabitant more than 70 years. Tate Regan,
authority on fishes in Britain in the first half
of this century, was of the opinion that under
artificial conditions a carp may attain 50
years but that 15 years would probably be
the maximum in the wild state.

Perhaps one reason for the excessive
claims is their hardiness when removed from
water. This is also the reason why the
fish could be spread over such a wide area
by man. Wrapped in damp moss or water
plants, it can survive transport over long
distances. If Pennant is to be believed, this
remark has the force of under-state-
ment. In his *British Zoology* he tells of a
carp wrapped in moss, with only its mouth
exposed, placed in a net and hung in a cel-
lar. It was fed with bread and milk and lived
over a fortnight. It is only fair to add that
it was 'often plunged in water'.

Carp usually grow to about 15 lb in the
United States but in Europe a fish of over 60
lb and a length of 40 in. has been recorded.
Claims have been made for 400 lb carp.
Frederick II of Prussia is said to have caught
one of 76 lb and a 140 lb carp is said to have

△ *Clarissa, the largest carp caught in Great Britain, was taken from Redmere Pool by R Walker in 1952. She was about 15 years old and weighed 44 lb. She lived in an aquarium until 1972.*

△ *The mirror carp is identified by rows of large scales along its back and sides.*

▽ *Some think carp found in Britain today came from carp cultivated in monastery stewponds.*

been caught at Frankfurt on Oder. There are several records of carp around 25 lb in Britain, but there is one for 44 lb taken by R Walker in 1952.

Historical uncertainty

The introduced form of the common carp was known to the Greeks and Romans, and has long been kept in ponds in parts of Europe. We know it is today found widely over England, the southern parts of Wales and in southern Scotland. The question remains: when was it first introduced into Britain?

Writers on the subject seem to have been fairly unanimous that all our carp must be regarded as descendants of fishes cultivated by the monks for centuries in their stewponds. Certainly, carp are still to be found in many of the surviving stewponds adjacent to ruins of monasteries and priories. That on its own is very little help in finding the date when they were first put there. Other than this, information comes from documentary evidence or guesswork, or a mixture of the two.

Eric Taverner, in his *Freshwater Fishes of the British Isles* (1957), suggested that carp were brought here from France and the Low Countries in the 14th century. Richard Fitter, writing in 1959, invokes an entry in *The Boke of St Albans* for dating their introduction prior to 1486. Emma Phipson, in *The Animal-Lore of Shakespeare's Time* (1883), speaks of Leonard Mascall, a Sussex gentleman, who has had the credit for importing the carp into England about the year 1514. She also points out that in the Privy Purse Expenses of Elizabeth of York, 1502, mention is made of a reward paid for the present of a carp. Izaak Walton, in *The Compleat Angler*, opined that the date was around 1530. Dr Albert Günther, celebrated authority on fishes in the last half of the 19th century, fixed the date at 1614.

The latest pronouncement is by Günther Sterba, in his *Freshwater Fishes of the World* (1962), that the carp reached England in 1512, Denmark in 1560, Prussia 1585, St Petersburg (Leningrad) 1729, and North America (California) 1872.

The dissolution of the monasteries began in 1535. A plan of a Benedictine monastery of the 12th century shows the site of a fishpond. Accepting the dates quoted here the fishponds of religious houses in England must have been stocked for at least two centuries with fish other than carp. Two of our seven authorities give dates about or after the dissolution of the monasteries, and three give dates only slightly before that event.

It is a romantic idea that English monks could supply themselves with carp to be eaten on fast days. But the evidence seems to be in favour of some other fish, probably the perch.

class	**Pisces**
order	**Cypriniformes**
family	**Cyprinidae**
genus & species	***Cyprinus carpio***

Swordtail

The swordtail is one of the more important as well as most popular of aquarium fishes, not only for its beauty but because it is a good subject for selective breeding. Swordtails are live-bearing tooth-carps, so they have the shape of that family. The dorsal fin is relatively large and so is the tailfin which is broad-based and rounded at the rear edge. The pelvic fins are at about the middle of the body. The females are up to 5 in., the males being up to 3¼ in. exclusive of the sword, which is formed from much elongated rays of the lower part of the tailfin. The outstanding feature of the swordtail is its colours.

Swordtails have been bred in so many colours and colour variations that a description of these in a small space would be impossible. What follows here can, however, be taken as a sort of standard colouring, the one most likely to be seen. The back is olive-green shading to greenish-yellow on the flanks and yellowish on the belly. The scales are edged with

them to take any food floating at the surface. They can also search on the bottom, the body held almost vertical with the head downward. They also snap at small swimming invertebrates. They are, in fact, omnivorous, taking anything small, both plant and animal, swimming or floating, and in the aquarium they spend much time grazing small algae growing on the glass or stones.

There seems to be a strong social hierarchy known as peck order in a community of swordtails which reveals itself in the aquarium by one of the males tending to bully the rest. Indeed, these fishes seem to be unduly spiteful, especially in small aquaria. Dominance in a community of any species is decided and maintained by fighting, or at least, by aggressive displays, and is closely linked with the strength of the sex hormones. Experiments with swordtails have shown, however, that a female maintains her position in the social hierarchy for 1–3 months after being spayed and a castrated male retains his for 1–6½ months. This is unusual because as a rule, when the gonads are removed, and with them the sex hormones, the individual usually drops more or less immediately to a subordinate rank in the social hierarchy.

brown so the whole body seems to be covered with a fine net. The fins are yellowish-green, the dorsal fin being ornamented with reddish blotches and streaks. From the tip of the snout to the base of the tailfin runs a rainbow band of colour made up of zigzag lines of carmine, green, cinnabar, purple or violet. The sword of the male is yellow at the base shading to orange, bordered with black above and below.

Swordtails live in the fresh waters of southern Mexico, British Honduras and Guatemala in Central America.

△ A male swordtail with a black-edged yellow 'sword' swims alongside a female.
◁ Red and green swordtails : two males with females and young.

Bullying males

As is usual with popular aquarium fishes more is gleaned about their way of life from individuals kept in tanks than from those living in the wild. They live the usual uneventful lives of small fishes, most of their time being taken up with searching for food – or bullying each other. Their mouth is inclined slightly upward making it easy for

Mystery of sex-reversal

Swordtails first became aquarium fishes about 1910, and not long after this the idea began to be current that these fishes undergo a remarkable sex-reversal. In 1926 Essenberg reported that females, after having had several broods, may become fully functional males. From the many reports that followed this the impression is gained that this is commonplace. There have, for example, been several authoritative books on freshwater or aquarium fishes written during the years since Essenberg's report was published, and all have given prominence to this idea. Gunther Sterba in his book first published in 1959 speaks of the quite remarkable and always astonishing sex-reversal in swordtails. He claims that in some strains as many as 30% of females later change into males. Yet in 1957 Myron Gordon, who had made a special study of the species, had already claimed that such changes were extremely rare, quoting a substantial report on swordtails by Friess, in 1933, in support of his claim.

Subjects for heredity study

If the supposedly remarkable sex-reversal is still in doubt there are other aspects of the breeding for which we have more reliable information. Swordtails have been almost domesticated and by selective breeding a wide range of colour varieties exist, usually named according to their colours, such as the green, the red, the red-eyed red, the red-wag, the black, the golden, and the albino. According to Dr Myron Gordon, quoted by William T. Innes, there are wild specimens comparable to all the selected varieties produced up to 1935 except the golden. There have, however, been others since then, including the one seen below.

Swordtails have been much used for the study of genetics, by crossing the colour varieties. In addition many hybrids with the platy have been produced, which increases still further not only the range of colours but also the materials for further studies on heredity. These fishes are particularly suitable for laboratory work of this kind. The sexes can be readily recognized, which is always a help in such studies. The males not only differ from the females in having the 'sword', they also have a gonopodium for the insertion of milt, fertilisation being internal. They also breed rapidly. A brood may number up to 200, each ¼ in. long at birth. The newly-born must rise to the surface for air to fill the swimbladder after which they can swim well and start to feed almost immediately. They also grow quickly. At first the sexes look alike but soon the males start to grow a sword. Swordtails live 2–3 years, so there is a rapid turn-over in populations. As a result swordtails, with their near relatives the platys, may be considered as a vertebrate equivalent of the fruit fly for genetical studies.

Hybridization

Probably the most remarkable feature of the sex life of the swordtail is the ease with which it hybridizes with platys in aquaria, yet although both species live virtually side by side in the fresh waters of Mexico and Guatemala no wild hybrids have been found. This is the more noteworthy since their breeding behaviour is so similar. There are, however, several small differences, hardly noticeable until close and critical study is made of them. To begin with, platys take about 5 minutes from the start of pre-mating behaviour to the actual mating, whereas swordtails take only one minute. The actual mating takes only half the time in platys that it does in swordtails and altogether the mating behaviour of platys is much the more vigorous. The differences are slight, and probably no one of them would be sufficient to form a barrier between the species, but taken as a whole they do. Under artificial conditions, as in an aquarium where the choice of mates is limited anyway, the barrier is readily overcome. In the wild, with a wide choice of mates, even small details count.

class	Pisces
order	Cypriniformes
family	Poeciliidae
genus & species	*Xiphophorus helleri*

▽ *Selective breeding results in a wide range of colour varieties: a recent breed is seen here.*

Zebra fish

There are several fishes with a common name that includes the word 'zebra'. The most noticeable of these is a small freshwater fish of Bengal and eastern India. Less than 2 in. long, it is called the zebra fish or zebra danio and is a member of the large carp family. It is an extremely popular fish with aquarists.

It is a slim fish with the body only slightly compressed. The single dorsal fin and the anal fins are fairly large, and it has a relatively large tailfin and small pelvic and pectoral fins. There are two pairs of barbels. The back is brownish-olive, the belly yellowish-white and the flanks are Prussian blue with four golden stripes from the gill cover to the base of the tail. The dorsal fin is also blue with yellow at its base and a white tip. The anal fin is again blue-gold barred, and so is the tailfin. The effect of the stripes is to make the fish look even more streamlined than it is, and to give an impression of movement even when the fish is stationary.

Beauty in repetition

As so often happens with a fish of outstanding colour, subsequently popular with aquarists, there is little that is zoologically striking in zebra fishes. They swim among water plants or in schools—it is when they are all aligned, swimming in formation, evenly spaced, and all travelling in the same direction that they most catch the eye. Almost certainly their attraction owes much to the repetition of their stripes—termed the 'beauty in repetition' by Dr Dilwyn John in 1947. In 1935, William T Innes came very near to saying this in his comprehensive book *Exotic Aquarium Fishes* when he described it as a fish 'to show to advantage moving in schools, it scarcely has an equal, for its beautiful horizontal stripes, repeated in each fish, give a streamline effect that might well be the envy of our best automobile designers'.

Special precautions

Zebra fishes are carnivorous, feeding on any small animals they can swallow, which usually means small insect larvae, crustaceans and worms. After their colour, their strongly carnivorous tendencies provide one of their more interesting features. They are egg-eaters, and those who breed zebra fish in aquaria need to take special precautions to achieve success.

There is little difference between the sexes except that the female, especially just before spawning, is more plump than the male, and her stripes are more silver and yellow than the golden stripes of the male. In the pre-spawning behaviour the male leads the female in among the water plants and the two take up position side by side, she to shed her ova, he to shed his milt over them to fertilise them. As the eggs slowly sink there is a tendency for the two to snap up the eggs. The first precaution for the aquarist is therefore to provide a breeding aquarium with water so shallow that the fish have no chance to catch the eggs before they sink to safety in the spaces between the gravel on the bottom. The correct size of gravel pebbles must be used or the adults may become trapped between them. Marbles have been used, or else some sort of trap. An early trap used was a series of slender glass rods held together at the ends with soft wire and raised just off the bottom of the aquarium. This was later superseded by fine metal mesh or nylon.

Each female lays about 200 eggs which hatch in two days. The larvae are at first fairly helpless and inactive, but two days later they can swim and start to feed on microscopic plankton animals. They begin to breed at a year old. At two years they are old-aged, and a zebra fish of three or more years old is an extreme rarity.

Question of stripes

The name 'zebra' is from an Amharic or Ethiopian word and first gained currency in Europe in 1600. By the early years of the 19th century its use had been extended not only to cover all manner of striped animals but also materials showing stripes, and especially to striped shawls and scarves. In the world of fishes there is the zebra shark of the Indian Ocean, with black or brown bars on the body, more like the stripes of a tiger. So we have the anomaly of the common name being zebra shark and the scientific name *Stegostoma tigrinum*. In the extreme south of South America is the zebra salmon *Haplochiton zebra*. In pisciculture there is a hybrid of the trout *Salmo trutta* and the American brook trout *Salvelinus fontinalis*, which is called the zebra hybrid. A foot-long marine fish of the Indo-Pacific *Therapon jarbua* is sometimes called the zebra or tiger fish. It is, however, among the aquarium fishes that the name is most used —the striped or zebra barb *Barbus fasciatus* of Malaya and the East Indies is an example. The common killifish *Fundulus heteroclitus*, of North America, is also called the zebra killie, while the zebra cichlid *Cichlasoma nigrofasciatum* is also—and more appropriately—called the convict fish. Some of these fish have horizontal stripes and others vertical, and there has been some disagreement over which are more correctly termed 'zebra'. However, since a glance at a photograph of a zebra shows that the stripes run in different directions on the different areas of the body, there seems no reason why the name should not be applied to all.

class	**Pisces**
order	**Atheriniformes**
family	**Cyprinodontidae**
genus & species	*Brachydanio rerio*

▽ *On the right lines: the popular zebra fish proves that parallel stripes never meet.*

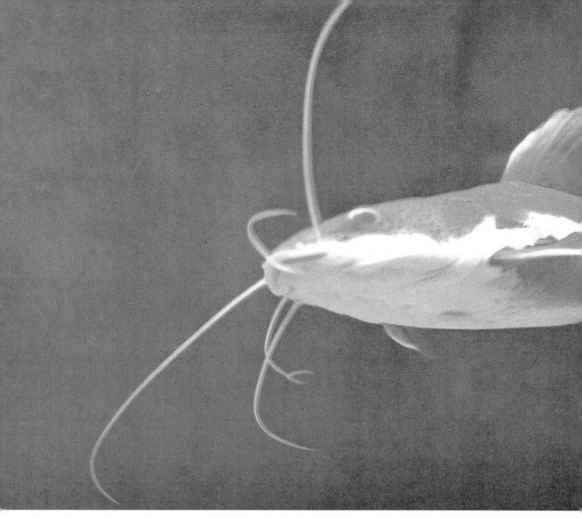

Catfish

*The European catfish, or wels, grows to
9 ft or more in the rivers of central
and eastern Europe and western Asia,
and is the most famous of a large group
called the naked catfishes. Its head is
large and broad, the mouth has a wide
gape and around it are three pairs of
barbels or 'whiskers', the feature of all
catfishes. In the wels the three pairs of
barbels can be moved about and one pair is
very long. The eyes are small. The body is
stout, almost cylindrical in front, and flattened
from side to side in the rear portion. The skin
is slimy and has no scales. The fins, except
for the long anal fin, are small. The
colour is dark olive-green to bluish-black*
on the back, the flanks being paler with a
reddish sheen, the belly whitish, the whole
body being marked with spots and blotches.

*The wels has many common names:
silurus, the name given it by the
Romans, glanis, sheatfish, or sheathfish,
said to be from a fanciful resemblance
to a sword scabbard, and waller. It has
been introduced to a number of lakes in
different parts of England.*

Night hunter

The European catfish lives in rivers or deep
lakes with plenty of water plants. It spends
the day under overhanging banks or on the
mud in deep water, foraging in the mud
with its barbels in search of small invertebrates. At night it hunts, feeding voraciously
on fish, crustaceans, and frogs. The larger
ones take small water birds and mammals.

In May to June, the breeding season, the
catfish moves into shallow water, where the
female lays her eggs in a depression in the
mud formed by lashing movements of her
tail. A large female may lay 100 000 eggs,
which are said to be guarded by the male.
The fry are black and tadpole-shaped.

Legendary criminal

It would be surprising if a large fish, with
hearty appetite, that lurks in dark places
did not gather an evil reputation. The wels
has been accused of swallowing lambs, even
children. Gesner, in the 16th century, reports that a human head and a hand bearing
gold rings were taken from the stomach of
one of these large catfish.

Many strange habits

Although related, the various naked catfishes show remarkable diversity in form
and habits. The banjo catfishes of South
America may live in rivers and brackish

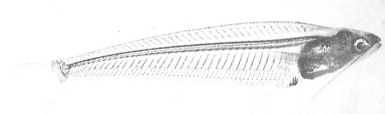

◁ *Most of the many different kinds of catfishes have three pairs of barbels round the mouth.*

△ *Glass catfish, like many catfishes, has no scales.*
▽ *The barbels are used to probe in mud for food.*

estuaries, some species in the sea. They are named for their flattened bodies with an unusually long tail. In one species *Aspredinichthys tibicen* the tail is three times the length of the body. In the breeding season, the females of this species grow a patch of spongy tentacles on the abdomen, and carry their eggs anchored to these.

Marine catfishes of the family Ariidae are mouth-breeders. That is, the male holds the eggs, which in some species are nearly 1 in. diameter, in his mouth, and when they hatch he continues to shelter the fry in the same way. For a month he must fast. Another name for these catfishes is crucifixion fish, because when the skull is cleaned, a fair representation of a crucifix is formed by the bones of the undersurface.

Another family of marine catfishes (Plotosidae) contains one of the most dangerous fishes of the coral reefs. The dorsal and the pectoral fins carry spines equipped with poison glands. Merely to brush the skin against these spines can produce painful wounds.

Equally dangerous are the parasitic catfishes. Some of this family (Trichomycteridae) are free-living but many attach themselves to other fishes using the spines on the gill-covers to hook themselves on, piercing the skin and gorging themselves on the blood. Others insinuate themselves into the gill-cavities, eating the gills. The candiru *Vandellia cirrhosa* is prone to make its way into the urethra of a naked person entering the water, especially, so it seems, if water is passed. A surgical operation may be necessary to remove the fish. Men and women in the unsophisticated areas of Brazil wear a special guard of palm fibres to protect themselves when wading into rivers.

North America has the flathead (family Ictaluridae), a useful catfish reaching 5½ ft long and 100 lb weight. The channel catfish is a most valuable foodfish. There are, however, the madtoms, 5 in. or less, but with pectoral spines and poison glands.

Mad in another sense are the upside-down catfishes of tropical African rivers. From swimming normally these catfishes may suddenly turn and swim upside-down, for no obvious reason. When courting, the male and female upside-down catfishes swim at each other and collide head-on, repeating this at half-minute intervals.

class	**Pisces**
order	**Siluriformes**
family	**Siluridae**
genus & species	***Silurus glanis*** *European catfish others*

Seahorse

The seahorse is a strange animal which looks like the knight of a chess set, but that is not the end of its oddities. It can wrap its tail round a seaweed or similar object, as a South American monkey wraps its tail round a branch. Each of its eyes is on a turret and can move independently. Although many other fishes can also move their eyes independently, this ability is more pronounced in seahorses. A final oddity is that the male carries the babies in a pouch.

A seahorse has a large head with a tubular snout, a moveable neck, a rotund body and a long tapering, slender tail, with a total length of not more than 8 in. The neck, body and tail are marked with circular and longitudinal ridges, on which there are bony bumps, so the fish looks almost like a wood carving. There is a pair of small pectoral fins and a single small dorsal fin. The colours vary widely but are mostly light to medium brown, scattered with small white spots, and often there are ornamental fleshy strands.

There are 20 species, half of which live in the Indo-Australian region. The others live off the Atlantic coasts of Europe, Africa and North America, with two species on the Pacific coast of America.

Swimming upright

Seahorses live in shallow inshore waters among seaweeds or in beds of eelgrass in estuaries. They swim in a vertical position, propelling themselves by rapid waves of the dorsal fin. When swimming at full speed this fin may oscillate at a rate of 35 times a second—which makes it look like a revolving propeller. The pectoral fins oscillate at the same rate, and the head is used for steering, the fish turning its head in the direction it wants to go. When a seahorse clings to a support with its tail it still keeps its body upright. If the fins are damaged they can be regenerated relatively quickly.

Tiny mouth

The seahorse eats any kind of swimming animal small enough to enter its tiny mouth. Prey is located by sight and quickly snapped up, or is sucked in from as much as $1\frac{1}{2}$ in. away. It is mainly tiny crustaceans such as copepods, but baby fishes are also eaten.

Male courts male

Breeding starts with males going through actions that look like a courtship, and a male seahorse of one species has even been seen to court a male of another species. This courtship probably brings him into condition to receive the eggs. He pairs up with a female, either swimming in front of her but without actually touching her or, in some species, the two may entwine tails. He seems to be bowing to her, but this is actually a pumping action to drive the water out of the pouch on his belly. The female inserts her long ovipositor into the opening of the pouch to lay her eggs, as many as 200 in

△ *Pregnant male seahorse **Hippocampus erectus**, his belly pouch extended with eggs.*
▽ *Proud parent with day-old young seahorses.*

▷ *The scene is set for the seahorse ballet; one wraps its prehensile tail round another.*
▽ *Young day-old seahorse (approx. × 7).*

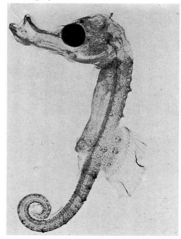

some species. During this time the mouth of the pouch is large but when laying is finished it closes to a minute pore, and stays like this until the baby seahorses are ready to be born, in 4–5 weeks. They are about $\frac{1}{2}$ in. long at birth, perfect miniatures of their parents and the first thing baby seahorses do is to swim to the surface to gulp air to fill their swimbladders. They feed ravenously on extremely small crustaceans, such as newly hatched brine shrimps, and grow rapidly. In the Steinhart Aquarium in the United States young seahorses *Hippocampus hudsonius* were found to grow from $\frac{3}{8}$ in. at birth to $2\frac{1}{2}$ in. in 2 months.

Placental fishes

The inside of the pouch changes just before and during courtship. The walls thicken and become spongy, and they are enriched with an abundant supply of blood vessels. As the female lays her eggs the male fertilises them and they become embedded in these spongy walls, which then act like a placenta. As the pouch is closed there must be some way by which oxygen reaches the eggs, and it is almost certain that the network of blood vessels in the wall of the pouch passes oxygen to the eggs and takes up carbon dioxide from them. Also food probably passes from the paternal blood into the eggs, just as it does from the mother's blood in the mammalian placenta.

Male labour

We are used to the idea that no matter what happens beforehand, in the actual bearing of offspring it is always the female that has the burden. In seahorses it is the reverse. As each batch of eggs is laid in his pouch the male seahorse goes through violent muscular spasms which work the eggs to the bottom of the pouch to make room for more. It seems also that there is a physiological reaction as the eggs sink into the spongy tissue, and he shows signs of exhaustion. When the young have hatched and are ready to leave the pouch, the mouth of the pouch opens wide. The male alternately bends and straightens his body in convulsive jerks and finally a baby seahorse is shot out through the mouth of the pouch. After each birth the male rests, and when all the babies are born he shows signs of extreme exhaustion. In aquaria the males often die after delivering their brood but this does not happen in a natural state, because the male soon looks around for another female to fill his pouch with eggs.

Seahorses have been described as having the head of a horse, the tail of a monkey, the pouch of a kangaroo, the hard outer skeleton of an insect and the independently moving eyes of a chameleon. It would, however, be difficult to find a suitable comparison for the labour pains of the father.

class	Pisces
order	Gasterosteiformes
family	Syngnathidae
genus	*Hippocampus brevirostris*
& species	*H. hippocampus, others*

Marine angelfish, **Holacanthus**, *living among the coral reefs of tropical seas, outstanding for its varied patterns and colours.*

Angelfish

The name 'angelfish' has been used commonly for two types of fishes. Both of these types are bony fishes, one of which is marine, the other freshwater. The latter has long been a favourite with aquarists who, perhaps to avoid confusion of names, developed the habit of using its scientific name, which is **Scalare**. *Since not everyone followed their example, however, at least part of the confusion remains. There is another perplexing usage. Some scientists 'lump' the marine angelfishes into the butterfly fish family (see page 10), but the butterfly fish is only distantly related to them and belongs to an entirely separate family.*

There is little to choose between these angelfishes and butterfly fishes. Most are brilliantly coloured, mainly coral-reef dwelling fishes; the angelfishes, however, have a sharp spine on the lower edge of the gill-cover which is lacking in the butterfly fishes.

It hardly needs explaining that these vernacular names are prompted by the enlarged flap-like or wing-like fins.

Most angelfish are small, up to 8 in. long, but the marine ones reach 2 ft in length. The outline of the body, because of the well-developed fins, has much the shape of a flint arrowhead.

Colourful and curious

The marine angelfishes, and the similar butterfly fishes, which together number more than 150 species, live mainly in shallow seas and a few enter estuaries. They live in pairs or small groups at most, around reefs, rocks or corals.

They are inoffensive as adults, they are peaceable, they do not dash away as most fishes do when, for example, a skin diver intrudes into their living space. They move away but slowly, every now and then tilting the body to take a closer look at the newcomer.

The outstanding feature of these fishes is the wide range and the beauty of their colours and patterns. In many of them the young fishes have the same colours as the adults, but in others the differences are so great that it looks as if there are two different species involved. Their behaviour tends to be different also. Quite small — that is, up to a few inches long — they tend to be solitary, and individuals are usually found in the same places day after day, in each case near a shelter into which the fish darts when disturbed. The shelter may be under a rock bed or among seaweed. A tin can lying on the sea-bed will readily be used for shelter. In an aquarium the sub-adults will be aggressive towards each other, but one kept on its own readily becomes tame and learns to feed from the hand.

Probably the most beautiful of the angels is the rock beauty, coloured jet black in front and yellow in its rear half, its fins bright yellow with red spots. It has a strong sense of curiosity that makes it draw near to the underwater swimmer. The queen angelfish, when small, is largely dark brown to black with three bluish vertical bands on the sides of the body and a bluish band along the dorsal fin. Adult, it is mainly a startlingly bright yellow with irregular and diffuse patches of violet or red on various parts of the body. The French angel is black with strongly contrasting bright yellow vertical bands and a yellow face (see illustration page 32).

Feeding

Angelfishes have small mouths armed with many small teeth and they use these when they browse on the algae and coral polyps or catch the small invertebrates on which they feed. In some species the snout is somewhat elongate, and may be inserted in cracks and crevices in rocks or coral to capture small animals for food.

In certain species of butterfly fishes, such as *Chelmon rostratus*, the snout is very long and tube-like with the small mouth at the end. This enables the fishes to probe even deeper into the crevices of coral rock for their food.

Parental care

Little is known of the breeding habits of marine angelfish, but they probably conform to the pattern of their better known relations in that they show quite close care of the eggs and fry.

Both fish clean a patch of flat rock, and the female lays her eggs on it, the male swimming close over them shedding sperm for fertilisation. The eggs are tended for 4−8 days by the parents, when the fry hatch, and sink to the bottom.

The parents guard them until they are sufficiently free-swimming to hide in crevices and weed. The fry are unlike the adults in that their bodies are long and slim. They do not not assume full adult shape before three or four months have passed.

Conspicuous colouring

All angelfishes and butterfly fishes are conspicuous. To the underwater swimmer

△ Angelfish are strongly territorial and use their colours both to advertise possession of their territory and to warn off an intruder of their own species. One of these freshwater **Scalare** is displaying at the other with a sideways flick of its bright pectoral fins like flashing signals.
▽ These freshwater angelfish, **Scalare**, are favourites with aquarists, being easy to care for and attractive to look at.

their colours stand out and 'hit the eye'. Especially striking are the patterns of the imperial angelfish or blue angelfish, with their inscribed patterns of white and black curves and half circles on a rich blue and violet background, dazzling to the eye when seen at close quarters.

We are used to the idea of colours and colour-patterns serving as camouflage to hide an animal from its enemies or enable it, if a predatory animal, to steal close to its prey undetected. We are used also to conspicuous colours, especially combinations of yellow, black and red, serving as warning colours, the wearer of these colours being poisonous or bad-tasting or having a sting. The colours of angelfishes certainly fail to hide their wearer. Although one writer has described angelfishes as nestling among coral heads like humming-birds among brilliant blossoms, most underwater swimmers agree you can see these fishes clearly at a distance. There is no indication that angelfishes are poisonous or unpalatable, or have a sting. They are eaten by the local peoples wherever they occur, although their skins are said to be tough.

Perhaps the comparison with humming-birds is not so far-fetched as it appears at first sight. Conspicuous colours in birds are associated with displays, especially aggressive displays, as they are in lizards such as the anole and the same may be true of angelfishes. Experimentally, a mirror was placed in an aquarium with a French angelfish. The fish drew near, nibbled at its reflection in the mirror, then threw itself sideways and flicked its bright blue pectoral fins like flashing signals. This suggests that angelfishes are strongly territorial and use their colours both to advertise possession of a territory as well as to warn off an intruder of their own species.

There was at least one angelfish that escaped attention for a long time despite its colouring, a bright orange head with a glowing dark blue contrasting body. This, the pygmy angelfish, was wholly unknown until 1908, when one was brought up in the trawl off Bermuda from a depth of 540 ft. It was dead when it reached the surface and its carcase was committed to a jar of alcohol to preserve it. It became something of a mystery fish and it was not until 1951 that it was given a scientific name, when one scientist examining it realized it was a new species of angelfish. The next year a second specimen was taken from the stomach of a larger fish, a snapper, caught in 240 ft of water off Mexico. In 1959, this fish, believed to be so rare, was caught in fair numbers by a skin-diver off the Bahamas, in 40 ft of water.

class	**Pisces**
order	**Perciformes**
family	**Chaetodontidae**

◁ *Marine French angelfish,* **Pomacanthus paru***, showing one of the bizarre shapes and patterns typical of these fish, which look quite different when they are seen from the side than they do from the front view.*

Pompadour fish

This fish from the rivers of the Amazon
basin has been described as the noblest
among aquarium fishes. Its name of
pompadour is then quite appropriate
although it is also known as the discus
from its shape. The pompadour fish and its
relative, which is divided into subspecies
known as the green discus, brown discus
and blue discus, are almost disc-shaped
when fully grown and up to 8 in. long. The
long dorsal and anal fins make the otherwise oval body look more nearly circular.
The body is covered with small scales but
the cheeks and gill covers are more
markedly scaly. The mouth is small, with
thick lips. There is a single row of small
conical teeth in the middle of each jaw and
instead of the usual two pairs, there is a
single pair of nostrils.

The colours are not easy to describe
because they change with age. A young
pompadour fish is brown with several
vertical dark bars down each side. At 6
months old, flecks of blue appear on the
head and gill covers, and these spread
until the sides are coloured with alternating bands of blue and reddish brown
and there are nine vertical dark bands, the
first running through the eye. The fins
become blue at their bases, pale blue and
orange on the outer edges, and there are
streaks of blue and orange between. The
pelvic fins are red with orange tips. The
green discus is mainly green with 9 dark
vertical bars, the brown discus mainly
brown with 9 dark bars and the blue
discus brown with 9 blue bars.

△ Turning blue with age, pompadour fish
Symphysodon aequifasciata. At 6 months the
head and gill covers become flecked with blue
and this gradually spreads across the sides.

Hanging by a thread

Pompadour fishes usually spend the day
sheltering in the shadows of water plants
when they are not feeding and they avoid
strong sunlight. They eat water insects,
especially the larvae of midges and small
dragonflies, small worms and similar invertebrates. There is a brief courtship,
during which the pair clean the surface of
a broad leaf of a water plant. When this is
ready, the female lays rows of eggs on it.
Sometimes the surface of a stone is used but
only after being meticulously cleaned. Once
the eggs are laid the male swims over and
fertilises them. The parents take it in turn
to fan them with their fins and they hatch in
about 50 hours. As each baby breaks out of

the egg it is removed in the parents' mouth and placed on a leaf, where each hangs by a short thread for the next 60 hours. The parents continue to fan with their fins and when, at the end of this time, the babies are about to swim, they swarm on the side of one of the parents and appear to hang there. After a time the parent gives a wriggle and the fry are shaken off towards the side of the other parent, who is swimming nearby. When 3–4 weeks old the fry become independent and feed on small animal plankton such as very small water fleas or their larvae. At first they are the normal fish shape, if a little plump in the body. The discoid shape comes with age.

Feeding the fry

There can be little doubt that baby pompadours get protection by swarming on the side of the parent, although sometimes they are eaten by the parents, at least in aquaria.

The question is whether they get something more. In 1959 Dr WH Hildeman reported observations that seemed to show that the babies fed on a slime secreted by the parents' skin. This seems to have been accepted by students of tropical fishes. In the 1969 edition of their book *All about tropical fish* Derek McInerny and Geoffry Gerard not only state that the parents secrete a whitish mucus over their bodies but that the fry will eat nothing else. They quote Mr R Skipper 'who has successfully raised several spawnings' and he claims they will not thrive on any alternative food. Indeed, he maintains the only hope of raising them is to leave them with their parents. Against this we have the words of Gunther Sterba, in his *Freshwater fishes of the world*, that not only do the young of some other cichlid fishes cling to the sides of their parents but that at least one aquarist has reared young pompadours away from

the care and protection of parents.

One reason why pompadours are not more often kept in aquaria is that young ones taken in the wild are infected with micro-organisms. The frequent changes of water necessary to keep them in captivity seem to favour the parasites, which get the upper hand and kill the pompadours.

class	**Pisces**
order	**Perciformes**
family	**Cichlidae**
genus & species	*Symphysodon aequifasciata* brown, green and blue discus *S. discus* pompadour fish

▽ *Floating discs of colour,* **Symphysodon discus** *swim in the shadows.*

34

In the ring: two wary males circle each other during a lull in combat, seeking an opening to attack.

Fighting fish

Many fish fight, but the celebrated species is the fighting fish Betta splendens of Thailand. This is one of 7 related species in southeast Asia, ranging from Thailand to Borneo. It has been selectively bred for fighting qualities and used for sport, with bets placed, in Thailand.

The wild ancestor is 2 in. long, yellowish-brown with indistinct dark stripes along the flanks. In the breeding season the male becomes darker and rows of metallic green scales on its flanks become brighter. Its dorsal fin is medium-sized, metallic green tipped with red. The anal fin is large and red edged with blue and the small pelvic fins are red tipped with white. The tail fin is rounded. The female is smaller, less colourful, mainly yellowish brown.

Short-lived

Fighting fish live in clear but weedy rivers and lakes, in irrigation ditches and ponds, and two species are also found in mountain streams. They mature rapidly and grow quickly, and they do not live much longer than two years. Because of their rapid growth they feed heavily on all kinds of small aquatic animals such as water fleas, mosquito larvae, worms or small pieces of dead flesh.

Endurance tests

Male fighting fish are pugnacious towards each other—one species has been named *Betta pugnax*—but to nothing like the extent of the selectively bred descendants. Wild fighting fish rarely keep up their fights for 15 minutes and usually it is much less. The cultivated varieties are considered to be poor samples if they fight for less than an hour and some will continue to attack for up to 6 hours.

A raft of bubbles

Mating is preceded by the male swimming around the female, with heightened colours and fins spread. There follows what can only be called dancing and embracing. Before this takes place, however, the male has built a nest, a raft of bubbles. He takes in bubbles of air at the surface and these become enclosed in a sticky mucus in his mouth, so the bubbles last a long time.

The courtship ends with the male turning the female on her side and wrapping himself round her. Then he tightens his grip, turns her upside down, and in a short while lets go and, as she remains in the upside-down position, he stations himself beneath her. She begins to lay 3–7 eggs at a time, to a total of several hundred. As these slowly sink the male catches each in turn in his mouth, coats it with mucus, then swims up to his raft and sticks it on the underside. This is repeated until all the eggs are laid, the male looping himself round the female each time to fertilise the eggs as she lays them. Finally, the male drives the female away. After that the male guards the nest. The young hatch 24–30 hours later, when the male's parental duties are at an end.

Head-on crash

The first *B. splendens* to be bred in Europe appeared in France in 1893 and in a very few years it was being kept by aquarists over a large part of the world. One of the earlier varieties was cream-coloured with flowing red fins. Then came the famous Cornflower Blue. After that there were various shades of blue, lavender, green and red ending in the best-known, the rich purplish-blue. All these varieties had flowing veil-like fins and, whatever their colour of body, all had red drooping pelvic fins.

There have been many stories, usually highly coloured, about the way the males fight. The facts are dramatic enough. When two males are put in an aquarium together their colours heighten and they take up position side by side, heads pointed in one direction, one fish slightly in advance of the other. Their fins are erected, their gill-covers expanded. Then, with lightning speed they attack. They try to bite each other's fins and in the end one may have some of its fins torn down to stumps. They may also bite patches of scales from each other's flanks. Sometimes they meet in a head-on clash with jaws interlocked.

Above: Male on the right surveys female. Below: Under the nest, a raft of bubbles, male mates with a female by wrapping himself round her.

The greatest damage is done when the cultivated fighting fish are unevenly matched. A small one matched against a large one is bound to suffer. So is a long-finned variety matched against a short-finned variety. Long flowing fins make it hard for their owner to turn quickly. More-over, the fishes attack the rear half of their opponents, where the flowing fins are.

Exploding with rage

One of the more exaggerated stories to be published was collected by the distinguished American fish specialist, Hugh M Smith. It is quoted in *Exotic Aquarium Fishes* by WT Innes. It tells how you go out and catch your fighting fish — assuming you live in Thailand — and bring it home in a bottle. Your neighbour does the same. You stand the two bottles together. The two fishes see each other, flash their colours at each other and blow themselves up. They hurl them-selves in vain at each other, until finally one of them becomes so angry it literally bursts. If this is your fish you lose your bet!

class	**Pisces**
order	**Perciformes**
family	**Anabantidae**
genus & species	***Betta splendens*** *B. pugnax* others

Kissing gourami

This is a popular aquarium fish that has achieved fame for a single trick of behaviour that looks uncommonly like a familiar human action. Other than this the species would have remained in relative obscurity. 'Kissing' is by no means confined to this gourami, which is chosen here to show an interesting facet of animal behaviour.

There are several species of gouramis, all from southeast Asia, where they grow to a foot or more and are used for food. The kissing gourami may grow to a foot long, but when kept in an aquarium it is usually well short of this. Its body is flattened from side to side, oval in outline, with a pointed head ending in a pair of thickened lips. The greenish to grey-yellow dorsal and anal fins are long and prominent and both slope upwards from front to rear. The normal colour of the body is silvery green with dark stripes on the flanks but there is another colour phase, pinkish-white and somewhat iridescent.

Thick lips for breathing and eating
The kissing and other gouramis belong to the labyrinth fishes, which means they have an accessory breathing organ in the gills for taking in air at the surface, as well as breathing by gills. The kissing gourami not only rises to the surface from time to time to gulp air, and therefore can live in water that is slightly fouled, but it also feeds at the surface. The thickened lips probably have an advantage in these two respects. The food consists of both animal and plant matter and in an aquarium kissing gouramis eat dried shrimps and powdered oatmeal, water fleas and dried spinach. To some extent they will feed on the small algae that grow on the sides of the aquarium.

Life history little known
There is still some doubt about their breeding habits. Many labyrinth fishes build bubble nests for their eggs but so far as we know kissing gouramis build no nest but lay 400–2 000 floating eggs. They seem to ignore these as well as the young which hatch in 24 hours. The baby fishes eat ciliated protistans for their first week, taking water fleas after this, graduating to the mixed diet as they grow older. They begin to breed when 3–5 in. long.

Mystery of the kiss
Nobody seems very clear whether this is an aggressive action or part of the courtship. Probably it enters into both. When several kissing gouramis are kept together in one aquarium the larger of them bother the smaller by 'sucking' at their flanks. They will do the same with fishes of other species. This is probably aggressive. When a pair are together, however, they can be seen to face each other, swaying backwards and forwards, as if hung on invisible threads, and then they come together, mouth to mouth, their thick lips firmly placed together in an exaggerated kissing action. Like other labyrinth fishes the male wraps himself around the body of the female when mating. This is preceded by the two swimming round and round each other in a circling movement, after which they again come together, lips to lips, in a seeming kiss.

A touching scene—like mirror images of each other two gouramis 'kiss'. It is not fully understood why this fish, a favourite among tropical fish fanciers, makes this familiar human action. It may be one of aggression but it also enters into the courtship ritual.

Mouth wrestling
The use of the mouth as a test of strength in fighting is common among the higher animals. It is frequently seen in aquarium fishes, especially among cichlids and labyrinth fishes. One fish butting another with its mouth is often used in courtship, especially by the smaller freshwater fishes, and it seems likely that the mouth-wrestling and the butting lead on to the kissing. At all events, A van der Nieuwenhuizen, in his book *Tropical Aquarium Fish*, takes the view that in the cichlid, known as the blue acara *Aequidens latifrons*, mouth-wrestling is used to defeat a rival as well as court a mate. He maintains that when a pair indulge in a bout of mouth-wrestling which ends in stalemate this means the two are physically and psychologically suited and the chances of their breeding are high. The mouth-tugging, as he calls it, may last for hours and be repeated day after day, to end in a genuine lovers' choice. The chances are that the kissing of the gourami has exactly the same importance, so it is a true lovers' kiss.

class	Pisces
order	Perciformes
family	Anabantidae
genus & species	*Helostoma temmincki*

37

The barracuda is one of the most feared and dangerous predatory fishes. Apparently they may be dangerous in one area and not in another.

Barracuda

Barracuda are pike-like fishes, not related to pike but having a similar long-bodied form, with a jutting lower jaw and a wicked-looking set of fangs. Fishermen, in handling even the dead fish, treat them with respect. There are more than 20 species, but most of them are harmless. The evil reputation of barracudas has perhaps been over-stated, and it is difficult to know what to believe. One eminent authority, speaking of the fear fishermen in the West Indies have for the barracuda, has referred to merciless struggles waged between man and barracuda in the shade of the mangroves. This is at variance with all that one hears from skindivers, as well as with what is said of the speedy attack by this fish. Nevertheless, there are a number of authentic records of attack, especially from the great barracuda, also called picuda, or becuna, the giant of the family, which ranges through tropical and subtropical waters the world over, and may reach a length of 8 ft or more. The northern barracuda, or sennet, of the western North Atlantic, reaches only 18 in., but the European barracuda, barracouta or spet, of the Mediterranean and eastern Atlantic, may reach 3 ft. Other species are the Indian barracuda and Commerson's barracuda, both of the Indian Ocean, and the California barracuda.

Most voracious fish

More fearful to some people than even the shark, the larger barracudas are among the most voracious of predatory fishes. Long and torpedo-shaped, the barracudas swim swiftly and feed voraciously, especially on plankton-feeding fishes, charging through their shoals, attacking with snapping bites. It is said that when a pack of barracuda has eaten enough, it herds the rest of the shoal it is attacking into shallow water and keeps guard over it until ready for another meal.

Small or half-grown barracudas swim in shoals, the larger individuals are solitary. A solitary barracuda attacks swiftly, bites cleanly and does not repeat its attack (shoaling barracuda seldom attack people). It hunts by sight rather than smell, as sharks do, and advice given to bathers and divers reflects this. For example, murky water should be avoided because the fish, aware of every movement you make through its keen sight, may over-estimate your size, thereby over-estimating the danger you represent to it, and attack. A metallic object flashing in clear water looks to a barracuda like a fish and stimulates attack. An underwater spear fisherman towing a fish may be in trouble also, and it is not unknown for a barracuda to snatch a captured fish from a skindiver's belt.

Virtually all the interest in this fish has been concentrated on its behaviour towards man, apart from its use for food. On two occasions American scientists have collected all reports of alleged attacks on human beings. It seems these amount to fewer than 40, making the barracuda less dangerous in aggregate than sharks. To a large extent the reputation of this fish is the result of what appears to be an insatiable curiosity. It will hang around a skin-diver, watching his movements and following him, generating in him a very uncomfortable feeling. There is evidence that a barracuda is most dangerous—some say only dangerous—when provoked. Even so, there are records of a person standing in no more than 1 ft of water having the flesh bitten from the lower leg, or the bone almost severed.

One feature of barracuda behaviour, for which there is as yet no explanation, is that the fish may be dangerous in one area and not in another. Barracuda in the Antilles, for example, should be avoided, but around Hawaii they seem to be harmless.

Barracuda spawn over deep water offshore in the Caribbean, ocean currents distributing the larvae and young.

Reputation prejudiced

All barracudas are regarded as good food-fishes, but there is some prejudice against the barracuda because its flesh is, on occasions, highly poisonous. This may be a seasonal danger, the flesh being poisonous at some times of the year and not at others, it may be due to the flesh being allowed to go slightly bad before being cooked, but it is also due to what is known as ciguatera, which is due to toxins, originating in toxic algae and diatoms, building up from plant-eating fish to predators, and concentrating. The toxin is the cause of sickness, and even death, in humans who eat the predator (for example the barracuda). In the Caribbean, some species of fish are safe to eat from only one side of an island.

Prejudice is not confined to the fish. Sir Hans Sloane, writing in 1707, maintained that barracudas were more fond of the flesh of dogs, horses and black men than that of white men. Père Labat, in 1742, carried this prejudiced statement further. He declared that, faced with a choice of a Frenchman and an Englishman, a barracuda would always choose the latter. He attributed this to the gross meat-eating habits of the Englishman, which produced a stronger 'exhalation' in the water, as compared with the more delicate exudations of a Frenchman, who is a daintier feeder.

△ The skull of the great barracuda showing its wicked-looking set of fangs and the jutting lower jaw.

class	**Pisces**
order	**Perciformes**
family	**Sphyraenidae**
genus & species	*Sphyraena barracuda* great barracuda
	S. borealis northern barracuda
	S. sphyraena European barracuda others

▽ School of barracuda swimming past coral of the Great Barrier Reef, Australia. Shoaling barracuda seldom attack people.

Plaice

The plaice is one of the best known of the flatfishes and commercially the most important. It has a flattened body, with the dorsal fin extending from the head almost to the tailfin, and the anal fin from behind the gill cover to the same point. The brownish, upper, or right side is marked with red spots, each of which is surrounded by a white ring in the adult. These may be pale when the fish has been resting on whitish pebbles. The underside is pearly white but can be partially or wholly coloured, a condition known as ambicoloration. It may take the form of scattered brown or black spots or patches on the white undersurface. Alternatively, only the hindend may be completely coloured as on the upper surface, including the red spots. When the pigmentation extends along the whole underside the undersurface of the head is usually white, but in exceptional cases even this may be coloured. The mouth is twisted, with the lower, or blind, side more developed and armed with a greater number of teeth. The small scales are embedded in the skin and there are bony knobs between the eyes. Plaice can grow to almost 3 ft long, but the usual size is much less.

They range from Iceland and the White Sea, along the coasts of Scandinavia, south through the North Sea to the coasts of France and the western Mediterranean. Plaice are not identical throughout their range but split into a number of races. They vary in area of distribution, time and site of spawning, and in their degree of pigmentation.

△ *Face to face with the adult plaice. With distorted mouth and transposed eye it now lives permanently at the bottom of the sea, lying on its left side.*

In this plaice the upper surface is mottled light grey to suit its background of shell-gravel. The plaice in the bottom picture has a brown mottling because it is lying on differently coloured sandy gravel. A plaice can change its colour and patterns to blend in with its background. A hormone is secreted which alters the shape of the pigment cells thus changing the colour of the plaice's body.

Living magic carpet

Plaice live on sandy, gravelly or muddy bottoms, slightly buried, swimming just off the bottom at intervals through the day and night. They are said to be demersal or bottom-living fishes. They swim with vertical undulations of the flattened body, like a living magic carpet, then, holding the body rigid, they glide down. On touching bottom they undulate the fins to disturb sand or mud, which then settles on the fins, disguising the outline of the body. In this position a plaice breathes with a suction-pump action of the gill-covers.

Young plaice seem to go into a state resembling hibernation in winter. They remain quiescent in shallow water, slightly buried in the sand. At the appropriate time they move from shallow to deeper water.

Chisel and grinder

The teeth in the jaws of a plaice are chisel-like, but the throat teeth are blunt crushers. The food is mainly small molluscs but other small bottom-living invertebrates, such as worms, are eaten. Plaice swim over the shore at high tide to feed on the cockle and mussel beds. They hunt by sight not raising the head much off the bottom, but shooting forward horizontally with great accuracy to take the prey. Very small molluscs are

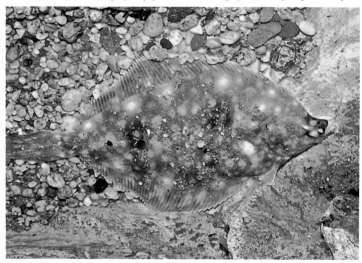

taken whole into the stomach. Larger ones are crushed by the throat teeth. They also bite off the siphons of molluscs or the heads of worms sticking out of tubes.

Prolific spawnings

There is little in their outward appearance to tell male from female, but if at any time they are held up to the light the female roe shows as a small dark triangle. The male roe is a curved rounded line. The males reach the spawning grounds first and are still there after the females have gone. Spawning time differs from one part of the sea to another. Off the east coast of Scotland it is

from early January to May, with a peak in March. In the Clyde estuary, on the west coast of Scotland, it is from February to June. In the southern North Sea it is from October to March.

To spawn, two plaice swim about $2\frac{1}{2}$ ft off the bottom, the female lying diagonally across the male, releasing a stream of eggs while he emits a stream of milt. Spawning lasts less than a minute, after which the two separate and return to the bottom. Each female lays 50–400 thousand eggs, the number depending, it seems, on the length of the fish. The transparent eggs, each in a tough capsule, are just under $\frac{1}{12}$ in. diameter.

They float at or near the surface, and many are eaten before they can hatch, which they do in 8–21 days, according to the temperature of the water. The larvae are about ¼ in. long, without mouth or gills, and with the remains of a yolk sac attached which supplies them with food. This is the most vulnerable part of the life of a plaice. Apart from those eaten by other animals only 1 in every 100 thousand survive the first few weeks of larval life, or 2–5 for every pair of parent plaice. Although this seems disastrous the figures are put in perspective by the knowledge that in one area alone, halfway between the mouth of the Thames and the coast of Holland, 60 million plaice come together each year to spawn. The adults are probably protected by their colour and their habit of lying buried, but seals find them, and predatory fishes, such as cod, eat the small ones.

Plaice are of great economic value but of the tens of millions of plaice eaten each year in Europe, few are eaten at the right moment. Plaice has the best flavour when it is cooked immediately after being caught. The sole however, develops its characteristic taste 2–3 days after death due to the decomposition of the flesh with the formation of different chemical substances.

Baby food

As the contents of the yolk sac are being used up, the larval plaice starts to feed on diatoms. At this stage it has the normal fish

larva shape, giving no indication of the adult shape to come. As it grows it graduates from small diatoms to larger diatoms then to larvae of small crustaceans, such as copepods, and molluscs. At this stage an important item is the planktonic food *Oikopleura*. After 2 months the larva gradually metamorphoses into a young flatfish, this takes about 2½ weeks. The body becomes flattened from side to side, the young plaice starts swimming on its side, the skull becomes twisted by growing more quickly on one side than the other, causing the left eye to be swung over to the right side. At the same time the young plaice leaves the upper waters for the seabed, settling on its left side, so its right side and both eyes are uppermost. As these changes have been taking place the young plaice (still only ½ in. long) has been carried by currents to its inshore nursery ground.

The account given above of the feeding of the larvae is only a generalization. The food taken varies in different places, the plaice taking whatever is available. In Scottish coastal waters they eat mainly worm larvae, crustacean eggs and larval molluscs. Off Plymouth, copepods and other small crustaceans are eaten, in the Irish Sea the larvae feed on small copepods, and spores of algae, and in southern North Sea it is mainly *Oikopleura*. The survival of the larvae can be seriously affected if supplies of these foods are low in the area where they form the staple diet of the larvae.

How they grow

After the ½in. young plaice has settled on the bottom it reaches 2¾ in. by the age of 1 year, 5 in. by 2 years, nearly 8 in. by 3 years, 10½ in. by 4 years and 13 in. by 5 years of age. These figures are for females, the males being smaller. On average, the males reach sexual maturity in 2–3 years, the females in 4–5 years. The figures must be read as approximations because average sizes of plaice have been found to vary: 17 in. in the North Sea, 15 in. in the English Channel, 13 in. in the Kattegat and 10 in. in the Baltic. These are, again, merely examples to show how size can vary, with environmental conditions. A 2ft plaice is 20 or more years old, and a 33in. plaice, which is one of the largest recorded, would be about 40 years old.

class	**Pisces**
order	**Pleuronectiformes**
family	**Pleuronectidae**
genus & species	***Pleuronectes platessa***

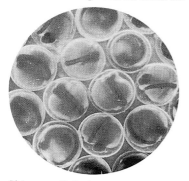

Plaice eggs with developing embryos.

Larva lives in plankton, off its yolk sac.

As yolk sac is used up the mouth develops.

Like many marine fishes the plaice lays a large number of eggs to offset heavy predation. The dramatic part of the life cycle occurs after 2 months in preparation for life on the seabed. The body becomes flattened from side to side; the skull is twisted by growing more quickly on one side than the other, causing the left eye to migrate to the right side; then the young plaice settles with both eyes uppermost.

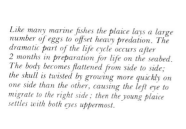

Left eye migrates as larva swims on its side.

Eye migration complete, plaice settles on bottom.

41

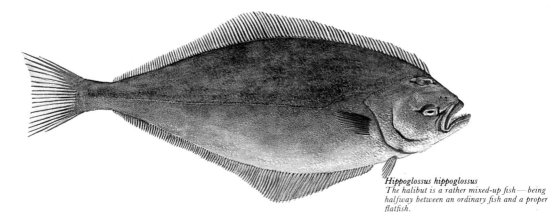

Hippoglossus hippoglossus
The halibut is a rather mixed-up fish—being halfway between an ordinary fish and a proper flatfish.

Halibut

The halibut is little more than halfway between an ordinary fish and a thorough-going flatfish. It is longer in the body and more plump than most flatfishes, such as the plaice and the flounder. Its jaws have kept their original shape instead of being distorted, with one jaw weaker than the other, and they are armed with sharp teeth. The fringing fins (dorsal and anal) are somewhat triangular and the tail and tail fin are well-marked and powerful. The upper surface, which is in fact the right side, is uniformly olive brown, dark brown or black, the underside being pearly white.

There are two species, one in the North Atlantic, the other in the North Pacific. Exceptional heavy-weights have reached a length of 12 ft and a weight of 700 lb. Small halibut live inshore but, as they mature, move into deeper waters, onto sandy banks for preference, at depths of 1 200 ft or more.

Matching its background

A halibut lies on the seabed where it can pass unnoticed by its prey because of its colour. It leaves the bottom to chase after smaller fishes. Most flatfishes swim by undulations of their fringing fins, but halibut do so by vigorous movements of the body and the powerful tail. While on the bottom the halibut's upper side is coloured like the seabed. Lying on mud a halibut will be black. If it moves onto a patch of sand it begins to grow pale. One with its head on a patch of sand and its body on mud will have a pale head and a black body. These changes are governed through the eyes. A flatfish blinded by injury remains the same colour whatever it is lying on. If we watch a flatfish in an aquarium we see the eyes standing well out on the head, each moving independently of the other, and commanding a view of the bottom all around its head.

Bludgeoning its prey?

Halibut eat crabs, molluscs, worms and other bottom-living invertebrates, but their main food is fishes, especially herring, also flounder, cod, skate, and many others. The fish evidently has a reputation as a killer with fishermen. Dr GB Goode, former Commissioner of Fisheries in the United States, has stated that fishermen declare a halibut kills other fishes with blows of its tail. Whether this is true or not, it tells us something of what fishermen think of the halibut.

Floating eggs

Spawning takes place in the Atlantic during May to July at depths of about 1 200 ft. The Pacific halibut spawns in winter at depths of 900 ft. The female roe is large. In a 250lb fish it may be 2 ft long and weigh 40 lb. A mature female may lay 2¾ million eggs, each ⅛ in. diameter and buoyant, so they float to the surface. The eggs hatch in a few days, the baby fish being the usual fish shape at first, with an eye on each side of the head. It remains at the surface and is carried by currents to inshore waters. After a while the left eye begins to migrate over the top of the head until it comes to lie close to the right eye. At the same time the young halibut turns more and more on to its left side while the dorsal and anal fins grow longer to become the fringing fins. As these changes are taking place the fish is sinking towards the bottom finally to rest on it, left side down. In about one in 5 000 it is the right eye that migrates and the fish then comes to rest on the right side. Until it comes to rest the young halibut is transparent, then it changes colour to become brown or black on the upper side. The halibut is fairly long-lived. One 4 ft long will be about 12 years old, and as much as 35 years of age has been recorded.

Evolution of flatfishes

In the Indian Ocean is one flatfish of the genus *Psettodes* that is more like sea perch to look at. The migrating eye stops short on top of the head, the dorsal fin begins farther back than in other flatfishes and both dorsal and anal fins have spiny instead of soft rays. They rest on their side on the bottom and, like the halibut, swim up to catch prey. Some sea perches also lie

on their sides on the bottom to rest, although their shape is normal, and they and *Psettodes* suggest how the flatfish condition probably arose during the course of evolution.

Enemies of halibut?

There are few details known about the enemies of halibut but we can be reasonably sure, by comparison with what is known about other fishes laying huge numbers of eggs, that there is a heavy loss of eggs, fry and young. Later, the growing halibut will suffer from fish-eaters among other species of fish, doubtless also from porpoises, dolphins and seals. There is a steady drain on their numbers from commercial fisheries, halibut being taken by trawl and long line.

Name is mediaeval

Halibut must have been fished for a very long time since the name dates from mediaeval times. It is believed to mean holy turbot, from the Scandinavian word *butta* used for turbot. Captain John Smith, founder of Virginia, wrote of 'the large sized Halibut, or Turbot', and followed this with the strange remark that some are so big 'that the fisher men onley eat the heads & fins, and throw away the bodies'. Later, the halibut became known as the workhouse fish. This may have been a term of contempt or a reference to the fact that one halibut could be large enough to feed many hungry mouths. The fish finally came into its own, not only for the table but for medicinal purposes, in the present century. As we know, the cod was finally recognized in the 1920s as a supplier of cod liver oil for medicinal purposes. A decade or so later halibut oil became popular and almost displaced cod liver oil.

class	**Pisces**	
order	**Pleuronectiformes**	
family	**Pleuronectidae**	
genus	***Hippoglossus hippoglossus***	
& species	*Atlantic halibut*	
	H. stenolepis *Pacific halibut*	

Anglerfishes

There are more than 350 species of anglerfish, the Pediculati, but because of the distinct differences between them it is convenient to consider them as two groups: anglerfishes (225 + species) and deep-sea anglers (125 species). All have developed the characteristic habits of anglers: they keep still most of the time, using a rod and line to catch small fishes. The rod of the anglerfish is a modified spiny ray of the dorsal fin. Habitual immobility means little expenditure of energy, and less need for breathing. This is reflected in the small gills of anglerfishes with only a small gill-opening.

'Pediculati', the old name for anglerfishes, means 'small foot', referring to the elbowed pectoral fins used like feet to move over the seabed in short jumps. The pelvic fins are also somewhat foot-like but they are small, usually hidden on the undersurface in advance of the pectoral fins. Because of their squat shape, bottom-living habits and method of locomotion the anglerfishes have been given a variety of descriptive vernacular names: goosefishes or monkfishes, frogfishes or fishing frogs (because of the wide mouth) and batfishes. One of the best-known is **Lophius piscatorius**, up to 4ft. long with a large head, about 2½ ft across, and a wide mouth. Although the fish is so ugly the flesh is highly palatable and is widely used as fried fish.

Camouflaged and immobile

Anglerfishes of one kind or another are found at all depths throughout tropical and temperate seas. Bottom-living for the most part, their bodies are ornamented with a variety of warts and irregularities, as well as small flaps of skin. These, with their usually drab colours arranged in a broken pattern, serve to camouflage the fish as it lies immobile among rocks and seaweed. The sargassum angler specializes more than most anglerfishes in camouflage. It lives exclusively among the weed of the Sargasso Sea, and uses its pectoral fins to grasp the weed, so that it is not easily shaken from its position.

Angling for food

The general method of feeding is to attract small fishes near the mouth with some form of lure. In the goosefishes or monkfishes this is a 'fishing rod' bearing a fleshy flap at its tip, which is waved slowly back and forth near the mouth. In others the rod lies hidden, folded back in a groove, or lying in a tube, and is periodically raised or pushed out and waved two or three times before being withdrawn. The lure at the end of the rod often is red and worm-like in shape. A small fish seeing it swims near and then suddenly disappears!

Breeding

Several deep-sea species of anglerfish show a peculiar relationship between male and

Anglerfish's body is camouflaged by flaps of skin resembling surrounding seaweeds.

Small fishes attracted to the anglerfish's mouth by a lure are snapped up. (⅓ natural size.)

female; the dwarf male, about ½in. long, attaches itself to the female (whose length is up to 45 in.) so securely that the two grow together, even sharing a blood system. The female is then, in effect, a self-fertilising hermaphrodite, the male being reduced to a mere sperm-producing organ.

Another outstanding feature of the breeding cycle of some anglerfishes is the size of the egg-masses. The female goosefish or monkfish lays eggs in a jelly-like mass, up to 40 ft long and 2 ft in width. This floats at the surface. The relatively large pear-shaped eggs are attached by the narrow end to a sheet of spawn, which floats at the surface, and may contain nearly 1½ million of them. The larva, even before it leaves the egg, begins to develop black pigment. Seen from above the spawn appears as a dark patch in the water, the enclosed larvae looking like currants in a cake. One of these masses, seen by rowers in a boat off Scapa Flow, was mistaken for a sea-monster and the rowers pulled away from it for dear life! The larva is in an advanced stage when hatched and already has the beginnings of its fishing rod. Later, other spines develop on the back and branched fins grow down from the throat, so the larva looks very unusual.

The compleat angler

It is an interesting pastime to list how many human inventions have been anticipated in the animal kingdom. Anglerfishes have used a rod and line (or a lure) long before man did. It is not surprising that both human and fish anglers should use similar methods because their aims are identical. But although attention is always drawn to this by writers on the subject, nobody seems to have commented on the other piece of apparatus the two have in common: the landing net. Both kinds of anglers play their fish but the anglerfish does not allow his quarry to take the bait. Instead, the lure is waved until a fish draws near, then it is lowered towards the mouth. As the victim closes in on it the rod and its lure is suddenly whipped away, the huge mouth is opened wide, water rushes into this capacious 'landing net' and the prey is sucked in, after which the mouth snaps shut. And it all takes place in a flash. Only when a fish is large, so that the tail protrudes

from the mouth after the first bite, can we see what has happened. The anglerfish's ability to snap up its prey like lightning is quite remarkable. One moment the small fish is there near its mouth, the next moment it is no longer there, and the speed with which the anglerfish moves its jaws is too fast for the human eye to follow.

The batfishes take their angling to even greater lengths. The whiskery batfish, of the Caribbean, for example, is covered with outgrowths of skin that look exactly like small seaweeds and polyps known as seafire, that coat rocks like so much moss. Small fishes are deceived to the point where they will swim near and try to nibble the flaps of skin. The final touch to this masterpiece of deception lies in the batfish habit of gently rocking its body, making the flaps of skin sway from side to side, just as polyps and seaweed gently sway as the slow currents in the sea move back and forth. This is so much an ingrained habit that a batfish, removed from its surroundings and placed in an aquarium, will periodically rock itself even although it is surrounded only by clear water and glass.

When the small fish, deceived in this way, swims near, out comes the rod with its lure, looking like a wriggling worm. With this the batfish 'plays' its quarry. It will dangle the lure in front of the fish then withdraw it to entice the little fish nearer. It will vary the wriggling of the lure, now waggling it in an agitated manner, now moving it slowly. Watching this one gets the impression of a fish 'playing cat-and-mouse' with a smaller fish until – 'snap' – and only the larger fish can be seen, motionless, and with a dead-pan expression.

class	**Pisces**	
order	**Lophiiformes**	
families	**Lophiidae** *anglerfishes*	
	Antennariidae *frogfishes*	
	Ogcocephalidae *batfishes*	

Amphibians and Reptiles

For reasons it would be difficult to define the custom has grown up of always speaking of amphibians and reptiles in one breath, as if the two must always be linked. Yet there is almost as much of a gulf between the living representatives of these two groups as between, say, birds and mammals. The features they have in common are that they are cold-blooded, air-breathing vertebrates typically living on land. The main differences between them are that amphibians, with rare exceptions, have a smooth scaleless skin whereas reptiles are scaly and that amphibians must go to water, or at least to a damp spot and this only exceptionally, to breed, whereas all reptiles have to come on land to lay their eggs.

The word 'amphibian' means more or less literally 'double life'. The typical amphibian spends the first part of its life in water and its adult life on land. There are plenty of exceptions to this, as there are to virtually every general statement made about living organisms. There are both salamanders and occasional toads that live their whole lives in water, examples being the salamander known as the olm and the Surinam toad. Conversely, there are frogs, the Stephens Island frog of New Zealand being one, that lay their eggs on land. The Stephens Island frog lives among boulders and its eggs are laid on damp earth. From them hatch fully formed froglets, the tadpole stage having been passed within the egg membrane.

The word 'reptile' is from the Latin *reptare* to creep and (very conveniently) *repere* to crawl. Therefore they should be, in fact, the 'creepy-crawlies' of modern vernacular, although this in practice embraces more commonly such creatures as centipedes, earthworms and slugs. Among reptiles the true creepers are the snakes and the few lizards, like the slow-worms, that are also legless. Tortoises and turtles may be said to crawl but most reptiles can employ a respectable walk, even a run, and it would tax the imagination to see in the Komodo dragon of today or the giant dinosaurs of past ages anything approaching a creepy-crawly.

Perhaps our habit of linking amphibians and reptiles dialectically is because of an intuitive feeling that both played an important part in the early colonization of the land masses by vertebrates. Among the diverse forms to emerge from among the multitudinous bony fishes were those that could breathe both by lungs and by gills. They were amphibious, and since they also had fins approximating to limbs, they could spend much time on land. There can be little doubt that it was from such pioneering fishes that the amphibians sprang.

The first fossil amphibians are found in the Lower Carboniferous rocks, 300 million years old. They are tailed amphibians of the type represented today by salamanders and newts. Tailless amphibians, the frogs and toads, did not appear for another 150 million years, in the Jurassic period. Meanwhile the first reptiles had put in an appearance in the Upper Carboniferous, and by the time frogs and toads had evolved reptiles were dominant on land and continued so into the Cretaceous period that followed, a period that was to become known as the Age of Reptiles.

The transition from an air-breathing fish to an undoubted amphibian is shown in one of the most complete series of fossils. A slightly less perfect series illustrates the development of reptiles from amphibian ancestors, but the indications that this was the true course of events are indisputable.

It is a common failing to think of the Age of Reptiles as including only the giant reptiles, the dinosaurs on land, the pterodactyls in the air and the plesiosaurs and ichthyosaurs in the water. In fact there were numerous other reptiles, small, medium and large, including the Rhynchocephalia, of which the tuatara is the only surviving representative, and the crocodiles and turtles, some of which also reached giant size. The lizards and snakes, by far the most numerous reptiles, came later, but meanwhile some groups of early reptiles had developed a temperature control and were partially warm-blooded (homoiothermic). One group gave rise to birds, the other to mammals, around 200 million years before the reptiles themselves achieved their domination in the Age of Reptiles.

The classification of Amphibians and Reptiles is as follows:

CLASS AMPHIBIA   3,000 species
Order Caudata or Urodela
  (salamanders, newts)
Order Anura or Salientia
  (frogs and toads)

CLASS REPTILIA   6,000 species
Order Rhynchocephalia (tuatara)
Order Crocodilia (crocodiles, alligators)
Order Testudines (tortoises, turtles)
Order Squamata
  suborder Sauria (lizards)
  suborder Serpentes (snakes)

Caecilian

The caecilian is a limbless amphibian with a long cylindrical body marked with rings, living wholly underground. The 158 species are worm-like or snake-like according to size, the smallest caecilian being only 4½ in. long, the largest, 4½ ft. Their colour is usually blackish but may be pale flesh-colour. The skin is smooth and slimy, but unlike that of other amphibians, it has small scales embedded in it, in most species, sometimes covered with skin, and usually useless. There is a peculiar sensory organ; a tentacle on each side of the head lies in a groove running from eyes to tip of snout.

As in snakes, one lung is large and long, the other is reduced to a small lobe.

Caecilians live in warm regions, in America from Mexico to northern Argentina, in southern and south-east Asia and in the Seychelles and parts of Africa. They live from sea-level to about 6 000 ft.

Ancient burrower

Caecilians are the sole surviving relatives of the earliest land animals, large fossil amphibians which roamed the earth 400 million years ago. Burrows are made in soft earth, and caecilians seldom come above ground except when heavy rain floods the burrows. One species, at least, is aquatic, and a few species live in leaf litter which is found on the floor of rain forests.

Feeding

Little is known for certain but earthworms are probably the main diet for most species, and a few may eat termites. The sticky caecilian, of southeast Asia, the best-known species, also eats small burrowing snakes.

They themselves are eaten by certain large burrowing snakes.

Life history

There is no difference between male and female externally. Fertilisation is internal and some species lays eggs, others bear live young.

More is known of the life history of the 15 in. sticky caecilian, the female of which lays some two dozen eggs, each about ¼ in. in diameter, connected in a jelly-like string. They are laid in a burrow near water, the female coiling her body around the egg-mass until they hatch. The larvae, which escape to water, have a breathing pore on either side of the head. This leads into internal gills, connected with the throat, as in fishes. External gills, present in the embryo, are lost before hatching. They have normal eyes, a flattened tail for swimming, and a head like a newt. At the end of its larval life the breathing pores close, lungs are developed and the young caecilian lives permanently on land, burrowing underground.

The aquatic species of caecilian has sometimes been observed swimming in an eel-like fashion.

Three-way links

The first mention of a caecilian was by Seba, in 1735, when he described it as a snake. Linnaeus, in 1754, also included it among the snakes. In 1811, Oppel put caecilians with frogs, toads and salamanders as amphibians, but these were generally regarded as reptiles as late as 1859. Then came a change, and the caecilians were thought to be degenerate salamanders. From 1908 on there followed studies of the anatomy, and it gradually became clear that caecilians provided an interesting link with the past.

Even now our knowledge of the caecilians is not extensive. They have always been regarded as rare animals, although it is now known that they are plentiful enough in suitable habitats. Yet, as with all animals living wholly underground, it is hard to find out anything about their way of life. What we can do, however, is study how they are made, and this is important, because it tells us that caecilians are a link with the large extinct amphibians that lived nearly 400 million years ago. Their large footprints are known from the Devonian rocks and their skeletons from the rocks of the next geological period, the Carboniferous (Coal Age). After that there is no trace of them, so they seem to have died out 300 million years ago. Some were crocodile-like, lived on land in the marshes where the coal measures were laid down, and they started life as aquatic larvae. They seemed to have been the first backboned animals to live permanently on land, and they almost certainly evolved from air-breathing fishes, the lobe-finned fishes which were the ancestors of the amphibians.

These ancient amphibians gave rise not only to the present-day amphibians but also to the reptiles. They link, therefore, the fishes, amphibians and reptiles, and the caecilians seem to be their direct surviving descendants. This relationship is seen not only in the degenerate scales found in the caecilian skin but also in the caecilian skull being so like that of these giant amphibians of 400 million years ago. It will be interesting to see if any fossil caecilians are found in the future and to compare them with the present day order. As yet no fossil caecilians have been found.

class	**Amphibia**
order	**Apoda or Gymnophiona**
family	**Caeciliidae**
genera	*Caecilia, Typhlonectes, Ichthyophis, others*

*Feeding habits of many caecilians are still unknown, but earthworms are probably important in their diet, as in this species **Siphonops annulatus.***

Newt

Newts are amphibians of the salamander family. They have a life history very similar to that of frogs and toads in that the adults spend most of their life on land but return to water to breed. They are different in form, however, having long, slender bodies like those of lizards with a tail that is flattened laterally. The name comes from the Anglo-Saxon **evete** which became **ewt** and finally a newt from the transcription of the 'n' in an **ewt**. In Britain, newt refers solely to the genus **Triturus** but in North America it has been applied to related animals which are sometimes, confusingly, called salamanders.

Newts of the genus **Triturus** are found in Europe, Asia, North Africa and North America. There are three species native to Britain. The most common is the smooth newt which is found all over Europe and is the only newt found in Ireland. The maximum length of smooth newts is 4 in. The colour of the body varies, but is mainly olive-brown with darker spots on the upper side and streaks on the head. The vermilion or orange underside has round black spots and the throat is yellow or white. The female is generally paler on the underside than the male and sometimes is unspotted. In the breeding season the male develops a wavy crest running along the back and tail. The palmate newt is very similar to the smooth newt, but about 1 in. shorter and with a square-sided body. In the breeding season the males of the two species can be told apart because black webs link the toes of the hindfeet of the palmate newts, and its crest is not wavy. In addition, the tail ends abruptly and a short thread, about $\frac{1}{8} - \frac{1}{4}$ in. long protrudes from the tip. The largest European newt is the crested or warty newt. It grows up to 6 in. long. The dark grey skin of the upperparts is covered with warts, while the underparts are yellow or orange and spotted with black. The distinguishing feature apart from its size is the crest of the male. From the head to the hips runs a tall, 'toothed' frill —its crest, which becomes the tail fin.

▽ A male smooth newt with its spotted front, as seen from below.

Hibernating on land

When they come out of hibernation in spring, newts make their way to ponds and other stretches of still water where water plants grow. They swim by lashing with their tails, but they spend much of their time resting on the mud or among the stems of plants. They can breathe through their skins but every now and then they rise to the surface to gulp air. Adult newts do not leave the water immediately breeding has finished but remain aquatic until July or August. When they come on land the crest is reabsorbed and the skin becomes rougher. The crested newt keeps its skin moist from the numerous mucus glands scattered over the surface of its body. A few individuals stay in the water all the year round, retaining their smooth skins and crests.

Hibernation begins in the autumn, when the newts crawl into crevices in the ground or under logs and stones. They cannot burrow but are very adept at squeezing themselves into cracks. Occasionally several will gather together in one place and hibernate in a tight mass.

Two rows of teeth

The jaws of newts are lined with tiny teeth and there are two rows of teeth on the roof of the mouth. These are not used for cutting food or for chewing but merely to hold slippery, often wriggling, prey. They feed on a variety of small animals such as worms, snails and insects when on land, and crustaceans, tadpoles and insect larvae while living in water. Unlike frogs and toads, newts do not use their hands to push the food into their mouths, but gulp it down with convulsive swallows. Snails are swallowed whole, caddis flies are eaten in their cases and crested newts eat smooth newts.

Internal fertilisation

The mating habits of newts are quite different from those of common frogs and common toads. Fertilisation is internal and is effected in a most unusual way. The male stimulates the female into breeding condition by nudging her with his snout and lashing the water with his tail. He positions himself in front of or beside her, bends his tail double and vibrates it rapidly, setting up vibrations in the water. The female is also stimulated by secretions from glands in the male's skin. At the end of the courtship the male emits a spermatophore which sinks to the bottom. The female newt positions herself over it, then picks it up with her cloaca by pressing her body onto it.

After fertilisation the 200–300 eggs are usually laid singly on the leaves of water plants, although some American newts lay their eggs in spherical clusters. The female newt tests the leaves by smell and touch. When she has chosen a suitable one she holds it with her hindfeet, then folds the leaf over to form a tube and lays an egg in it. The jelly surrounding the egg glues the leaf firmly in place to protect it.

The eggs hatch in about 3 weeks and a more streamlined tadpole than that of a frog or toad emerges. It is not very different from the adult newt except that it has a frill of gills and no legs. Development takes longer than in frog tadpoles but the young newts are ready to emerge by the end of summer. A few spend the winter as tadpoles, remaining in the pond until spring, even surviving being frozen into the ice.

Unpleasant secretion

Newts have many enemies: the young are eaten by aquatic insects and the adults by fishes, water birds, weasels, rats, hedgehogs and many other animals. The crested newt has an unpleasant secretion that is produced in the glands on the back and tail and is exuded when they are squeezed. Grass snakes are known to be dissuaded from eating crested newts because of this.

Newt's nerve poison

The poison of the crested newt is not only unpleasant, but men who have tasted it have found it to be burning. A far more potent poison is that of the California newt. The poison is found mainly in the skin, muscles and blood of the newt, as well as in its eggs. Analysis showed that the poison is a substance called tetrodotoxin, which is also found in puffer fish. Tetrodotoxin extracted from newts' eggs is so powerful that $\frac{1}{5000}$ oz. can kill 7 000 mice. It acts on the nerves, preventing impulses from being transmitted to the muscles. Somehow, in a manner that is not understood, California newts are not affected by their own posion. Their nerves still function when treated with a solution of tetrodotoxin 25 000 times stronger than that which will completely deaden a frog's nerves.

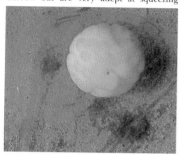

△ *Left: Segmenting embryo of a crested newt. Right: The legless tadpole of the crested newt.*
▽ *Alpine newt* **Triturus alpestris.**

class	**Amphibia**	
order	**Caudata**	
family	**Salamandridae**	
genera & species	***Taricha torosa*** *California newt*	
	Triturus cristatus *crested newt*	
	T. helveticus *palmate newt*	
	T. vulgaris *smooth newt*	
	others	

Common toad

Despite a superficial resemblance to the common frog, few people have difficulty in recognising a common toad, even if they recoil in horror on seeing it. It has a flatter back and relatively shorter legs. Instead of the moist, bright skin of the frog, the toad has a dull, wrinkled, pimply skin. Its movements are slow and grovelling, and, although it can jump a short distance on all fours, it usually walks laboriously over the ground.

The rough skin blends well with the earth, so a toad can easily be over-looked as a clod of earth. This impression is heightened by the dark

Common toads mating.

brown or grey colouring which can change, although only a little and slowly, to match the surroundings, becoming almost red in a sand pit, for instance. Its jewel-like eyes are golden or coppery-red, and behind them lie the bulges of the parotid glands that contain an acrid, poisonous fluid.

Male toads measure about 2½ in. and the females 1 in. longer.

The common toad ranges over Europe, north and temperate Asia and North Africa.

Hibernating toads

The common toad, like the common frog, hibernates from October to February, but in drier places. Dry banks and disused burrows of small mammals are chosen, and hibernating toads are sometimes found in cellars and outhouses. In the spring they migrate to breeding pools, preferring deeper water than frogs. Where the two are found in the same ponds, the frogs will be in the shallows and the toads in the middle.

The migrations of these toads are more spectacular. Toads give the impression of being slower movers and the migration route becomes littered with the remains of toads that have fallen foul of enemies. The route is especially well marked where it crosses a road and passing cars have run over the toads.

Although the migration may be long and arduous, perhaps covering 2 or 3 miles at

a rate of $\frac{3}{4}$ mile in 24 hours, the toads are very persistent, and laboriously climb stone walls and banks.

Outside the breeding season toads live in hollows scooped out by the hindlegs. In soft earth they bury themselves completely, otherwise the hole is made under a log or stone. These homes are usually permanent, the toad returning to the same place day after day. One toad was recorded as living under a front-door step for 36 years until it was attacked by a raven. Occasionally the retreats may be in places that must cost the toad some effort to reach. One is known to have made its home in a privet hedge, 4 ft above the ground, and others have been found in birds' nests.

Every now and then there are stories of toads being found in even odder places. Quarrymen and miners tell of splitting open a rock or lump of coal revealing a cavity in which lies a toad that leaps out hale and

with glass plates. The toads in the compact sandstone soon died but the ones in the porous limestone lived for a year or more. These rather macabre experiments suggest that the toads found in rocks and tree trunks could not have been there for long. It is most likely that either they had crawled into a crack or cavity which had later been filled in, or perhaps the miner or quarryman had hit a rock that happened to have a cavity in, thereby causing a toad hidden nearby to leap out suddenly, so creating the impression that it had come out of the hole.

Prey must be moving

At night and during wet weather, toads come out to feed on many kinds of small animals, but they must be moving because toads' eyes are adapted to react to moving objects. Any insect or other small invertebrate is taken, ants being especially favoured, and the stomach of one toad was found to

Spawn in strings

There is little to distinguish the breeding habits of common frogs and common toads. Both breed at roughly the same time of year and may be seen in the same pools. Male toads start arriving before the females but later the males may arrive already in amplexus on the females' backs. There is no external vocal sac and, unlike many of its relatives, a male common toad has a very weak croak.

The spawn is laid in strings rather than in a mass. The eggs are embedded three or four deep in threads of jelly that may be up to 15 ft long. Each female lays 3–4 thousand eggs, which are smaller than those of a frog, being less than $\frac{1}{16}$ in. in diameter. The jelly swells up but the spawn does not float, because it is wrapped round the stems of water plants.

The eggs hatch in 10–12 days and the tadpoles develop in the same manner as

The coppery-golden eye of the toad, its most attractive feature, shown with pupil expanded (left) and contracted (right).

hearty. Another story is told of two sawyers working in a saw pit, some 90 years ago. They were sawing the trunk of an oak into planks when they noticed blood dripping out of the wood. Examination revealed the now grisly remains of a toad in a cavity in the trunk. In every story there is speculation as to how the toads came to be imprisoned. It is hardly likely that they were trapped when the coal or rock was first formed millions of years ago, as was once believed. They could not have lived that long, as was shown by the following experiments performed over a century ago. Holes were drilled in blocks of sandstone and limestone, toads put in and the holes sealed

contain 363 ants. Some distasteful animals such as burnet moth caterpillars or caterpillars covered with stiff hairs are left well alone, but toads are known to sit outside beehives in the evening and catch the workers as they come back home. Snails are crunched up and earthworms are pushed into the mouth by the forefeet which also scrape excess earth off them. Young newts, frogs, toads and even slowworms and grass snakes are eaten. One toad had five newly-hatched grass snakes in its stomach, while another had the head of an adder in its mouth. Toads will often return to a favourite retreat after hunting and will use the same home for years.

frog tadpoles, becoming shiny, black, $\frac{1}{4}$ in. toadlets in about 3 months. Sexual maturity is reached in 4 years, before the toads are fully grown.

Poisonous toads

Toads suffer from all the enemies to which frogs fall prey, despite the poisonous secretions of the parotid glands. The poison is certainly effective against dogs, that salivate copiously after mouthing a toad, and show all the signs of distress.

Toads react more strongly to danger signals than frogs do, possibly because, not being leapers, they are more vulnerable and need added protection from enemies. One

Strings of spawn rope through the water during mating, to be wrapped around the stems of water plants and convenient pebbles.

reaction is to inflate the lungs more than usual, so increasing the volume of the body by as much as 50%. Snakes, their chief enemies, know fairly accurately when an object is more than they can swallow, but how far the inflated body of the toad deceives them has never been tested.

Unless the snake is only small, the swelling of the toad will make little difference to the outcome if attacked by a constricting or a poisonous snake.

The defence mechanism of the toad of inflating itself against enemies is instinctive. This is seen by the following experiment. Any long cylindrical object, such as a length of thin rubber tubing, moved across its field of vision, will cause it to blow itself up. This reaction becomes progressively weaker when the experiment is repeated, and in a short time no reaction is produced.

In old age, toads fall victim to flesh-eating greenbottle flies, which lay their eggs on them. The larvae then crawl into the nostrils, hampering breathing, and eat their way into the toad's body, eventually killing it.

Many superstitions

Toads are often regarded with horror, and in folklore they generally play an unpleasant role. Their mere presence was said to pollute the soil, but one method of preventing this from happening was to plant rue, which toads could not abide. Without it, tragedies could occur of the kind that befell a mediaeval couple strolling in the garden. The young man plucked some leaves of sage, rubbed his teeth with them and promptly fell dead. His young woman was charged with murder and, to prove her innocence, took the judge and court to the garden to demonstrate what had happened, and fell dead too. The judge suspected the cause and had the sage dug up. There was a toad living in the ground beside it.

By contrast, 'the foule Toad has a faire stone in his heade', as the 16th-century writer John Lyly declared. To obtain this jewel the toad was placed on a scarlet cloth which pleased the toad so much that it cast the stone out. The toadstone was then set in a ring, for it had the valuable property of changing colour in the presence of any poison that an enemy might put in food and drink. It was also effective as a cure for snakebite and wasp-stings.

class	**Amphibia**
order	**Salientia**
family	**Bufonidae**
genus & species	***Bufo bufo***

50

Arrow-poison frog

Arrow-poison frogs are found only in Central and South America where the Indians have long extracted poison from their bodies for use on arrow-heads. Many amphibians have at least a trace of poison in their bodies or secrete poison from glands in the skin, and quite a few can cause a good deal of pain to any human that handles them. Only the arrow-poison frogs and one or two others secrete such a strong poison as to cause rapid death.

Most arrow-poison frogs can be distinguished by the nail-like plate on each toe. Many species are brilliantly coloured. The two-toned arrow-poison frog is brick red with patches of blue-black on its legs. More brilliant is the three-striped arrow-poison frog, which is yellow with stripes of black running lengthways down the head and body and around the limbs. Some species have 'flash colours' which are suddenly exposed as the frog jumps. It is thought that the bright colours, especially the 'flash colours' are warnings to other animals that they are not fit to eat.

A Cuban member of the family, **Sminthillus limbatus** *is the smallest frog in the world, measuring less than ½ in.*

Each female lays only one egg. The egg is large in comparison with the size of the mother's body and is laid in a moist spot on land, the larva completing its development and undergoing metamorphosis before hatching. This particular frog is by no means uncommon and its slow rate of breeding is in striking contrast to most frogs that ensure the perpetuation of the species by laying large numbers of eggs.

Habits

The various species of arrow-poison frogs are found in forests of different parts of Central and South America, some living in trees, others living on the forest floor.

Feeding

Arrow-poison frogs conform to the usual amphibian diet. As adults all amphibians are carnivorous. They take insects or other small invertebrates which are full of protein to restore worn-out tissue, and salts, fats, vitamins, and water needed for their metabolism. They also need carbohydrates which can be rebuilt from surplus protein.

Male carries the tadpoles

There are several peculiar features about the breeding habits of arrow-poison frogs. Courtship or courtship rituals are rare amongst frogs and toads, and the golden arrow-poison frogs, and probably other species, 'play' together for as much as two or three hours. They repeatedly jump at each other, sometimes landing on one another's backs, as if fighting. Following the 'play', the eggs are laid, but there is no 'amplexus', the process in which the male, as in the common frog, perches on the female's back and fertilises the eggs as they

are laid. The female arrow-poison frog lays her eggs on the ground and the male, who has been waiting nearby, comes over and fertilises them.

The absence of amplexus may be linked with the occurrence of the courtship play, because in frogs using amplexus it is often the pressure of the male hugging the female that causes the eggs to be extruded. When there is no amplexus, it may be necessary for another stimulus, in this case leaping about with the male, to initiate egg-laying. Both methods ensure that there is a male present to fertilise the eggs which is the primary purpose of animal courtship.

When the eggs have been fertilised, the male carries them on his back where they become attached to his skin although how this is done remains to be discovered. After they hatch, the tadpoles remain on their father's back, getting no moisture except from rain. Up to twenty tadpoles can be found on one arrow-poison frog, and, as they grow, their father has to seek larger and larger holes in which to rest. Eventually he takes them down to the water and they swim away to lead an independent life.

Predator deterrent

Snakes, predatory birds and some carnivorous mammals will often prey on the majority of frogs. The arrow-poison frogs, however, possess the ultimate deterrent of the animal world—their flash colours give a warning to the predator, not to attempt to eat them because of their poisonous nature, giving the frogs a much safer life in their hazardous jungle existence.

It is very usual for an animal that carries a venom, or is in some other way unpleasant or unpalatable, to be brilliantly coloured in red, yellow or black or in some combination of these colours. Among arrow-poison frogs which are so highly poisonous these colours tend to predominate and are accentuated by the use of flash colours, as we have seen. This makes it even more puzzling that one species, *Dendrobates pumilio* should be dark blue and very difficult to see in the dark forests which are its home. The warning colours, red, yellow and black are very conspicuous, and it is their purpose to be conspicuous, because they are advertising a warning to predators. Yet *Dendrobates pumilio* seems to be doing its best to efface itself although it has eight times more poison in its skin than those arrow-poison frogs that are bright red and very conspicuous.

Self-effacing relative

Although it is usual to speak of the Dendrobatidae as the family of arrow-poison frogs, not all its members are poisonous. It is of interest to compare the case of a Brazilian species *Dendrophryniscus brevipollicatus* with other members of the family being discussed here. Apparently this particular species has no venom or very little of it. It is coloured brown, tan and buff, it lives among the leaf litter of the forest floor, and when molested its flattish body becomes stiff and the front part of the body bends upwards and backwards so that it looks like a dried leaf.

Poison arrows

The Indians of South America are renowned for their use of poisoned-tipped arrows,

△ *Golden arrow-poison frog (*Dendrobates auratus*).*
Overleaf: Arrow-poison frog **Dendrobates leucomelas.** *The poison secreted by these amphibians is so strong it kills very rapidly. Their bright colours give other animals warning of their poisonous nature so they are not eaten.*

which are reputed to cause death if they do no more than scratch the skin of their target. The best known of the poisons is curare, which is extracted from certain plants, but even this is a mild poison compared with that of the arrow-poison frogs. The Indians collect the poison by piercing the frog with a sharp stick, and holding it over a fire. The heat of the fire forces the poison through the skin where it collects in droplets. These are scraped off into a jar. The amount collected from each frog, and its potency, varies with the species. The kokoi frog of Colombia secretes the most powerful poison known. This is a substance called batrachotoxin which has recently been shown to be ten times more powerful than tetrodotoxin, the poison of the Japanese puffer fish which had previously held the record as the most powerful known animal venom. 1/100,000 oz. of batrachotoxin is sufficient to kill a man.

One kokoi frog, only 1 in. long, can supply enough venom to make 50 lethal arrows. But the arrow-poison frogs are now being sought for more peaceful purposes. In the same way as curare has become an important drug because of its muscle-relaxing properties, so the venom of arrow-poison frogs is now being used in the laboratory for studies on the nervous system. It has been found that it acts in the same way as the hormones secreted by the adrenal gland, blocking the transmission of messages between nerves and muscles. Large amounts rapidly cause death, but in tiny doses it could well have medicinal value.

class	**Amphibia**	
order	**Salientia**	
family	**Dendrobatidae**	
genera	*Sminthillus*	
	Dendrobates, Phyllobates	

△ *African bullfrog,* **Pyxicephalus adspersus,** *can puff out its vocal sacs to bellow like a calf.*

△ *With its powerful back legs, the bullfrog can leap over 3 ft. This ability helps in catching its prey; it lies in wait and leaps out on passing prey, catching it while it is in the air.*

Bullfrog

The bullfrog is a large species of North American frog. The adult grows to be about 8 in. long. Its skin is usually smooth like that of a common frog but sometimes it is covered with small tubercles. The colour varies; on the upper parts it is usually greenish to black, sometimes with dark spots, the underparts are whitish with tinges of yellow. The females are browner and more spotted than the males. The best way of telling them apart is by comparing the size of the eye and the eardrum. In females they are equal, but in males the eardrum is larger than the eye.

The natural home of the bullfrog is in the United States, east of the Rockies, and on the northern borders of Mexico. They have also been introduced to the western states of America, as well as to Cuba, Hawaii, British Columbia, Canada.

The bullfrog's damp world

Bullfrogs are rarely found out of the water, except during very wet weather. They like to live near ponds and marshes or slow-flowing streams, lying idly along the water's edge under the shade of shrubs and reeds. In winter they hibernate, near the water, under logs and stones or in holes on the banks. How long they hibernate depends upon the climate. Usually they are the first amphibians in an area to retire and, in the spring, they are the last to emerge. In the northern parts of their range they usually emerge about the middle of May, but in Texas, for example, they may come out in February if the weather is mild enough. In the southern areas of their range they may not bother to hibernate at all.

A voracious appetite

The bullfrog gets most of its food from insects, earthworms, spiders, crayfish and snails. Many kinds of insects are caught including grasshoppers, beetles, flies, wasps and bees. The slow-moving larvae and immobile pupae, as well as the active adults, are taken. The unfortunate dragonfly is usually caught when it is in the middle of laying its eggs.

The bullfrog captures small, active prey like this by lying in wait and then leaping forward as the prey passes. Its tongue flies out by muscular contraction and wraps around the prey like a whiplash wrapping itself around a post. The frog then submerges to swallow its victim.

Its diet of insects, however, is usually supplemented by bigger prey. This can include other frogs and tadpoles and small terrapins and alligators. The bullfrog even eats snakes, including small garter and coral snakes. The fact that it eats these snakes is a measure of its voracity. Garter snakes themselves feed largely on amphibians and coral snakes are venomous. There is one case on record of a 17 in. coral snake being taken by a bullfrog. It can even capture small animals like mice and birds and especially ducklings. Even swallows, flying low over the water, are not safe from its voracious appetite and leaping ability.

Unusual mating call

When the water temperature reaches about 21°C/70°F mating takes place. This can be about February in the south of its range, to June or July in the northern parts. At night the males move out from the banks to call, while the females stay inshore. They join the male only when their eggs are ripe.

Find an empty barrel somewhere and shout into it, as deeply as possible, the word 'rum' and, according to Clifford Pope, the American herpetologist, the hollow, booming sound which will emerge is very like the mating call of the bullfrog. The call has also been described as sounding some-thing like 'jug o' rum' or 'more rum' and the alcoholic allusion is carried a bit further in some parts by referring to the bullfrog as 'the jug o' rum'.

The bullfrog makes this extraordinary sound 3 or 4 times in a few seconds. Then, after an interval of about 5 minutes, it repeats it. The sound is made by air being passed back and forth along the bullfrog's windpipe, from lungs to mouth, with the nostrils closed. Some of the air enters the airsacs in the floor of the mouth and they swell out like balloons and act as resonators, amplifying the sound so that the noise can be heard half a mile away.

After the mating the female bullfrog lays 10—25 thousand eggs which float in a sheet on the surface of the water, in among the water plants. With its envelope of jelly, each egg is just over ½ in. It is black above and white below. The eggs usually hatch within a week of being laid. If the temperature is low, however, they may take 2 years, sometimes more, to change into an adult frog, by which time they are 2–3 in. long. They feed on algae and decaying vegetation with occasional meals of small pond animals. After about another 2 years the young bullfrogs are almost fully grown and are ready to breed.

Many enemies

Both the tadpole bullfrog and the adult have a lot of enemies. Fish, snakes, birds and mammals, such as skunks and raccoons, all take their toll. A particular enemy of the tadpoles is the backswimmer, which grapples with a tadpole, inserts its 'beak' and sucks out the body fluids. All the bullfrog can do to protect itself from any enemy, apart from hiding at the bottom of the pool or stream, is to use its tremendous jumping powers to leap several feet clear.

Man is another enemy of the bullfrog. Men hunt them for their legs which are considered as much of a delicacy as those of the edible frog. In California, where they multiplied rapidly after their introduction half a century ago, limits had to be set on the numbers that could be collected in an attempt to prevent them being wiped out altogether. The usual method of killing them is to search for them after dark, dazzle them with a flashlight and then shoot before they can leap clear.

The jumping-frog

There are many ancient legends about 'jumping-frogs' and how their owners have been double-crossed. Mark Twain tells one of the best versions in a short story about one Jim Smiley of Angel's Camp, Calveras County, California. In the story Jim Smiley catches a frog. He calls it Dan'l Webster. The frog is a terrific jumper and Jim makes a lot of money betting on it in contests with other frogs. Then a stranger arrives in the camp and says that he does not think that Dan'l, the frog, is that good a jumper. He's quite prepared to back his word with 40 dollars. The trouble is that, being a stranger, he does not have a frog. Unwilling to let 40 dollars slip by so easily Jim Smiley goes off to find a frog. He leaves his frog with the stranger.

Eventually the new frog is lined up alongside Dan'l Webster. The starting signal is given and both frogs are prodded. The new frog leaps away. Dan'l Webster doesn't move an inch. The stranger collects his 40 dollars and smugly takes his leave. Jim Smiley is baffled and furious.

He can't imagine what's happened to his champion frog. Maybe it's ill. So he picks it up to have a look.

'Why, bless my oats,' he exclaims, 'if he don't weigh a double handful of shot!' So he turns Dan'l Webster, the champion frog, upside down and out pours a couple of pounds of lead shot.

Mark Twain's story was a roaring success. In 1928 when a celebration was held in Angel's Camp, to mark the paving of the streets, the ceremonies included, naturally, a frog-jumping contest. The winner was an entrant called 'Jumping Frog of the San Joaquin' with a leap of 3 ft 4 in.

The contest became very popular and it is now held every year. Allowances are even made for the unpredictable natures of the frogs. Because the first jump might be short and the second record-breaking the contest is judged on the distance travelled by the frog in three consecutive leaps. The record now stands at over 16 ft. So many entries are attracted every year that a stringent set of rules is enforced. One can surely presume that all entries are weighed before jumping so that competitors are spared the embarrassing experience of Jim Smiley—whose tortured ghost is said still to haunt the arena.

class	**Amphibia**
order	**Salientia**
family	**Ranidae**
genus & species	*Rana catesbeiana* *bullfrog*

54

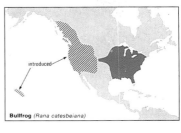

Bullfrog (Rana catesbeiana)

◁◁ *Bullfrog,* **Rana catesbeiana**. *It will take quite large prey including other frogs, small terrapins and alligators, and even coral and garter snakes.*
◁ *Australian bullfrogs,* **Limnodynastes dorsalis**. *The female lays eggs in a mass of jelly which she beats up as the eggs are extruded so the eggs are coated and given protection.*
▽ *The bullfrog rarely leaves the water except during very wet weather. It lives in ponds, marshes or slow-flowing streams, and is often seen lying idly along the water's edge under the shade of reeds and shrubs.*

Mouth-breeding frog

Also known as the vaquero, in Argentina, and as Darwin's frog and Darwin's toad, the mouth-breeding frog is probably the most remarkable of all the amphibians. First discovered by Darwin, it is only 1 in. long and its tadpoles mature to tiny froglets inside the father's vocal sacs.

This midget frog is an inconspicuous greenish brown with darker stripes and patches and a dark line running from behind each eye to the hind end of the body. There are many warts arranged in irregular rows on the body and legs. In front of the large eyes the snout rapidly narrows to a pointed, false nose, the nostrils lying halfway between the eyes and the tip of this 'proboscis'. The front legs are fairly short with long, slender toes, the hindlegs being long as in a normal frog.

The mouth-breeding frog was found by Darwin in the Argentine during his famous **Beagle** *voyage, and has since been found to range through southern Chile as well as southern Argentina.*

Weak voice
The home of this frog is in the beech woods where it hops around in a lively manner, rising well up on its hindlegs before making a short hop forward. The male has a small bell-like voice—weak for the size of the

The mouth-breeding frog was first found by Darwin and so is named after him. It is just over 1 in. long and has a peculiar false nose.

vocal sacs which, as we shall see, have a more important function. These form a large pouch under the throat which extends backwards under the belly to the groin and upwards on each side, almost to the backbone. Inside the mouth is a pair of slits, one on each side, that lead into the vocal sacs, which lie between the skin and the muscles of the body.

Strange nursery
In the breeding season the females lay 20–30 eggs over which the males stand guard for 10–20 days. As the eggs are about to hatch the males pick them up with their tongues, several at a time, and they slide through the slits into the vocal sacs which have now become much swollen. Each male may have anything up to 17 large eggs in his vocal sacs, and quite naturally he now becomes silent. The males do not have to fast while the tadpoles develop. The tadpoles can take no food, however, except for the yolk contained in the eggs which becomes enclosed in their intestines. When about ½ in. long, and with just a stump of a tail left, they leave the vocal sacs. Everything now goes back to normal in the male parent's body. The vocal sacs shrink and his shoulder girdle and internal organs, which had become distorted to make room for the growing tadpoles, go back to their former shape.

The males do not necessarily tend their own offspring; the females lay their eggs in masses and the males take whichever eggs are nearest at the time.

The colouring and patterning of the skin of this tiny frog varies tremendously from one frog to another as pictures 1, 2 and 3 show.

The earliest voice
The first voice in the history of the earth was probably that of a frog, and it may have sounded some 200 million years ago. Plenty of other animals made sounds, the crickets and grasshoppers, for example, as well as many fishes, but a voice-box in the throat came first in the tailless amphibians. Even the tailed amphibians, the salamanders and newts, who can hear, although they were once thought to be deaf, use only a very weak voice, though they have a larynx. By recording the calls of frogs and toads and playing these back to the animals during the breeding season and at other times the value of the voice was discovered. First and foremost, it seems, the voice is used as a mating call. The frogs and toads react most to calls when they are ready to breed. Males move towards any source of calls as a potential breeding site. Once the females have spawned, the voices of the males have no charms for them. So the mouth-breeding males suffer little from having to fall silent, as the females have already spawned. When the voice is used outside the breeding season it is to keep individuals spaced out.

class	**Amphibia**
order	**Salientia**
family	**Rhinodermatidae**
genus & species	***Rhinoderma darwinii***

The tadpoles, picture 4, develop in the swollen vocal sac of the male. This sac is opened, picture 5, showing the tadpoles inside.

1

2

3

4

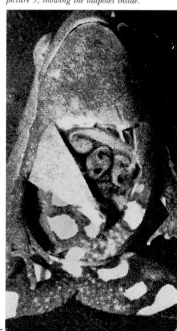

5

Terrapin

The name terrapin is derived from an American Indian word for 'little turtle' and is one of those common words about which there is confusion as to the precise meaning, in the same way as there is confusion about 'turtle' and 'tortoise' (see tortoise, page 59). In Britain 'terrapin' is often used as the name for any small freshwater member of the order Testudines, particularly those kept as pets in aquaria. West of the Atlantic, however, the word has a more restricted meaning and some writers insist that terrapin should refer only to the diamondback terrapin **Malaclemys terrapin**. This is a very sensible idea and will certainly save the confusion that occurs when American natural history books are published in British editions with no explanation of the terms 'turtle', 'tortoise' and 'terrapin', and vice versa. The diamondback terrapin is well known

gastronomically as the basic ingredient of 'Terrapin à la Maryland', and because of its economic importance as food, its biology has been studied in detail. It is so named because of the bold, rhomboidal or whorled markings etched in each plate of the carapace. The small plates that border the carapace like the scalloping on a pie crust, are hollowed and lighter in colour. The plastron is yellow and is speckled and lined with small black dots, as is the skin of the head and limbs. Female diamondback terrapins grow up to 8 in., the males to 6 in. and they weigh up to 2 lb. They range from Cape Cod, Massachusetts to Florida, Texas and Mexico.

Other freshwater turtles or tortoises sometimes known as terrapins, are the red-eared terrapin or pond terrapin **Pseudemys scripta**, the Spanish terrapin **Clemmys leprosa** of Spain, Portugal and North Africa and the geographic or map terrapin **Graptemys geographica** of the St

Lawrence, the Great Lakes and the Missouri. Confusingly, the box turtles of North America are in the genus **Terrapene**.

Salt essential for health
The diamondback terrapin is never found far from the coast and is restricted to brackish waters, such as tidal estuaries and salt marshes, or the sea, where it may be found in bays. It is found up rivers only as far as the tide penetrates. It seems strange that diamondbacks should be restricted to brackish water but if captive terrapins are kept in fresh water they develop a fungus on the skin, which is cured by adding some salt to the water.

Terrapins come onto rocks to bask in the sun but they spend most of their time swimming with their webbed feet. They have the habit of floating with their shells hanging vertically with only the snout showing above water and with the hindfeet slowly moving to keep them steady. During the winter months terrapins hibernate under the mud of their habitat.

The diamondback terrapin, so called from the bold sculpturing of the plates of the carapace, is famous as a delicacy in the southern USA.

Crushed food

Apart from a few water plants, terrapins feed mainly on small animals such as fiddler crabs, periwinkles, insects and worms, which are crushed in the powerful jaws.

Males not always needed

Most of our knowledge of the breeding habits of diamondbacks comes from observations at terrapin farms where they are bred commercially for their flesh. In the wild, however, they lay their eggs in nests not far above the high water mark. The females, and probably the males as well, mature when about 7 years old. They may lay 1–5 clutches a year, younger terrapins laying fewer, and each clutch consists of 7–24 elliptical white eggs, 1½ by ¾ in. The laying season depends on the climate, being from early May to late July in North Carolina. The young hatch in about 90 days.

Observations at terrapin farms showed that female terrapins can lay fertile eggs although they have been separated from males for several years. In one test 10 females laid 124 eggs one year after being separated from males. Only one failed to hatch. After 3 years they laid 130 eggs and 91 failed to hatch but in the fourth year only 4 out of 108 hatched. It seems that the live sperms are stored in the ovaries and it is now known that this also occurs in other turtles and in snakes.

Gourmet's turtle

The diamondback terrapin has had a varied career as human food. During the 18th century it formed a cheap source of food for slaves, then over the course of the 19th century its fortunes changed as some whim of fashion decided its taste was superior to any other turtle. 'Terrapin à la Maryland' is a rich dish of terrapin meat cooked with vegetables, wine and eggs, with sherry added before serving. By 1920 diamondbacks were fetching $90 a dozen. As a result their numbers decreased so protection laws were passed and they were reared artificially. In recent years, however, there has been a decrease both in demand and price for terrapins.

class	**Reptilia**
order	**Testudines**
family	**Emydidae**
genus & species	***Malaclemys terrapin*** *diamondback terrapin*

▽ *Horny lips, goggle eyes and spotted wrinkled chin and throat – close-up of the diamondback terrapin.*

Tortoise

Tortoises are well known for their slowness of movement and for their long life span. They live longer than any other animal today; and they are about the most heavily armoured. There is a difference between American and British usage. In the United States the name 'tortoise' is used only for land-living chelonians belonging to the family Testudinidae. In British usage some water-living chelonians, such as the European pond tortoise, are also given the common name of tortoise.

There are about 40 land tortoises, the best known of which are the so-called garden tortoises and the giant tortoises. Since the way of life of all of them is much the same, most attention will be given here to the Iberian or Algerian tortoise and the Greek or Hermann's tortoise, both garden tortoises. They have high domed shells, up to 1 ft long. The legs are covered with hard scales which often have bony cores and the five toes on the forefoot and the four on the hindfoot all have stout claws. When disturbed a tortoise pulls its head and limbs into the shelter of the bony box covered with horn which is usually spoken of as its shell. The head is completely withdrawn. The front legs are pulled back to make the elbows meet in the middle, protecting the entrance with their scaly skin. The hindlegs and tail are similarly withdrawn, the soles of the hindfeet sealing the entrance.

Tortoises live in tropical and subtropical regions. The Iberian or Algerian tortoise is found in northwest Africa and Spain, the Balkans, Iraq and Iran. The Greek tortoise ranges from southern France through parts of Italy to the Balkans. The star tortoise of southern Asia has pale star-shaped markings on its shell. The gopher tortoises of the southern United States get their name from the French gaufre, a honeycomb, an allusion to their burrowing. There are other land tortoises in southern Asia, Africa, Madagascar and other islands of the Indian Ocean, South America and the Galapagos Islands.

The warmer, the faster
Tortoises live in sandy places or among rocks or in woodlands. They are active by day and generally slow in their movements, yet they can at times reach a speed of 2 mph over short distances. This may be slow compared with the speed of most quadrupeds but it is nearly the walking speed of a man and is faster than we normally consider tortoises' speed. The behaviour of a tortoise is geared to the temperature of the surrounding air. Its movements are faster in warmer temperatures but like other reptiles it is intolerant of the higher air temperatures. Tortoises spend some time every day basking. In

△ A leopard tortoise **Testudo pardalis** about to enjoy a refreshing mouthful of cactus.

temperate latitudes garden tortoises hibernate from October to March, fasting for a while prior to digging themselves into soft earth or under dead vegetation.

Seedlings a favourite meal
It was once widely believed that the smaller tortoises fed on insects and slugs and for this reason people, in England at least, bought tortoises to keep in their gardens. The idea is not yet wholly dead. It may be that a garden tortoise will sometimes eat the smaller garden vermin, but anyone who has seen a tortoise travel along a row of seedlings just showing through the ground will need little convincing that tortoises are wholly or almost exclusively vegetarian, eating low growing vegetation such as seedlings, succulent leaves, flowers and fallen fruits, and only occasionally insects.

Battering ram courtship
Males and females look alike but in most species there is some small difference in shape. In Hermann's tortoise, for example, the plastron, or underside of the shell, is flat in the female, concave in the male. In the Iberian tortoise the tail shield is flat in the female, curved in the male. Another

sign is that a male in breeding condition butts the female in the flank, at the same time hissing slightly. Male garden tortoises, when there is no female around, will butt the shoes of people sitting in the garden or the legs of garden chairs. The female lays 4 – 12 whitish spherical eggs, each 1½ in. diameter, in a hole which she digs in soft ground. The eggs hatch 3 – 4 months later.

Man the enemy today . . .
The solid box of bone with its horny covering and the tortoise's habit of withdrawing into this fortress at the slightest disturbance, seem the best possible protection against enemies. The Bearded Vulture is a traditional enemy, flying to some height with a tortoise and then letting it drop to the ground to crack its shell. Rats attack and eat tortoises. Apart from these the natural enemies must be limited. On the other hand, tortoises are probably very vulnerable to the elements, especially to such catastrophes as grass and woodland fires. After a grass fire the number of dead tortoises of all sizes, and especially the small ones, gives an indication of how numerous these animals can be in places where normally little is seen of them. The greatest danger today is the

trade in tortoises for pets. Once a tortoise has been bought and installed in a garden it will be treated with the greatest care. The method of packing them for transport has meant, however, that in recent years there has been a hideously high mortality between their being collected, mainly in North Africa, and their reaching the dealers.

. . . and in the past

The four species of gopher tortoises, which may be up to 13 in. long, have also suffered from the pet trade. Two, the Texas tortoise and the desert tortoise, are now protected by law but the Mexican is very rare and may be extinct. The giant tortoises which live on the islands of the Galapagos and on islands in the Indian Ocean have also suffered in numbers, but in a different way. The largest of them have reached nearly 5 ft long, stood 2½ ft high and weighed 200 – 300 lb. Those of the Galapagos especially were taken by the crews of whalers, sealers and buccaneers for fresh meat. Between 1811 and 1844, a mere 105 whalers took 15 000. The giant tortoises of the Indian Ocean suffered even more, and in recent years a population on Aldabra Island was threatened through a proposal by the British Ministry of Defence to make the island an air staging post.

A ripe old age

Keeping tortoises as pets has been the only reliable way of estimating how long they can live.

The longest authentic record we have is for one of the giant tortoises, Marion's tortoise. It was taken to Mauritius, when full grown, by Marion de Fresne in 1766. In 1810 the British captured the island and the tortoise continued to live in the artillery barracks until 1918. It was, therefore, at least 152 years old, and probably 180 years or even more. Another famous giant was the Tonga tortoise, presented by Captain James Cook in 1774, when it was already 'a considerable age'. There is some doubt about this tortoise, largely because in Tonga the records are oral, not written, but there seems no reason why the present tortoise should not be the same as the one Captain Cook handed over.

class	**Reptilia**
order	**Testudines**
family	**Testudinidae**
genera & species	**Gopherus agassizi** *desert gopher tortoise*
	G. berlandieri *Texas*
	G. flavomarginatus *Mexican*
	Geochelone elephantopus *Galapagos giant*
	G. gigantea *Indian Ocean giant*
	Testudo graeca *Iberian or Algerian*
	T. hermanni *Greek, others*

▷ *Galapagos giant tortoises: some of the few remaining members of a species once numerous enough to give its name to the islands but numbers are now greatly diminished. In the 19th century they were easy prey for the crews of passing ships, and their hardiness enabled them to be kept on board as a live source of meat.*

Early morning and the leathery turtle completes her task of egg-laying by filling in the nest hole. This rare sea turtle spends more time in deep water than any other turtle. The females come onto land only to lay eggs. Each comes ashore, usually late at night, about four times a season.

Leathery turtle

The leathery or leatherback turtle or luth is the largest sea turtle, and also differs from the others in the structure of its shell. The upper shell or carapace is made up of hundreds of irregular bony plates covered with a leathery skin instead of the characteristic plates of other turtles. There are seven ridges, which may be notched, running down the back, and five on the lower shell, or plastron.

Leathery turtles are dark brown or black with spots of yellow or white on the throat and flippers of young specimens. They grow to a maximum of 9 ft, the shell being up to 6 ft, and may weigh up to 1 800 lb. The foreflippers are very large; leathery turtles 7 ft long may have flippers spanning 9 ft.

Rare wanderer

The leathery turtle is the rarest sea turtle and lives in tropical waters, probably spending more time in deeper water than other turtles. Little is known about its habits and even its breeding haunts are not well known. Leathery turtles are known to breed in the West Indies, Florida, the north-eastern coasts of South America, Senegal, Natal, Madagascar, Sri Lanka and Malaya. The breeding populations are quite small and predation of eggs by men and dogs endangers the populations of some beaches. Although generally restricted to warm waters, leathery turtles are occasionally found swimming in cooler waters or washed up on beaches, especially when carried by adverse winds or currents. They have been seen off Newfoundland and Norway in the north, occasionally straggling as far south as New Zealand.

Unlike some other turtles leathery turtles do not carry encrustations of barnacles and seaweeds. This may be due to the very oily skin. The oil has been found to have anti-biotic properties but it is not known whether this prevents other organisms settling on the skin. Also, like the other turtles without barnacles, they are fast swimmers. Leathery turtles are regularly escorted by pilot fish, which are more commonly associated with other fishes, such as sharks.

Although the leathery turtle is described here as the rarest of the turtles, it is of interest to note that it has been increasingly reported in recent years, especially in the North Atlantic. One reason for this, possibly the main reason, is that fishermen have switched to faster, motorized vessels.

A soft diet

The stomach contents of leathery turtles show that they feed on jellyfish, salps, pteropods (planktonic sea snails) and other soft bodied, slow-moving animals, including the amphipods and other animals that live in the bodies of jellyfish and salps. Leathery turtles have been seen congregating in shoals of jellyfish and the 2–3in. horny spines in the mouth and throat are probably a great help in holding slippery food.

Breeding in bands

Female leathery turtles come ashore in small bands to lay their eggs, usually late at night. They come straight up the shore to dry sand, stop, then start to dig the nest. They do not select the nest site, by digging exploratory pits and testing the sand, as in green turtles. A hollow is excavated with all four flippers working rhythmically until the turtle is hidden. She then digs the egg pit, scooping out sand with her hindflippers until she has dug as deep as she can reach. About 60–100 eggs, 2–2¼ in. diameter, are laid, then she fills the nest with sand and packs it down. Finally she masks the position of the nest by ploughing about and scattering sand, then makes her way back to the sea. Each female comes ashore to lay about four times in one season. The eggs hatch in 7 weeks and the babies emerge together and rush down the shore to the water.

The Soay beast

In September 1959 a large animal was seen in the sea off Soay, a small island off the Isle of Skye, western Scotland. There was much speculation at the time about what it could be. The two men who saw it gave a description and each made a rough sketch of it. The interest was increased by the fact that on at least one occasion many years previously a similar animal had been reported from these same waters. So the Soay Beast, as it came to be called, passed into history as an unsolved mystery, possibly a sea monster, probably one of the several different kinds of sea-serpent reported at various times. All these things seemed possible when one looked at an artist's impression published at the time. In due course Professor LD Brongersma had little difficulty in showing that, beyond reasonable doubt, the animal was nothing more than a large leathery turtle. In this he confirmed the opinion of Dr JH Fraser of Aberdeen, expressed in May 1960, a few months after the sighting was reported.

If the artist's impression was misleading we cannot blame him. He had only the verbal statements to go upon, together with two crude sketches. The real moral is that one should pay more attention to Occam's Razor. William of Occam (now Ockham) was a 14th century English scholar and philosopher who expounded the principle that if there are two or more theories to account for something, choose the simplest.

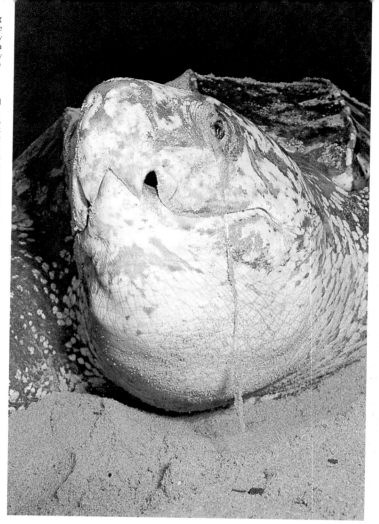

△ Why do leathery turtles cry? The answer might be to remove sand from its eyes on the rare occasions when the turtle comes ashore to nest and lay eggs. The accepted theory is that the tears a turtle sheds get rid of the excess salt that has been swallowed with gulps of sea water.
▽ The leathery turtle belongs to tropical waters, but sometimes ranges into temperate seas in summer.

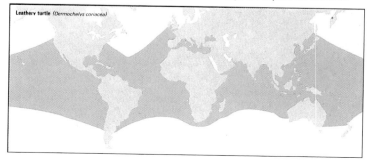

Leathery turtle (Dermochelys coriacea)

class	**Reptilia**
order	**Testudines**
family	**Dermochelidae**
genus & species	***Dermochelys coriacea***

With a shell length of little more than 4 in. this tiny turtle, the common mud turtle, is one of the smallest freshwater turtles of North America.

The common musk turtle has a much reduced plastron without hinges. The shields of the plastron are separated along the mid-line by soft skin.

Mud turtle

The mud turtles and musk turtles of the family Trionychidae are some of the smallest North American turtles: the adult eastern mud turtle has a brown or olive shell which is little more than 4 in. long. The young of this species has three ridges on the carapace, the upper part of the shell, but these disappear as it grows up. The plastron, or underpart of the shell, is light brown or yellow and the turtles have yellowish green spots on the head. The central part of the plastron is joined to the carapace while its front and rear portions are hinged to this central portion by strong connective tissues forming movable lobes. When the turtle withdraws its head, limbs and tail it draws these lobes over the openings, completely sealing itself in. Musk turtles are similar to mud turtles except that the plastron is very much smaller in proportion to the carapace and is without hinges, but the two kinds of turtles are alike in having musk glands along the sides of the body. The musk is much stronger in the musk turtles which are often called stinkpots as a result. Male mud turtles differ from females in having larger heads and longer tails and, when adult, their plastrons are concave. They also have patches of horny scales on the hindlegs, which are used to hold the female in mating.

There are about 17 species of mud turtle, 4 or 5 in the United States, and the rest in Central and South America. One large South American mud turtle has enlarged lobes on the plastron that make a perfect fit with the edges of the carapace, so the turtle inside is fully protected. The musk turtles live in the United States.

Quiet life

Mud and musk turtles live in pools and sluggish streams where there are plenty of water plants. They crawl over the bottom and occasionally wander out over the land or bask on banks and tree stumps. The

Stinkpot — a three day old common musk turtle.

common musk turtle is rarely seen out of water but the keel-backed musk turtle of the southeastern United States often comes out to bask in the sun. The mud turtles are more likely to be found on land and they often live in very small pools and roadside ditches.

An unpleasant catch

Mud turtles and musk turtles feed on tadpoles, snails, worms, water insects and fish. They also eat a large amount of carrion and are unpopular with anglers because they often take their bait. After giving an angler the impression that he has hooked a large fish the turtle adds insult to injury by discharging its foul-smelling musk when lifted from the water.

Leisurely courtship

The courtship of mud turtles usually takes place in the water but the female comes on land to lay her eggs. To mate the male approaches the female from behind and noses her tail to confirm her sex. He then swims beside her, nudging her just behind her eye. She swims with him for some distance then stops suddenly. This is a signal for the male to climb onto her back, grasp the edges of her carapace with his toes and hold her tail to one side with the scaly patches on one of his hindlegs. Several fertile clutches may result from one mating and females isolated for 3-4 years have laid fertile eggs.

The eggs are laid under rotten logs and stumps or in nests dug in the earth. The musk turtles sometimes lay their eggs in muskrat nests. Up to 7 eggs with hard, brittle shells are laid in each clutch. They hatch in 60–90 days, depending on the heat provided by the sun and the decaying vegetation around them. The newly-hatched turtles have shells about 1 in. long. Males mature in 4–7 years and the females in 5–8 years. In captivity mud turtles have lived for 40 years but in the wild they fall prey to several predators; crows attack the adults, while king snakes, raccoons and skunks eat the eggs.

The turtle frame

It is natural to assume that the plastron is no more than a breast plate to protect the underside of a turtle or tortoise, but in some species it is so small that it can offer very little protection. Even so, it still has an important part to play. In all turtles and tortoises the ribs are incorporated into the carapace and the plastron takes over to some extent the work of the ribs in bracing the body and in providing an anchoring surface for the muscles of the shoulders and hips. In the snapping turtle, for instance, in which the plastron is very much reduced, scientists have calculated that this small plastron is just sufficient to give the necessary strength and support to the body. It is much the same in the mud and musk turtles when they are young; they have a soft carapace and a rigid plastron which braces the carapace. As the turtles grow older and the carapace hardens the plastron is freed from this duty. Then, in mud turtles, it develops the hinges which, acting like lids, close over the turtle when it withdraws into its shell so giving it maximum protection from its enemies.

class	**Reptilia**
order	**Testudines**
family	**Trionychidae**
genera & species	***Kinosternon subrubrum*** common mud turtle ***Sternotherus carinatus*** keel-backed musk turtle ***S. odoratus*** common musk turtle others

Crocodile

The crocodiles and their close relatives alligators, caimans and gharials are the sole survivors of the great group of reptiles, the Archosauria, that included the well-known and awe-inspiring dinosaurs. The crocodile family itself includes the dwarf crocodiles and the false gharial as well as the dozen or so species of true crocodiles.

Crocodiles are often distinguished by the shape of the snout. This is long and broad in the Nile crocodile, the best-known species, short in the Indian marsh crocodile or mugger, and long and narrow in the false gharial. The differences between crocodiles and alligators are set out under alligator, page 70.

As with many large, fearsome animals, the size of crocodiles has been exaggerated. There is reliable evidence for the Nile crocodile reaching 20 ft and American and Orinoco crocodiles have measured 23 ft. At the other extreme the Congo dwarf crocodile has never been found to exceed 3 ft 9 in. Now that crocodiles have been hunted too intensively, large ones have become extremely rare.

Cold-blooded lover of warmth

Crocodiles are found in the warmer parts of the world, in Africa, Asia, Australia and America. Unlike alligators, they are often found in brackish water and sometimes they even swim out to sea. Estuarine crocodiles swim between the islands of the Malay Archipelago and stray ones have been found in the Fijis and other remote islands.

▽ *Smaller relative, different jaw structure: the broad-fronted crocodile of West Africa only grows to 5 – 6 ft and does not attack man.*

△ *Saltwater or estuarine crocodile: one of the world's most dangerous crocodiles, it can reach lengths of over 20 ft.*

Reptiles are said to be cold-blooded because they cannot maintain their body temperatures within fine limits, as can mammals and birds. A reptile's body temperature is usually within a few degrees of that of its surroundings. It cannot shiver to keep warm or sweat to keep cool. Many reptiles, however, can keep their body temperatures from varying too much by following a daily routine to avoid extremes of temperature. Crocodiles do this. They come out of the water at sunrise and lie on the banks basking in the sun. When their bodies have warmed up, they either move into the shade or back into the water, escaping the full strength of the midday sun. Then in the late afternoon they bask again, and return to the water by nightfall. By staying underwater at night they conserve heat, because water holds its heat better than air.

Stones in their stomachs

When crocodiles come out of the water they generally stay near the bank, although occasionally they wander some distance in search of water, and can cause great consternation by appearing in towns. They are generally sluggish, but, considering their bulky bodies and relatively short legs, they are capable of unexpected bursts of speed. They have three distinct gaits. There is a normal walk, with the body

lifted well off the ground with the legs under the body – a gait most unlike the popular conception of a crocodile walking. More familiar is the tobogganing used when dashing into the water. The crocodile slides on its belly, using its legs as paddles. The third method is used by a young crocodile which will occasionally gallop along with the front and back legs working together, like a bounding squirrel.

In the water, crocodiles float very low, with little more than eyes and nostrils showing. They habitually carry several pounds of stones in their stomachs, which help to stabilise their bodies. The stones lie in the stomach, below the centre of gravity and work as a counterpoise to the buoyant lungs. This is particularly useful when the crocodiles are fairly young. At that age they are top heavy and cannot float easily at the surface.

Maneaters: myth and fact

For the first year of their lives, young crocodiles feed on small animals, frogs, dragonflies, crabs and even mosquito larvae. Young crocodiles have been seen cornering the larvae by curving their bodies and tails around them. Larger animals are stalked. The baby crocodile swims stealthily towards its prey then pounces, snapping at it with a sideways movement of the jaws, necessary because the crocodile's eyes are at the side of its head.

As a crocodile grows the amount of insects in its diet falls, and it turns to eating snails and fish. The adult crocodiles continue to catch fish but turn increasingly to trapping mammals and birds. They capture their prey by lying in wait near game trails or waterholes. When a victim approaches the crocodile will seize it and drag it underwater or knock it over with a blow from its tail or head. Once the victim is pulled into the water the crocodile has a definite advantage. Drowning soon stills the victim's struggles, and, grasping a limb in its jaws, the crocodile may roll over and over so that the victim is dismembered.

Crocodiles are well-known as maneaters — but how true is this reputation? The maneating habit varies and it may be that only certain individuals will attack man. In parts of Africa, crocodiles are not regarded as a menace at all, while elsewhere palisades have to be erected at the water's edge to allow the women to fetch water in safety. It seems that crocodiles are likely to be more aggressive when their streams and pools dry up so they cannot escape, or when they are guarding their young.

In the crocodile's nest

The Nile crocodile breeds when 5 – 10 years old. By this time it is 7 – 10 ft long. The full-grown males stake out their territories along the banks and share them with younger males and females. They defend the territories by fighting, which may sometimes end in one contestant being killed.

A male crocodile approaches a female

Like an extra for a film on the first amphibious reptiles, a small saltwater crocodile comes ashore in Queensland, Australia. Unlike alligators, crocodiles can be found in brackish waters, estuaries, and swimming out at sea.

crocodile and displays to her by thrashing the water with his snout and tail. They swim in circles with the male on the outside trying to get near her so he can put a forelimb over her body and mate.

Up to 90 eggs are laid during the dry season. They hatch 4 months later, during the rainy season when there are plenty of insects about for the babies to feed on.

The Nile crocodile and the marsh crocodile dig pits 2 ft deep for their nests, but the estuarine crocodile of northern Australia and southeast Asia makes a mound of leaves. The nests are built near water and shade, where the female can guard her brood and keep herself cool. During the incubation period she stays by the nest defending it against enemies, including other crocodiles, although in colonies they sometimes nest only a few yards apart.

The baby crocodiles begin to grunt before hatching. This is the signal for the mother to uncover the nest. The babies climb out and stay near her, yapping if they get lost. They follow her about like ducklings and forage for insects, even climbing trees, and grunting and snapping at one another. They disperse after a few days.

The young Nile crocodiles are about 1 ft long at hatching and for their first 7 years they grow at a rate of about 10 in. a year.

Cannibals

The mother crocodile has to be on her guard all the time as many animals will wait for their chance to eat the eggs or the baby crocodiles. Their main enemy is the monitor lizard. They are bold enough to dig underneath the crocodile as she lies over her nest, and once a male monitor was seen to decoy a crocodile away from the nest while the female stole the eggs. Other crocodiles, herons, mongooses, turtles, eagles and predatory fish all eat baby crocodiles. Adult crocodiles have been killed by lions, elephants, and leopards, and hippopotamuses will attack crocodiles in defence of their young.

Crocodiles are cannibals, so basking groups are always sorted out into parties of equal size and the smaller crocodiles keep well away from the bigger ones.

Crocodile tears

If we say that someone is shedding crocodile tears it means that they are showing grief or sympathy that they do not really mean. The idea that crocodiles are hypocrites is an ancient one, and is described in TH White's translation of a 12th century bestiary: 'Crocodiles lie by night in the water, by day on land, because hypocrites, however luxuriously they live by night, delight to be said to live holily and justly by day.' The hypocrisy seems to be manifested in the form of tears, and malicious or misunderstanding comparisons are made with women's tears. Thus when Desdemona weeps, Othello complains:

'O devil, devil!
If that the earth could teem with woman's tears,
Each drop she falls would prove a crocodile.'

John Hawkins explains crocodile's tears as meaning 'that as the Crocodile when he

△ Hatching out: while still in the egg, baby Nile crocodiles grunt a signal to the mother to uncover the nest.

▽ Prelude to feeding: prey trapped in its vice-like jaws, a crocodile returns to the water where it will take its meal at leisure.

crieth, goeth then about most to deceive, so doth a woman commonly when she weepeth'. The deception practised by the 'cruell craftie crocodile' is that it lures unwary travellers into drawing near to find out what is the matter.

The story, like many myths and legends, may have a basis of truth. It could have sprung from the plaintive howling that crocodiles make. Crocodiles, however, do have tear glands to keep their eyes moist and tears, or water trapped in their lids, may run from the corners of their eyes. This, with the permanent grin of their jaws, could have led to their legendary reputation as hypocrites.

class	**Reptilia**
order	**Crocodilia**
family	**Crocodylidae**
genera & species	***Crocodylus niloticus*** *Nile crocodile*
	C. porosus *estuarine crocodile*
	C. palustris *marsh crocodile*
	Osteolaemus *dwarf crocodiles*
	Tomistoma schlegeli *false gharial*

▷ *'African crocodiles at home': a romanticized print shows waterfowl scattering in panic from the threat of an evil-looking flock of crocodiles.*

▽ *Although in parts of Africa crocodiles are not regarded as maneaters, the Nile crocodile has a very bad reputation. One crocodile (15ft 3ins long) shot in the Kihange River, Central Africa, was reported to have killed 400 people over the years.*

When annoyed, alligators open their vast jaws and roar. Male alligators also roar during their quarrels in the breeding season and to attract females.

Alligator

Two species of reptiles which, with the caimans, belong to a family closely related to the crocodiles. Alligators and crocodiles look extremely alike: the main distinguishing feature is the teeth.
In a crocodile the teeth in the upper and lower jaws are in line, but in the alligator, when its mouth is shut, the upper teeth lie outside the lower. In both animals the fourth lower tooth on each side is perceptibly larger than the rest: in the crocodile this tooth fits into a notch in the upper jaw and is visible when the mouth is closed, whereas in the alligator, with the lower teeth inside the upper, it fits into a pit in the upper jaw and is lost to sight when the mouth is shut. In addition, the alligator's head is broader and shorter and the snout consequently blunter. Otherwise, especially in their adaptations to an aquatic life, alligators are very similar to crocodiles.
One of the two species is found in North America, the other in China. The Chinese alligator averages a little over 4 ft in length and has no webs between the toes. The American alligator is much larger, with a maximum recorded length of 19 ft 2 in.
This length, however, is seldom attained nowadays because the American alligator has been killed off for the sake of its skin; whenever there is intense persecution of an animal the larger ones are quickly

eliminated and the average size of the remainder drops slowly as persecution proceeds.
It is sheer accident that two such similar reptiles as the alligator and the crocodile should so early have been given different common names. The reason is that when the Spanish seamen, who had presumably no knowledge of crocodiles, first saw large reptiles in the Central American rivers, they spoke of them as lizards – **el largato** in Spanish. The English sailors who followed later adopted the Spanish name but ran the two into one to make 'allagarter' – which was later further corrupted to 'alligator'.

Long lazy life
Alligators are more sluggish than crocodiles; this may possibly have an effect on their longevity. There is a record of an American alligator living for 56 years. They spend most of their time basking on river banks.
The American alligator is restricted to the south-eastern United States and does not penetrate further north than latitude 35. The Chinese alligator is found only in the Yangtse River basin.

Meat eaters
Alligators' food changes with age. The young feed on insects and on those crustaceans generally known as freshwater shrimps. As they grow older they eat frogs, snakes and fish; mature adults live mainly on fish but will catch muskrats and small mammals that go down to the water's edge to drink. They also take a certain amount of waterfowl. Very large alligators may

occasionally pull large mammals such as deer or cows down into the water and drown them.

Alligator builds a nest
It seems that the female alligator plays the more active role in courtship and territorial defence. The males apparently spend much of the breeding season quarrelling among themselves, roaring and fighting and injuring each other. The roaring attracts the females to the males, as does a musky secretion from glands in the male's throat and cloaca. Courtship takes place usually at night, the pair swimming round faster and faster and finally mating in the water with jaws interlocked and the male's body arched over the female's.
A large nest-mound is made for the reception of the eggs. The female scoops up mud in her jaws and mixes it with decaying vegetation; the mixture is then deposited on the nest site until a mound 3 ft high is made. The eggs are hard-shelled and number 15 – 80; they are laid in a depression in the top of the mound and covered with more vegetation. The female remains by the eggs until they hatch 2 – 3 months later, incubated by the heat of the nest's rotting vegetation.
The hatchling alligators peep loudly and the female removes the layer of vegetation over the nest to help them escape. Baby alligators are 8 in. long when first hatched and grow 1 ft a year, reaching maturity at 6 years.

The biter bitten
Young alligators fall an easy prey to carnivorous fish, birds and mammals, and at all stages of growth they are attacked and eaten

by larger alligators. This natural predation was, in the past, just sufficient to keep the numbers of alligator populations steady. Then came the fashion for making women's shoes, handbags and other ornamental goods of alligator skin. So long as these articles remain in fashion and command a high price, men will be prepared to risk both the imprisonment consequent on the laws passed to protect alligators and the attacks of the alligators themselves.

There is also another commercial interest, detrimental both to the alligator and to the fashion industry. For, while the fashion for skins from larger individuals shows no sign of abating, a fashion for alligator pets also persists—though it may have dropped in intensity since its inception. Baby alligators are still being netted in large numbers for the pet shops, but—as so commonly happens with pets taken from the wild—not all those caught are eventually sold. Of a consignment of 1,000 hatchlings that reached New York City in 1967, 200 were already dead and putrefying, and many others were in a sorry condition and unlikely to survive.

In addition to persecution, land drainage has seriously affected the numbers of the American alligator. The Chinese alligator is an even worse case. Its flesh is eaten and the various parts of its body are used as charms, aphrodisiacs and for their supposed medicinal properties. The New York Zoological Park has recently announced plans to try and breed the Chinese alligator and so protect it from complete extermination.

Unwanted pets

The fashion for alligator pets has its disadvantages for owners as well as the alligator populations. Even setting aside the largest recorded lengths for the American species of 19 ft upwards, it still achieves too large a size to be convenient in the modern flat, and people who invest in an alligator often find it necessary to dispose of it. Zoos have proved unable to deal with the quantity offered them—Brookfield Zoo near Chicago has built up an enormous herd from unwanted pets—and it is widely said that unfortunate alligators are disposed of in such a way that they end up in the sewers. One result of this is that every now and then, despite official denials, reports have appeared in the press to the effect that the sewers of New York are teeming with alligators that prey on the rats and terrorise the sewermen.

△ *A female alligator builds a nest of rotting vegetation for her clutch of 15—80 eggs. She stays for 2—3 months by the nest until they hatch.*

▽ *Alligators spend much of their time basking on the banks of jungle rivers. Here they have made a lagoon by their thrashing about.*

class	**Reptilia**
order	**Crocodilia**
family	**Alligatoridae**
genus & species	***Alligator mississipiensis*** American alligator
	A. sinensis Chinese alligator

Gecko

Geckos form a family of lizards noted for the large number of species, the structure of their feet, their voices, the differences in the shape of their tails, and for the ease with which some of them will live in houses. The smallest is 1⅜ in. long; the largest—the tokay—may be 14 in. long.

Geckos are found in all warm countries: 41 species in Africa, 50 in Madagascar, about 50 in Australia, the same in the West Indies, with others in southern and southeast Asia, Indonesia, the Pacific islands and New Zealand, and South America. There are geckos in the desert regions of Mexico and southern California. Several have been introduced into Florida from the Caribbean islands. Spain and Dalmatia, in southern Europe, have the same wall gecko as North Africa.

A liking for houses

The majority of geckos live in trees, some live among rocks, others live on the sandy ground of deserts. Tree geckos find in human habitations conditions similar to, or better than, those of their natural habitat: natural crevices in which to rest or take refuge and plenty of insects, especially at night when insects are attracted to lights. Because geckos can cling to walls or hang upside-down from ceilings they can take full advantage of these common insect resting places, and so many of them are now known as house geckos.

Hooked to the ceiling

Most geckos can cling to smooth surfaces. Their toes may be broad or expanded at the tips with flaps of skin (lamellae) arranged transversely or fanwise. The undersides of the toes bear pads furnished with numerous microscopic hook-like bristles that catch in slight irregularities, even in the surface of glass, or have bristles ending in minute suckers. So a gecko can cling to all but the most highly polished surfaces. The hooks are directed backwards and downwards and to disengage them the toe must be lifted upwards from the tip. As a result, a gecko running up a tree or a wall or along a ceiling must curl and uncurl its toes at each step with a speed faster than the eye can follow. Some of the hooks are so small the high power of a microscope is needed to see them, yet a single toe armed with numbers of these incredibly small hooks can support several times the weight of a gecko's body. In addition to the bristles, most species have the usual claw at the tip of the toe which also can be used in clinging. In one species there are microscopic hooks on the tip of the tail which enable the animal to cling.

△ *Close pursuit. As firm as the flies it is hunting, a diurnal gecko* **Phelsuma vinsoni** *pauses on a vertical tree-trunk, unaware of the apparent impossibility of its position.*
▷ *Living crampons. Geckos get a grip from tiny hooks in the flaps of skin on their feet.*
▷▷ *After partial loss, regrowth and healing, the result is a three-tailed gecko.*

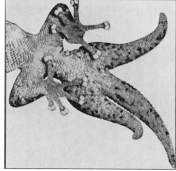

Leaf-like tail

The tail is long and tapering, rounded or slightly flattened and fringed with scales, according to the species, or it may be flattened and leaf-like. A South American gecko has a swollen turnip-shaped tail. It has been named *Thecadactylus rapicaudus* (*rapi* for turnip, *caudus* for tail). The flying gecko of southeast Asia has a leaf-like tail, a wide flap of skin along each flank, a narrow flap along each side of the head and flaps along the hind margins of the limbs. Should the gecko fall it spreads its limbs, the flaps spread and the reptile parachutes safely down.

Geckos can throw off their tails, like the more familiar lizards, and grow new ones. In some species 40% have re-grown tails.

Sometimes the tail is incompletely thrown and hangs by a strip of skin. As a new tail grows the old one heals and a 2-tailed gecko results. Even 3-tailed geckos have been seen. Temperature is important in growing a new tail. It has been found that when the wall gecko of southern Europe and North Africa grows a new tail with the air temperature at 28°C/82°F it is short and covered with large overlapping scales. With the temperature around 35°C/95°F the new tail is long and is covered with small scales.

Cat-like eyes

One difference between snakes and lizards is that the former have no eyelids. In most geckos the eyelids are permanently joined and there is a transparent window in the

△ *Pinhole sight: pupils shrunk to four tiny holes, to keep out excessive glare of the sun.*

lower lid. The few geckos that are active by day have rounded pupils to the eyes. The rest are active by night and have vertical slit-pupils like cats. In some species the sides of the pupils are lobed or notched in four places, and when the pupils contract they leave four apertures, the size of pinholes each one of which will focus the image onto the retina.

Surprisingly small clutches

All geckos except for a few species in New Zealand, which bear live young, lay eggs with a tough white shell. Usually there

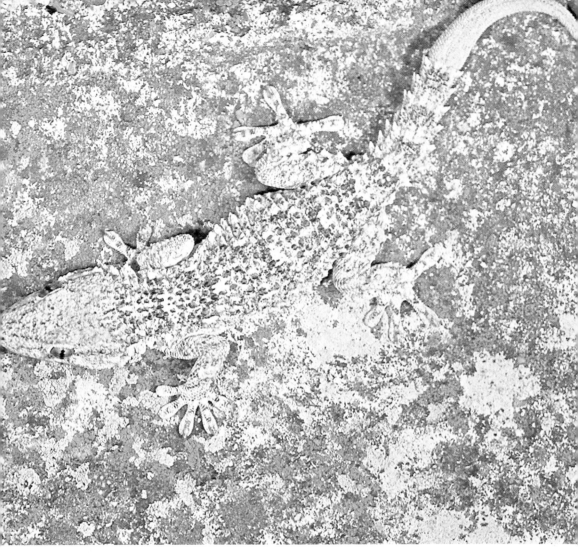

are two in a clutch, sometimes only one. The eggs are laid under bark or under stones and take several months to hatch.

Harmless creatures

Geckos eat only insects. They are harmless and wholly beneficial to man, yet among the people of Africa, South America, Malaysia and the aboriginals of Australia there are widespread beliefs that their bite makes them dangerous to handle. Possibly such beliefs spring from some of the more remarkable species, like the gecko that stalks insects as a cat does a mouse, even lashing its tail from side to side just before the final pounce. Then there are the web-footed geckos living on the sand dunes of Southwest Africa. They not only use the webbed feet to run over loose sand but also to burrow. They scrape the sand away with the forefoot of one side and shovel it back with the hindfoot of the same side while balancing on the feet of the other side. Then they change over. They walk with the body raised high and the tail held up and arched.

One web-footed gecko has a delicate beauty. It is pinkish-brown with a lemon yellow stripe along its flank. Its eye has brilliant yellow lids, the iris is black, patterned with gold and coppery tints, while the edges of the vertical pupil are chalky white. Its skin is so transparent the spine and some internal organs can be seen clearly. In *African Wild Life*, GK Brain claims its two ear openings are almost in direct connection; by looking into one earhole light coming in

△ *A regrown tail shows that, despite excellent camouflage, only desperate measures saved this gecko's life.*

through the other can be seen.

class	**Reptilia**
order	**Squamata**
suborder	**Sauria**
family	**Gekkonidae**
genus & species	*Gekko gecko* others

it passes to an aggressive display. The lizard steps boldly towards the intruder, keeping its mouth open and frill fully extended, and from the mouth comes a low hiss. The remarkable thing is that people who know very well the lizard can do nothing to harm them, tend nevertheless to be intimidated by all this show. Even a dog used to attacking larger lizards will retreat before it.

Meals of ants and eggs
The frilled lizard eats insects, including large quantities of ants, as well as spiders and small mammals. It is also said to be an egg thief. One of the many difficulties found in keeping this animal in captivity is that of getting enough of the right kind of food. In 1893, when the time it took to travel from Australia to Great Britain was much longer than it is today, the naturalist W Saville Kent brought a frilled lizard to London, the first to reach Europe alive. When it was exhibited before an audience of learned gentlemen one eminent zoologist is said to have followed it, in his excitement, on hands and knees, to watch it careering round on its hind legs and displaying its frill. Unfortunately, there is no record of how Saville Kent managed to feed his pet, but, like many reptiles, the frilled lizard can probably go without food for months.

Umbrella trick
Neither does history record whether any of the learned gentlemen noticed a comparison between the lizard and a lady. At that time ladies carried parasols and it was not uncommon for a lady, confronted by a cow as she crossed a field, to frighten the cow away by suddenly opening her parasol in its face. Konrad Lorenz, in *King Solomon's Ring*, tells how his wife kept geese from devastating her newly-planted flower beds. She carried a large scarlet umbrella and this she would suddenly unfold at the geese, with a jerk, causing the geese to take to the air with a thundering of wings. It is almost instinctive for a woman carrying an umbrella to use it in this way against a powerful and persistent opponent. It is a matter of no small interest to find that this same effective defence should have been evolved by a lizard.

△ *Defiance: a cornered lizard unfurls its frill.*

Frilled lizard

One of the so-called dragons of Australia, the frilled lizard grows to about 3 ft long, with a slender body and long tail. It is pale brown, either uniformly coloured or with patches of yellow and darker brown. Its most conspicuous feature is the frill around the throat, like the ruff fashionable in Europe in the Middle Ages.

Apart from its size the only remarkable thing about this lizard is its frill. Normally this lies folded over the shoulders like a cape. It is a large area of skin supported by cartilaginous rods from the tongue bone which act like the ribs of an umbrella. In moments of excitement, muscles pulling on these raise the frill to 8 in. or more across, about as wide as the length of the head and body together.

It lives mainly in sandy semi-dry areas of northern and northeastern Australia.

Hindleg sprinter
The frilled lizard lives in rough-barked trees, coming to the ground after rainstorms, to feed. When disturbed on the ground it runs on its hindlegs with the frill laid back over the shoulders, tail raised, and the forelegs held close into the body. It may sprint for a considerable distance, or it may seek safety by climbing a tree. When brought to bay it turns, opens its mouth wide and extends its frill. The best description of what happens next is given by Harry Frauca in *The Book of Australian Wild Life*. It does not raise its tail, as it has often been reported to do, and as some other similar lizards are known to do, but keeps it flat on the ground. It sways from side to side and with its open mouth, coloured dark blue inside edged by pinkish yellow, surrounded by the greenish-yellow frill splashed with red, brown, white and black, it looks like a large flower among broad leaves. The colours of the lizard vary from one region to another. In Queensland the general colour is a sombre grey, in the Northern Territory it is pinkish, often with a black chest and throat. The colours of the mouth and frill also vary.

The open mouth and spread frill are a warning display. If the warning is ignored

class	**Reptilia**
order	**Squamata**
suborder	**Sauria**
family	**Agamidae**
genus & species	***Chlamydosaurus kingii***

Frilled lizard *(Chlamydosaurus kingii)*

Chameleon

The chameleons are a family of lizards renowned for several unusual features. The body is high in proportion to the length and is flattened from side to side. The tail in most species is prehensile, is often held in a tight coil, and can be wrapped round a twig for extra grip. The toes of each foot are joined, three on the inside of the front feet and on the outside of the hindfeet, resulting in feet like pairs of tongs that can give a tenacious grip on a perch. Above all, a chameleon is remembered for three things: its ability to change colour, its eyes set in turrets that can move independently of each other, and its highly extensible tongue which can be shot out at speed to a length greater than the chameleon's head and body. To add to their bizarre form, some species have rows of tubercles down the back or a 'helmet' or casque like the flap-necked chameleon or horns like Jackson's chameleon.

A few species grow to 2 ft long, while dwarf species measure less than 2 in.

There are about 80 species of chameleon most of which live in Africa south of the Sahara and including Madagascar. One species, the common chameleon, ranges from the Middle East along the coast of North Africa to southern Spain. Two others live in the southern end of the Arabian peninsula and a third in India and Sri Lanka.

Chameleons live in slow motion

Chameleons live mainly in forests, and seem to spend most of their time virtually rooted to the spot, the only movement being of the eyes, each independently sweeping from side to side searching for food or danger. When they move they creep slowly along a twig. Sloth-like, a fore foot is released on one side and the hind foot on the other, and both are slowly moved forward to renew their grip on the twig while, equally stealthily, the other two advance. Although most chameleons keep to the trees as much as possible, the stump-tailed chameleons can often be found on the ground.

Periodically chameleons shed their skins. Before it comes off the old skin comes away from the new skin under it, leaving an air-filled gap that gives the chameleon a pale, translucent appearance as if it were neatly wrapped in polythene. Then the old skin splits, first just behind the head, and chunks of it flake off exposing the brilliant new skin.

Extensible tongue

Chameleons eat the usual food of small reptiles, that is, insects and other small invertebrates, but the larger species will also catch small birds, lizards and mammals. The similarity with other reptiles ends here, for the method of capture is unique except in frogs and toads. Chameleons capture their prey by shooting out their long tongue, trapping the victim on the tip and carrying it back to the mouth. The whole

△ Portrait of **Chamaeleo bitaeniatus** taken on Mt Elgon, Kenya. It lives above 9 000 ft.

◁ A chameleon in the later stages of shedding its skin. A new skin has first grown under the old. Notice that it even sheds the skin on its eyelids.

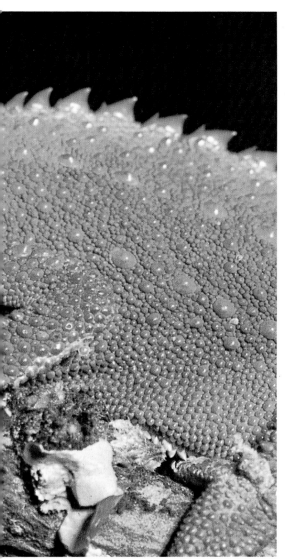

△ *Stage one: lining up on the target with tongue protruding. Note the spider in the top right corner.*
▽ *Stage two: muscles shoot the tongue to its full extent.*

▽ *Stage three: muscles contract, withdrawing the tongue. Despite its speed, the spider was quicker!*

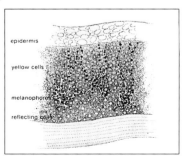

◁ *Simplified diagram of section through skin: colour change is mainly due to melanophores moving dark pigment into or out of upper layers.*
▷ *Catapult mechanism of the chameleon's tongue: special bone with its own muscles pushes tongue forward and circular muscles squeeze it out. Longitudinal muscles withdraw the tongue.*

epidermis

yellow cells

melanophores

reflecting cells

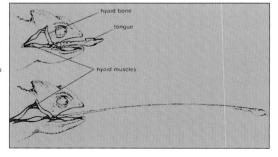

hyoid bone

tongue

hyoid muscles

action is so rapid that high-speed photography is needed to show the mechanism at work. By using a ciné camera it has been found that a $5\frac{1}{2}$ in. tongue can be extended in $\frac{1}{16}$ second and retracted in $\frac{1}{4}$ second. Without such aids all one sees is the chameleon watching its prey from its perch, or slowly edging towards it, for chameleons only take sitting prey. When in range it directs both eyes at its victim and rocks from side to side, improving its stereoscopic vision and range-finding capacity by looking at the target from different angles. While doing this the tip of the tongue protrudes from the mouth like a wad of chewing gum, then suddenly the insect disappears from its perch and is seen to be crushed in the chameleon's jaws. Young ones begin eating insects when a day old, and with a little practice become expert.

How the chameleon shoots out its tongue has been deduced by a careful study of its anatomy. Two mechanisms throw the tongue forward, both of them activated by powerful muscles. At the back of the jaw lies a V-shaped bone with the point of the V pointing backwards. Attached to this bone by a flexible joint is the tongue bone, over which the tongue fits like a glove on a finger. When the chameleon is about to shoot the V-bone is moved forward slightly to push the tip of the tongue out of the mouth. Then, the circular muscles in the thick tip of the tongue contract violently so that the tongue is forced out in the same way as an orange pip squeezed between the fingers, and simultaneously the V-bone is thrust further forward, giving added impetus.

The end of the tongue is sticky with saliva but an insect can settle on a chameleon's head and walk across its protruding tongue with no difficulty. On the other hand some people who have kept chameleons as pets report that the end of the tongue does feel adhesive, but this may be due to the minute hooks or hairs or other roughenings of its surface. Finally, there are photographs that show the tongue apparently grasping an insect. It may be that a combination of all three may be operating as in toads.

Breeding poses problems
Male chameleons hold territories which they guard against other males, keeping them out by bluff. The lungs of chameleons have branches spreading through the body and by inflating its lungs a chameleon can blow itself to a most impressive size. Females, of course, are allowed to enter the territories and the males chase after them and mate with them, unless dissuaded by a female already pregnant.

Some chameleons lay eggs, others bear their young alive. The former course has some disadvantages for chameleons lay up to 50 eggs in a clutch, each has a diameter of perhaps $\frac{1}{2}$ in. Places to hide such a large clutch must be rare in a tree and the chameleon, who is bulky and ungainly when carrying her eggs, has to climb down the tree and dig a hole in the ground. A common South African chameleon has been described as digging the hole with her head and front feet, pushing the loose soil away with her hind feet. It takes a long time that eventually she has a hole nearly the length of the body. She then backs into it and lays

Independently-swivelling eyes and palsied gait.

her eggs, pressing each one into place with her hind legs. When she has finished she fills in the hole, tamps it down, camouflages it with sticks and pieces of grass and leaves it. In due course the young hatch out and fight their way to the surface.

Other chameleons bear their young alive. Before the birth the female's body becomes greatly distended. The young are born in a translucent membrane. As each one is due the mother presses her cloaca against the twig on which she is perching and the membrane sticks to it. After a short interval the baby chameleon struggles out and walks off down the twig. The mother takes no more interest in her offspring, except that, if she is very hungry, she may eat them. The young start to feed when a day old, and with a little practice become expert at catching insects.

Quick colour change
Although other reptiles, as well as many fish and squid, can change colour, it is the chameleon that is renowned as a quick change artist. This is epitomised by the story of the chameleon put on a red cloth that changed to red, then when put on a green cloth turned to green, but had an apoplectic stroke when placed on a Scottish tartan. This greatly exaggerates the chameleon's power of colour change. The truth is that most species of chameleon have a basic colour and pattern that suits their particular habitat and do not really change colour to resemble the background but in response to

light intensity, temperature, or emotional state. Thus, colour change serves two purposes: to camouflage the chameleon and to act as a signal telling other chameleons its mood. An angry chameleon, for instance, goes black with rage. How the colour change is controlled is still not properly known. There is evidence for control by nerves and also by the secretion from the brain of chemicals which act on the colour cells; probably both act in different circumstances.

What is better known is the mechanics of colour change. The specialised colour cells lie under the transparent skin in four layers. The outermost is made up of xanthophores or yellow-bearers, together with erythrophores, the red-bearers. Under this layer are two reflecting layers, one reflecting blue light, the other white light. Beneath is the most important, and most complicated, layer of melanophores. These contain a dark brown pigment called melanin, the same substance that colours human skin brown or black. The main body of each melanophore lies under the reflecting layers but it sends tentacle-like arms up through the other layers.

To alter the colour of the skin, the colour cells alter in size, so that by variation of the amounts of yellow, red and dark brown, different colours are produced by mixing. The reflecting layers modify these effects. When the blue layer is under yellow cells, green is produced and where the blue layer is missing, light reflected from the white layer enhances the yellow or red coloration. The melanophores control the shading of the colours. When the colours are bright all the melanin is concentrated in the bodies of the melanophores. If the melanin spreads along the 'tentacles' to obscure the white layer, greens and reds become darker and if the melanin is dispersed completely, the chameleon becomes dark brown.

class	**Reptilia**
order	**Squamata**
suborder	**Sauria**
family	**Chamaeleontidae**
genera & species	*Chamaeleo chamaeleon* common chameleon
	C. dilepis flap necked chameleon
	C. oweni three horned chameleon
	C. jacksoni Jackson's chameleon
	Brookesia spp. stump tailed chameleons others

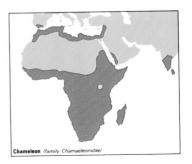

Chameleon *(family Chamaeleonidae)*

Iguana

The iguana family contains lizards such as the anole, the basilisk, the horned toad and many others, some of which are called iguanas in everyday English. The marine iguana is discussed under a separate heading; here we are dealing with the green iguana, the ground iguana, the land iguanas and the desert iguana or crested lizard.

The ground iguana is one of the most primitive members of the family. It has a crest like the teeth in a comb running down its back starting behind the head and petering out in the middle of the heavy tail.

One kind, the rhinoceros iguana, has two or three hornlike scales on its head and a large swelling on either side of the chin. Ground iguanas reach a length of 4 ft, 2 ft shorter than the green iguana which has been introduced to the Virgin Isles and the Lesser Antilles where it has driven out the ground iguana. The native home of the green iguana is Central and northern South America. It is pale green in colour, has a crest similar to that of the ground iguana and an erectable sac under the throat. The males are larger than the females, their crests are longer and their bodies are more orange or yellow compared with the females' light green. The males

△ Flowers on the menu: although it eats mainly insects when young, this green iguana seems to be interested in the more adult diet of tender young buds. They often clamber in trees.

also have a row of pores on the underside of each thigh, whose function is unknown.

The desert iguana lives in the deserts of North America. It measures 1 ft and is cream coloured with brown or black lines and spots. The land iguana of the Galapagos islands grows up to 5 ft. It is yellow with brown spots on the sides and legs.

High diver

The green iguana is an agile climber and adults are rarely found far from the trees of the tropical forests in which they live. It can scramble from one tree to another providing the twigs are interlaced to give reasonable support for iguanas cannot leap far. Green iguanas will, however, throw themselves from a branch 40 – 50 ft up and land on the ground unhurt, sprinting away to the undergrowth with barely a pause for breath. For an animal that appears so clumsy, with a heavy tail and legs splayed sideways, an iguana is remarkably fast and is extremely difficult to catch. Its reflexes are very rapid and unless one has nets the only way to catch an iguana is to throw oneself at it and even then a fullgrown iguana will be very hard to hold, as it can inflict nasty bites and scratches. Iguanas often take refuge in water and their favourite haunts are in trees overhanging pools and rivers. If disturbed they leap from the branch where they were lying and dive into the water. They swim underwater, propelling themselves with their tails, and surface under cover of vegetation along the bank.

The green iguana comes down to the ground in cold weather and hides under logs or in holes, but the other iguanas are usually ground-living and only occasionally climb trees. The desert iguana is a very fast runner and races about on its hindlegs.

Vegetarian lizards

As adults green iguanas eat a variety of plant foods, including young shoots, fruits, flowers and leaves, but the young ones also eat insects. Other iguanas are also vegetarian. The desert iguana prefers the yellow-flowered creosote bush but also eats other flowers, and after the flowering season is over it eats insects and carrion. Land iguanas feed on cactus and the larger species eat small rodents.

Eggs need constant temperature

Male land iguanas of the Galapagos form territories which they defend against other males. Each keeps watch from a rock and if another male intrudes he climbs down from his vantage point, walks slowly over to his rival and displays at him, pointing his snout at the sky and jerking his head up and down. If this does not scare the intruder into running away a fight breaks out, each trying to grab the loose skin on the other's flanks.

The female land iguanas live in the same burrows as their mates or in separate burrows alongside. Iguanas generally lay their eggs in nests well separated from each other but on a small island in Panama green iguanas were found nesting in great numbers close together on a sandy beach. Each female spent up to 2 weeks on the shore. For the first few days she probed the sand and dug small holes seeking a suitable site. Then she dug a large burrow 1 – 2 yd long and 2 – 3 ft deep. Because the beach was so crowded some were seen digging up other nests and scattering the eggs. Eggs were laid at the bottom of the burrow which was

▷ *The Barrington Island iguana of the Galapagos* **Conolophus pallidus**. *Local people prize its flesh, goats destroy its home.*

◁◁ *The aptly named rhinoceros iguana, with
two horn-like scales on the top of its nose.*
◁ *A green iguana pauses, throat sac down and
crest erect, to fight or flee an intruder, its
partly missing tail witness of a past escape.*

filled in afterwards. The females spent some
time filling the hole and at the same time
filling in adjacent holes. Sometimes this
meant filling in the burrows of other females who might be trapped and buried.

The green iguana lays 20—70 eggs in a
clutch. The eggs are spherical, white and
about 1½ in. diameter. They hatch in 3
months and it has been found that an almost
constant temperature is needed for their
development. A few degrees too high or too
low and they fail to hatch. Although the
female abandons her eggs after they are
laid she ensures their survival by burying
them in a suitable part of the beach. She
chooses a spot where the temperature
fluctuates only 1°—2° either side of 30°C/
86°F. The young iguanas measure about
10 in. when they hatch and grow to 3 ft in
one year.

Fooling the iguanas

Man and his domestic animals are the
iguanas' worst enemies. Their flesh is
relished in many parts of the world. Hawks
are also serious enemies, for they catch
iguanas as they lie basking in trees. In parts
of South America iguanas are hunted by
men imitating the screams of hawks. The
iguanas' reaction to the cries is to 'freeze'
and they are then easily caught. Snakes also
hunt iguanas; a 6 ft boa constrictor has been
found with an adult green iguana in its
stomach.

Vanishing iguanas

When Charles Darwin visited the Galapagos
islands in 1835 land iguanas were extremely
abundant. Darwin wrote 'I cannot give a
more forcible proof of their numbers than
by stating that when we were left at James
Island, we could not for some time find a
spot free from their burrows to pitch our
single tent.' Since then man has settled on
the island, bringing with him dogs, cats,
pigs, rats, goats and other animals and the
iguana population is now a fraction of its
former size. On some islands, however,
where there are no goats, there are still
large numbers of iguanas. The link between
goats and iguanas is that goats strip the vegetation, depriving iguanas of cover. Some
islands seem to be populated by adult
iguanas only. They can survive in the open
but young iguanas need cover to protect
them from the Galapagos hawk. Without
this cover they are killed off, and when the
old lizards die there will be none left.

class	**Reptilia**
order	**Squamata**
suborder	**Sauria**
family	**Iguanidae**
genera & species	***Conolophus subcristatus*** land iguana ***Cyclura cornuta*** rhinoceros iguana ***Dipsosaurus dorsalis*** desert iguana ***Iguana iguana*** green iguana

Skink

Skinks have none of the frills or decorations found in other lizard families; they all have an ordinary 'lizard shape' with a rather heavy tail and very often limbs that are reduced or missing. These are adaptations to the burrowing way of life which is characteristic of skinks and many spend most of their lives underground. Skinks are usually only a few inches long, the largest being the giant skink of the Solomon Islands, which is 2 ft long. The skink family contains over 600 species, and they are found all over the warmer parts of the world. In some areas, such as the forests of Africa, they are the most abundant lizards.

Within the skink family there are all gradations from a running to a burrowing way of life. The little brown skink of the southeastern United States has well-developed legs and toes and is a surface dweller; the burrowing Florida sand skink is almost limbless. In the **Scelotes** *genus of Africa there is a whole range of limb reduction. Bojer's skink of Mauritius has well-developed legs; the black-sided skink of Madagascar has very short legs; others have lost their forelegs altogether and have a reduced number of toes on the hindlegs; and the plain skink of South Africa has completely lost all its legs.*

Other adaptations for burrowing include the streamlining of the scales, the provision of a transparent 'spectacle' over the eye and the sinking of the eardrum into a narrow tube.

Diverse habits

Skinks are found in a variety of habitats, both on the ground and beneath the surface, from the damp soil of forests to the sands of deserts. A few live in trees, but only one has any adaptation for aboreal life. This is the giant skink which has a prehensile tail. Some skinks, such as the keel-bearing skinks, named after the projections on their scales, live on the banks of streams and dive into the water if alarmed. Some of the snake-eyed skinks live among rocks on the shore and feed on sea creatures such as small crabs and marine worms.

▷ *A young* **Eumeces skiltonianus.** *Like many other lizards skinks can shed their tails when they are attacked by a predator. The young of some skinks, including the type shown, have bright blue tails as an added safety device. When attacked the tail is broken off and it bounds continually; as it is the most conspicuous thing in sight, the predator is confused and the skink can scuttle safely away while the predator pursues the bounding tail. The tail is bright blue only when the skink is young, when the hazards of life are greatest. The blue-tailed Polynesian skink is exceptional in retaining its blue tail throughout its life.*

◁ *Foot-long mother **Tiliqua rugosa** and enormous newly-born.*

◁ ▽ *The largest of the skinks – the prehensile-tailed giant skink of the Solomon Islands.*

Teeth to fit the diet

The main food of skinks is insects and other small animals, including young mice and birds' eggs. The insect-eating skinks have pointed teeth with which they crush their hard-bodied prey and some types of skink which feed on earthworms have backwardly curving teeth which prevent the worms from escaping as they are being swallowed. The larger skinks are vegetarians and have broad, flat-topped teeth used for chewing.

Some lay eggs

Skinks lack the wattles and fans which other lizards use to display their superiority to rivals, but some male skinks develop bright colours during the breeding season. When they meet the males fight vigorously and may wound each other. Courtship is simple: the male follows a female, who allows him to catch her if she is ready to breed.

About half the skinks lay eggs; the others bear their young alive, the eggs being hatched just before they leave the mother's body. The eggs are usually laid under a log or rock and some skinks such as the five-lined skink of North America guard their eggs. The female curls around the eggs and stays with them until they hatch 4–6 weeks later, only leaving them to feed. As with other reptiles which stay with their eggs, it is difficult to decide what function they are performing. There is no evidence that skinks incubate the eggs and they desert them if disturbed, but it is known that skinks regularly turn their eggs which may be to prevent them from rotting.

Swimming in the sand

Some of the desert skinks are called sand-fish from the way they appear to swim through the sand. Their legs are well-developed but they are held close into the body when moving. Propulsion comes from the flattened tail which is reminiscent of the tails of amphibians or aquatic reptiles such as the marine iguana. Another adaptation is a sharp chisel-like snout that can cleave a way through the sand. Like other lizards, skinks have flexible skulls but their heads are strengthened for sand-swimming and burrowing by the fusing of the scales on the head.

class	Reptilia
order	**Squamata**
suborder	**Sauria**
family	**Scincidae**
genera & species	***Corucia zebrata*** *giant skink*
	Eumeces fasciatus *five-lined skink*
	Lygosoma laterale *little brown skink*
	Neoseps reynoldsi
	Florida sand skink
	Scelotes bojeri *Bojer's skink*
	S. inornatus *plain skink*
	S. melanopleura *black-sided skink*
	others

Green lizard

This is the second largest lizard in Europe; the male is 15 in. long, of which 10 in. is tail. Europe's largest lizard is the eyed lizard, 24 in. long of which 16 in. is tail, and there are records of 36 in. total length. The eyed lizard is often dark green spotted with yellow and black. There are blue spots forming rosettes on the flanks.

The head of the green lizard is large, its legs stout and the toes, especially on the hindfeet, long. The length of the toes is most marked in the males although the females are usually slightly larger than the males in total body size. The colour varies and while usually bright green in the male it may be yellowish-green or brown and yellow on the flanks of the female. Males are noticeably thick at the root of the tail.

Green lizards range across southern Europe from northern Spain and the south of France to southwest Russia and northwards to parts of Germany. They are also found in the Channel Islands, but attempts to acclimatize them a few degrees farther north, in southwest England, have failed.

△ Green lizards fighting.
▽ The second largest lizard in Europe.

Lovers of dampness

Green lizards live among rocks and on rough ground especially along the margins of woods, where the ground is not too dry. They are particularly found on river banks, but they may also occur in meadows, especially where there are damp ditches. They climb well and are reputed to be good swimmers and to take readily to water when disturbed and seek refuge on the bottom. They are active by day, hunting or basking, but seek the shade when the sun is hot. Hibernation is from October to March, in holes in the ground, under buttress roots of trees or under vegetation litter, the period of hibernation being shorter in the southern than in the northern parts of the range.

Shell-cracker jaws

Green lizards feed on insects, spiders, woodlice, earthworms and other small invertebrates but also eat smaller lizards and small rodents. They sometimes take birds' eggs, cracking the shells with their powerful jaws which can give a strong but non-venomous bite on the hand. They occasionally eat fruit.

Submissive females

The breeding season starts in late April and continues into May. The male's throat goes cobalt blue, and is used as a threat in the many contests that take place between males. He also uses the same intimidating displays towards females and it is the fact that she responds submissively, that is, she does not return his menacing attitude, which tells him she is a female. A short time after mating the female lays 5−21 dull white oval eggs, about ¾ in. long, in soft earth. She stays near her eggs and will come back to them even after being driven off. They hatch 2−3 months later, the newly-hatched young being 2−3½ in. long, brown with one or two rows of yellowish-white spots. They gradually turn

△ *A meal of a brimstone butterfly.*
▽ *A male in the mating season.*

green as they reach maturity. Green lizards may live for 10 years in captivity although their life in the wild is doubtless generally less than this.

Victims of pet-keepers

This lizard is attacked by the usual enemies of lizards, particularly the larger birds of prey, and it has the usual lizard defence of casting its tail and growing a new one. The chief danger to the green lizard, as with several other southern European reptiles, notably the Greek tortoise and the wall lizard, is their export for pet-keeping. Thousands each year find their way northwards to central and northern Europe to be kept in vivaria, to be used in laboratories, or to re-stock the many zoos.

Unsuccessful habitat

Some idea of the traffic in these attractive reptiles can be gained from the attempts to naturalize them in England. In 1899 an unspecified number of green lizards were liberated in the Isle of Wight and for a while they bred there. The last were seen in 1936. In 1931 some were introduced into Caernarvonshire, in North Wales. These did not breed and survived for only 4 years or so. In 1937, 100 green lizards were set free at Paignton, in south Devon. A few were still alive in 1952.

The wall lizard, a medium-sized European lizard, 8 in. long, was also introduced at Paignton in 1937, 200 being set free. They lasted only a few years, yet the wall lizard is a more northerly species than the green lizard, ranging from Jersey, in the Channel Isles, across Holland, Germany and Poland to the southern European mountain ranges.

South Devon is only a few degrees farther north than the Channel Islands, but it seems this is enough to make the difference between survival and extinction for the green lizard. Subtropical plants grow well in south Devon so, while temperature may be important, there must be other factors working against the lizards. An animal set down in a foreign environment must find suitable hiding places, suitable food and other necessities for successful living. Everything around is strange and, far more than for a plant, it is a gamble whether an animal will settle down. Nevertheless, we have the instances in which one group of green lizards survived in the Isle of Wight for at least 37 years and another group in South Devon continued for at least 15 years. The climate of the British Isles is said to be slowly getting warmer. It may well be that future attempts at acclimatization might prove more successful, provided there is then more sunshine than is usual now. Experience with captive green lizards shows that without sufficient sunlight they are prone to skin complaints that shorten their lives.

class	**Reptilia**	
order	**Squamata**	
suborder	**Sauria**	
family	**Lacertidae**	
genus	***Lacerta viridis*** *green lizard*	
& species	*L. **lepida*** *eyed lizard*	

Anaconda

The largest snakes are to be found in the boa family, and the largest of these is **Eunectes murinus**, *the anaconda or water boa. Probably no animal has been the subject of such exaggeration in respect of size. The name itself is said to come from the Tamil words* **anai** *for elephant and* **kolra** *for killer. Properly this name must have originally referred to the anaconda's relative, the Indian python. Claims for 140-ft anacondas have been made and 40 ft often occurs in travel literature. The famous explorer, Colonel Fawcett, claimed to have killed a 62-ft anaconda and was pronounced 'an utter liar' by London opinion. In fact, a 20-ft anaconda is a large specimen, although it must be presumed that larger individuals do occur. It is difficult to find an authentic record for the largest anacondas. The measurement of 37½ ft for one specimen has been widely accepted by scientists but not by all. Long ago, the New York Zoological Society offered a prize of 5,000 dollars for a 30-ft anaconda. This has never been won.*

The anaconda is olive green with large, round black spots along the length of its body and two light longitudinal stripes on the head. It lives throughout tropical South America, east of the Andes, mainly in the Amazon and Orinoco basins, and in the Guianas. It extends north to Trinidad. The species is variable in colour and size giving rise to numerous sub-specific names. However, these can be regarded as merely geographical variations. The closely related **Eunectes notaeus** *of Paraguay is known as the Paraguayan or southern anaconda.*

Life by jungle streams and swamps

Water boa is a good alternative name for the anaconda, the most aquatic of the boas. It is apparently never found far from water; sluggish or still waters being preferred to rapid streams. It is this preference that limits the species to the basins east of the Andes. Swamps are a favourite haunt.

Anacondas have, as a rule, fixed hunting grounds and generally live alone, but they are occasionally seen in groups.

Largely nocturnal in habit, anacondas lie up during the day in the shallows or sun-bathe on low branches, usually over water. On land they are relatively sluggish, but they are able to swim rapidly and often float motionless, allowing the current to carry them downstream.

Killing by constriction

Anacondas usually lie in wait for their prey to come down to the water's edge to drink, whereupon they strike quickly with the head, grabbing the luckless prey and drag-ging it underwater so that it drowns. At other times anacondas may actively hunt prey on land.

The usual prey caught by lying in wait are birds and small mammals – deer, peccaries

Anaconda is the largest of snakes, reaching up to 37 ft, although exaggerated claims give lengths of 140 ft. They kill their prey by constricting. Each time the victim breathes out, the anaconda tightens its coils until the animal dies of suffocation.

and large rodents such as agoutis. Fish also form a large part of the diet, a fact not surprising in so aquatic an animal. More surprisingly, turtles and caimans are some-times attacked. There is a record of a 25-ft anaconda killing a 6-ft caiman. The special jaw attachment that snakes have allows an anaconda to swallow such a large victim. After a meal of this size, which will suffice an anaconda for several weeks, the snake rests for a week or more until digestion has taken place. Normally the diet will consist of more frequent smaller meals.

Most snakes are adapted for swallowing prey wider than themselves: the upper and lower jaws are only loosely attached, and the brain protected from pressure by massive bones. Also a valve on the breathing tube allows the snake to breathe while swallowing.

The method of killing the prey is the same as in other constricting snakes such as the pythons. The prey is not crushed, but merely contained; each time the victim exhales, the coils of the anaconda tighten around its chest so that the ribs cannot expand, thus preventing inhalation until it suffocates. Stories in travelogues refer to anacondas' prey having every bone in the body broken and being squashed to pulp. In reality, bones are rarely broken during the process just described, which is one of strangulation. The fallacy is due to con-fusion between freshly-killed and regurgi-tated prey. This is covered with mucus, which gave rise to the story that anacondas smear their prey with saliva to facilitate swallowing.

Breeding

Few observations have been made on the breeding cycle of the anaconda. Males of southern anacondas studied in captivity were apparently aroused by the scent of the females. The male moves up alongside the female, flicking his tongue over her, until his head is resting over her neck. When in this position, he erects his spurs, two claw-like projections which are the last visible remnants of the hind limbs. The spurs are moved backwards and forwards against the female's skin and when the cloacal regions are in opposition, a hemipenis is inserted and copulation takes place.

Anacondas, like other boas, are viviparous. From 20—40, sometimes up to 100 young are born in the early part of the year. Each baby is 2—3 ft long.

Anacondas in folklore

It is not surprising that such a large, and malevolent-looking creature should be the subject of folklore and fallacy. The South American Indians have numerous stories about the anaconda, from the belief that it turns itself into a boat with white sails at night, to the mythology of the Taruma Indians who claimed to be descended from an anaconda. Several factors have led to tales of giant snakes. For one thing size is notoriously difficult to estimate unless a comparison can be made with something of known dimensions. Exaggeration is more likely if the animal is moving and writhing around, or if the observer has had a shock, as he might well have on suddenly seeing an anaconda Secondly, snake skins stretch very easily when being prepared so that the length of a skin gives no concrete evidence. It is not therefore difficult to see how stories of giant snakes could have arisen, and, once started, how this has led to unwitting or deliberate embroidery. Along with stories of venomous qualities and body size, there is exaggeration about the danger involved in meeting an anaconda. This is not unique; all large carnivorous animals become surrounded by stories of their man-eating habits. Many accounts are pure fiction. Only a few years ago a book was published describing a 140-ft anaconda, and how the author narrowly escaped from a 45-ft specimen by shooting its head off. Other stories are reported truthfully but are not evidence of man-eating habits, but of self-defence, for when man blunders into an animal it is not surprising that it tries to defend itself. There are, however, remarkably few authentic stories of people killed and eaten. Rolf Blomberg, who has made many searches for record-sized specimens, has been able to find only two fairly definite instances of anacondas killing human beings. In only one case was it claimed that the victim, a 13-year-old boy, was eaten. Even this was somewhat doubtful because the story goes that he disappeared while bathing with friends. On discovering his absence, one of them dived down to search and saw an anaconda. The victim's father then hunted down the snake and shot it. Blomberg states that the boy's body had been vomited up but does not say whether,

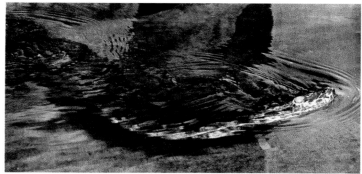

△ *An alternative name for the anaconda is water boa as it is never found far from the sluggish forest streams or swamps. Anacondas move relatively slowly on land but can swim rapidly and often float motionless, allowing the current to carry them downstream.*

▽ *Anacondas often lie up during the day in branches over the water's edge and wait for their prey to come down at night to drink, when they strike quickly with the head, grab the prey in their coils, often dragging it down into the water, to drown.*

in fact, it was recovered or whether this was only surmise. In the other incident a grown man was captured by an anaconda while swimming and was drowned. His body, when later found, had distinct marks of having been subjected to a powerful squeeze, but there was no indication of his having been swallowed.

Here then are two reports of the death of human beings, caused by anacondas. As we have seen, there is some doubt about one of them and in the second the man may have been killed but there is nothing to show he was eaten. In fact, few anacondas would be large enough to swallow a man. Nevertheless, such stories, perhaps in a garbled form, would travel through the country, so giving the impression that anacondas are man-eaters. After this, anyone who disappeared

and was last seen at the water's edge would be presumed to have been eaten by the anaconda, especially if one of these large snakes was seen in the vicinity. Such stories are so sensational that nobody asks for details or unequivocal evidence and the travellers would then take home a supposedly authentic story to relate to eager and uncritical audiences.

class	**Reptilia**
order	**Squamata**
suborder	**Serpentes**
family	**Boidae**
genus & species	***Eunectes murinus*** ***E. notaeus***

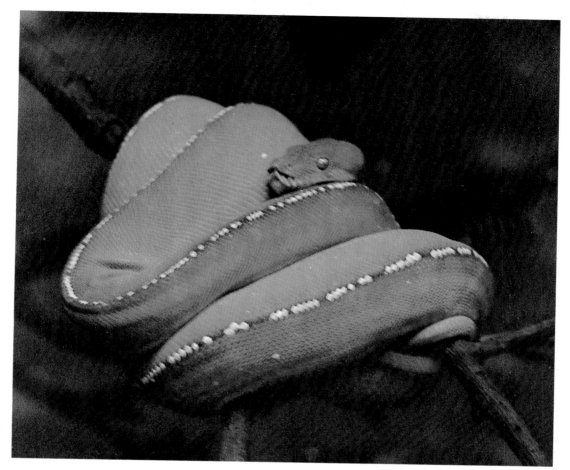

Python

Pythons are the Old World equivalent of the New World boas. Like the boas they have small spurs that represent the vestiges of hind limbs. The largest and best-known pythons belong to the genus **Python**. Not only are these large pythons at home in jungles, climbing trees, but they are often found near water. The African rock python which reaches about 32 ft long is not quite as long as the accepted record figure for the anaconda ($37\frac{1}{2}$ ft.), the largest of the boas. It lives in most parts of Africa in open country except the deserts. The other African pythons are the ball python and Angolan python of West Africa. There are no pythons in southwest Asia but several species are found from India to China and the East Indies. The Indian python reaches about 20 ft and ranges through southeast Asia from India to China and on some of the islands of the East Indies. The reticulated python,

reaching a length of 33 ft, has a more easterly distribution, from Burma to the Philippine Islands and Timor. The short-tailed python lives in the Malayan Peninsula, Borneo and Sumatra and the Timor python lives on the islands of Timor and Flores in Indonesia.

As well as the true pythons there are several other genera of pythons, including the carpet snake, that are found in the East Indies and Australia. Of the rock pythons the largest is the 20ft amethystine rock python or scrub python. A smaller group is the Australian womas which eat other snakes. The green tree python of New Guinea hunts in trees. The burrowing python, which lives in West Africa, in Liberia and throughout the rain forest of Zaire, spends its time underground chasing rodents and shrews.

Good travellers

The large pythons are often found near water and the Indian python is almost semi-aquatic. They also live in jungles and

△ A green tree python wraps its coils around itself as it waits for some unsuspecting prey which it grasps with its enlarged front teeth. Its leaf-green colour with white spots along its back and its extremely prehensile tail, make it admirably adapted for life in the trees.

climb trees, except for the African python which prefers open country. The reticulated python shows a preference for living near human settlements. At one time it was a regular inhabitant of Bangkok, hiding up by day and coming out at night to feed on rats, cats, dogs and poultry. One individual was caught in the King's palace. This habit of associating with buildings must account for its turning up in ships' cargoes. One reached London in good condition; but it is a good traveller under its own steam. It swims out to sea and was one of the first reptiles to reach the island of Krakatoa in the Malay archipelago, after it erupted in 1888, destroying all life.

Any live prey accepted

Pythons kill their prey by constriction, wrapping themselves around the body of the

prey so that it cannot breathe. The coils then hold the body steady while the python works it into its mouth. Prey is caught by ambush; the python lies in wait then springs out knocking the animal with its head and seizing it with its jaws until it can wrap its body round it. The list of animals eaten by pythons is too long to enumerate. Mammals are preferred, followed by birds, but young rock pythons have been caught in fish traps. African pythons eat many small antelopes such as dassies, gazelle, impala and bushbuck A large python can swallow prey weighing up to 120 lb but this is exceptional and usually smaller animals are taken such as dassies, hares, rats, pigeons and ducks. Jackals and monkeys are sometimes eaten and one 18 ft African python is known to have eaten a leopard, with very little damage being sustained in the process of catching it. Pythons sometimes suffer from their meals. They have been found with porcupine quills and antelope horns sticking through their stomach wall. Usually such dangerous projections are digested before causing any serious damage.

A large animal will last a python for a long time but they sometimes kill several small animals in quick succession. An African python has been credited with capturing and eating three jackals and a small python was seen to kill two sparrows in quick succession, then pin down a third with its tail.

There are a few authentic accounts of men being attacked by pythons, and there is good reason to believe the case of the 14 year old Malay boy attacked and eaten on the island of Salebabu.

Devoted mother pythons

The courtship of pythons is less lively than that of smaller snakes. The male crawls after the female, trying to climb over her and sometimes they rear up and sway to and fro. The spurs or vestigial limbs that lie either side of the cloaca are used by the male to scratch the female and stimulate her to raise her body so that he can wrap his body around hers and bring the two cloacas together. The eggs, 100 in a single clutch, are laid 3–4 months after mating. The female gathers the eggs into a pile and wraps herself around them, brooding them throughout the 2–3 month incubation period, only leaving them for occasional visits to water and more rarely to eat. Most pythons merely guard their eggs but the Indian python incubates them by keeping her body a few degrees above that of the surrounding air. Reticulated pythons are $2-2\frac{1}{2}$ ft long when they hatch and for the first few years they grow rapidly at a rate of about 2 ft or more a year. An Indian python nearly trebled its length in its first year of life. Pythons may live for over 20 years.

Courageous otters

Even the great snakes are not free from enemies. Young pythons have many enemies but as they grow larger fewer animals can overcome them. Crocodiles, hyaenas and tigers have been found with the remains of pythons in their stomachs and Jim Corbett writes of finding a 17ft Indian python killed by a pair of otters which had apparently attacked from either side, avoiding harm by their agility. When the ball python of Africa is molested it rolls itself into a tight, almost uniformly round ball, its head tucked well inside.

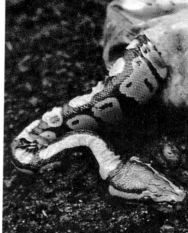

Beating elephants

Both African and Indian pythons were well known to the Greeks and Romans and have taken their place in folklore and religion. They are, for instance, responsible for one of the many dragon legends. Dragon is derived from the Greek word for snake, and the ancient writers were obviously talking about big snakes. It was mediaeval naturalists who turned them into fabulous creatures. Edward Topsell has left us a delightful description of how dragons capture elephants. In his *Historie of Serpentes* 1608 he writes how they 'hide themselves in trees covering their head and letting the other part hang down like a rope. In those trees they watch until the Elephant comes to eat and croppe off the branches, then suddainly, before he be aware, they leape into his face and digge out his eyes, and with their tayles or hinder partes, beate and vexe the Elephant, untill they have made him breathlesse, for they strangle him with theyr foreparts, as they beat him with the hinder.' Apart from the impracticability of an elephant being attacked, this is a reasonable account of a python killing its prey.

◁ *Strangled! A flying fox, caught in the jaws of a scrub python, is being strangled to death by the python's tightening coils.*

△ *A carpet python* **Morelia spilotes** *curls over and around her eggs, rarely leaving them. The temperature within her coils is up to 12F warmer than the surrounding atmosphere.*

▷△ *A ball python emerges from its egg, after an incubation period of up to 80 days. It may be one of a hundred snakes in the clutch.*

▷ *Superfluous legs. The two claws (arrowed) on either side of the anal vent of this African python are vestigial hind limbs, reminding us that snakes evolved from legged reptiles.*

▽ *The African python's skull shows the typical arrangement of teeth of a non-poisonous snake. The even sized teeth all point backwards, which ensures a firm and fatal grip on their prey.*

class	**Reptilia**
order	**Squamata**
suborder	**Serpentes**
family	**Pythonidae**
genera & species	***Calabaria reinhardti*** *burrowing python* ***Chondropython viridis*** *green tree python* ***Liasis amethystinus*** *amethystine rock python* ***Morelia argus*** *carpet snake* ***Python anchietae*** *Angolan python* **P. curtus** *short-tailed python* **P. molurus** *Indian python* **P. regius** *ball python* **P. reticulatus** *reticulated python* **P. sebae** *African python* **P. timorensis** *Timor python*

Cobra

Immortalised in Kipling's story of the hardy mongoose Rikki-Tikki-Tavi, the true cobras of the genus **Naja**, from the Sanskrit word 'naga' for snake, are medium-sized snakes. Several species average 6 or 7 ft. The Indian cobra has a dark body encircled by a series of light rings, and like all cobras, it has the characteristic hood behind the neck. The neck is flattened horizontally by long, moveable ribs being swung out to stretch the loose skin of the neck, rather like the ribs of an umbrella stretching out the fabric. The cobra rears up and expands the hood when frightened or excited, and, in the Indian cobra, this displays the distinctive spectacled pattern the hood has the typical 'spectacle' markings, but towards the eastern side of India a single ring-like marking becomes more common, while in the Kashmir and Caspian region the hood is marked with black transverse bars.

There are four species in Africa, the black-and-white cobra, the Cape cobra, the spitting cobra and the Egyptian cobra, which is also found in Asia.

Some cobras, such as the Egyptian cobra, are diurnal, others nocturnal like the Indian cobra, retiring by day to a favoured shelter in a burrow or under rocks. Some are found only near water.

Inoculating nerve-poisons

The cobra's venom is secreted from glands which lie just behind the eyes. It runs down

The Indian cobra is regarded by many experts as being one of the most dangerous snakes and death has been recorded as little as 15 minutes after the bite. Figures of 10 000 deaths a year have been given for India, which represents 1 in 30 000 of the population. Snakebite is so common in Asia and Africa because so many of the country people go about barefooted. Some cobras, notably the spitting cobra, of Africa, defend themselves by spitting venom over a distance of up to 12 ft. They aim for the face and the venom causes great pain and temporary blindness if it gets in the eyes.

Cobra venom has a different effect on the body than that of vipers which acts principally on the blood system, destroying tissues. Some tissue damage is done by cobra venom causing swelling and haemorr-

One of the four African species, the Cape cobra eats snakes as well as rodents, and is not averse to cannibalism.

Indian cobra, with its distinctive pattern. A cobra's hood works like an umbrella, with long, flexible ribs spreading the thin skin.

as the scales slide apart. The pattern is on the back of the neck but it can be seen from the front as the stretched skin is translucent.

Another well-known species is the Egyptian cobra, depicted on Ancient Egyptian headdresses rearing up with its hood inflated. Average length of adults is $5\frac{1}{2}$–6 ft and there are reports of their reaching 10 ft, although the longest reliable measurement is over 8 ft. The body is yellowish to almost black, the lighter forms often having darker spots.

Cobras are found in Africa and Asia, although fossils have been found in Europe, presumably dating from a time when the climate was warmer. There are two or four species in Asia, the number depending on different authorities' methods of classification. One of these is the Indian cobra that is found from the Caspian across Asia, south of the Himalayas to southern China and the Philippines, and south to Bali in Indonesia. Throughout its range, the markings vary. In the west

ducts to the fangs that grow from the front of the upper jaw. Each fang has a canal along the front edge, and in some species the sides of the canal fold over to form a hollow tube like a hypodermic needle, so resembling the hollow fangs of vipers. The cobra strikes upwards, with the snout curled back so that the fangs protrude. As soon as they pierce the victim's flesh, venom is squirted down the fangs by muscles that squeeze the venom gland. When a very aggressive cobra tightens these muscles too early venom dribbles from its mouth.

Cobras' fangs are fairly short, but after it has struck the snake hangs on, chewing at the wound and injecting large quantities of venom. The seriousness of the bite depends very much on how long the cobra is allowed to chew. If it is struck off immediately, the bite will probably not be too serious. It is always difficult to assess the dangers of snake bite. Even where good medical records are kept, some of the less severe cases will probably not be reported, and the severity depends so much on the condition of the victim. Young and old people and those who are sick, especially with weak hearts, are most likely to succumb.

hage, but the principal ingredients are neurotoxins acting on the nervous system causing paralysis, nausea, difficulty in breathing and, perhaps, eventually death through heart and breathing failure.

Rat-catching snakes

Cobras eat mainly rodents, coming into homes after rats, which is a cause of many accidents. Frogs, toads and birds are also eaten, the cobras climbing trees to plunder nests. The Egyptian cobra often raids poultry runs. The Cape cobra often eats snakes, including its fellows, and the black-and-white cobra is reported to hunt fish. When food is short they will eat grasshoppers and other large insects.

Cobras' mating dance

Before mating, the pair 'dance', raising their heads a foot or more off the ground and weaving to and fro. This may continue for an hour before mating takes place, when the male presses his cloaca to the female's and ripples run through his body.

The Cape cobra mates between September and October and the eggs are laid a month later. These dates vary through the cobras' range as they mate and lay eggs at the season most likely to provide abundant food for the young. Eggs number 8–20, and are laid in a hole in the ground or in a tree. The female may stand guard and during the breeding period is irritable and aggressive. She is liable to attack without provocation with dire results for passers-by if her nest is near a footpath. Newly-hatched cobras measure about 10 in.

Enemies

The traditional enemies of cobras are the mongooses, but genets also attack them. The mongoose's tactics are to leap backwards and forwards, around the cobra, keeping it continually on the alert until it tires and cannot hold its body raised in striking position. The mongoose is protected by the speed of its movements and by being very resistant to the cobra's venom. Mongooses do not always win, however. It has been suggested that the inflated hood serves as a protection, making it difficult for any enemy to bite the cobra's neck. Cobras also sham dead, going limp until danger passes.

Snake-charmer's bluff

Cobras, especially the Indian and Egyptian species, are the favourite performers in the snake-charmer's act. It is perhaps fairly common knowledge now that the snakes are not reacting to the music but to the rhythmic movements of the charmer. The pipe is merely a stage prop, and is not used by all performers, because snakes are deaf, or, in other words, they cannot perceive airborne vibrations. They have no eardrum that in most other terrestrial animals vibrates in time to the airborne waves, and

The legendary 'asp' or Egyptian cobra may grow to a length of 8 ft; and length for length it is much heavier than the Indian cobra.

they do not have the systems of bones and ducts that convey the vibrations from the eardrum to the sense cells of the inner ear. They can, however, detect vibrations through the earth.

The explanation of the cobras' dance is that the basket is suddenly opened, exposing the snakes to the glare of daylight. Half-blinded and somewhat shocked, they rear up in the defensive position with hoods inflated. Their attention is caught by the first moving object they see, which is the swaying snake-charmer, whose actions they follow.

Part of the act consists of the cobras being handled and even kissed on the head. This is not such a dare-devil act of bravado as it may seem for it is said that cobras cannot strike accurately in the full light of day, and, anyway, their fangs will have been

drawn or their lips sewn up. If this has not been done, the chances are that the charmer is immune to their venom.

class	**Reptilia**
order	**Squamata**
suborder	**Serpentes**
family	**Elapidae**
genus & species	*Naja naja* Indian cobra *N. haje* Egyptian cobra *N. nivea* Cape cobra *N. nigricollis* spitting cobra *N. melanoleuca* black-and-white cobra others

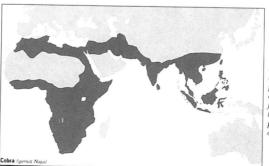

Cobra (genus Naja)

△ When cobras 'dance' for snake-charmers it is because, shocked and half-blinded by sudden exposure to daylight, they rear into their typical defensive position with their attention fixed on the first moving object they see—the hand or pipe of the snake-charmer.

Adder

A snake, member of the viper family, the adder has a relatively stout body and a short tail. The average male is 21 in. long, the female 2 ft – the record length is 2 ft 8 in. The head is flat, broadening behind the eyes to form an arrow-head shape.

The colour and body-markings vary considerably; adders are among the few snakes in which male and female are coloured differently. Generally the ground colour is a shade of brown, olive, grey or cream; but black varieties in which all patterning is obliterated are fairly common. The most characteristic marking is the dark zig-zag line down the back with a series of spots on either side; the head carries a pair of dark bands, often forming an X or a V.

It is often possible to distinguish the sex of an adder by its colour. Those which are cream, dirty yellow, silvery or pale grey, or light olive, with black markings, are usually males; females are red, reddish brown or gold, with darker red or brown markings. The throat of the male is black, or whitish with the scales spotted or edged with black; females have a yellowish-white chin sometimes tinged with red.

Distribution and habits

The adder ranges throughout Europe and across Asia to Sakhalin Island, north of Japan. In the British Isles it is absent from Ireland and the northern isles. It is usually to be seen in dry places such as sandy heaths, moors and the sunny slopes of hills where it often basks in the sun on hedge-banks, logs and piles of stones. It is, however, also found in damp situations.

Its tolerance of cold allows the adder to live as far north as Finland, beyond the Arctic Circle. It escapes cold weather by hibernation, which starts when the shade temperature falls below 9°C/49°F. It emerges again when the air temperature rises above 8°C/46°F – even coming out onto snow –

△ *The adder's tongue looks menacing but is harmless. It is a smell-taste organ, picking up particles from the air and withdrawing them for analysis in the mouth.*

▽ *The hedgehog is one of the adder's arch-enemies. It is protected by its spines while it alternately bites and rolls up, until the adder is dead.*

but a cold spell will send it in again. The duration of hibernation depends, therefore, on climate: in northern Europe it may last up to 275 days, whereas in the south it may be as little as 105 days. In Britain, adders usually hibernate for about 135 days in October-March, depending on the weather.

Unlike many other snakes adders do not burrow but seek out crevices and holes where they lie up for the winter. The depth at which they hibernate depends, like duration, on the climate: in Britain the average depth is 10−12 in., but in Denmark, where winters are more severe, adders are found at depths of 4 ft.

Very often many adders will be found in one den, or hibernaculum. As many as 40 have been found coiled up together, along with a number of toads and lizards. This massing together is a method of preventing heat loss, but it is not known how the adders come to congregate in the hibernacula, which are used year after year. It may be that they can detect the scent left from previous years.

It is uncertain whether adders are nocturnal or diurnal. Their eyes are typical of nocturnal animals in that they are rich in the very sensitive rod cells: such eyes will see well at night, but during the day they need protection, and the adder's slit pupils cut down the intensity of light. On the other hand, despite these adaptations, adders are often active during the day. Courtship and some feeding are definitely diurnal; feeding depends on how hungry the adder is.

Rodent killer

The adder's main prey is lizards, mice, voles and shrews. Young adders subsist at first

A black adder. Adders range in colour from cream, through dirty yellow to silvery grey or olive (male); and from red to gold (female).

on insects and worms. Larger victims are killed by a poisonous bite, the effects of which vary with the size of the prey. A lizard will be dead within a few minutes, or even within 30 seconds; but an adder's bite is rarely fatal to humans. There were only seven authenticated records of fatalities through snakebite in England and Wales in the first half of this century, and four of these were children.

The adder's method of hunting is to follow its prey by scent, then poison it with a quick strike of the head. While the venom acts, the victim may have time to escape to cover, in which case the snake will wait for a while then follow to eat its dead prey.

Dance of the adders

The mating period is from the end of March to early May, though it has been known to last until autumn. In the north of Europe the summer is too short for the eggs to mature in one year, so breeding takes place in alternate years.

At the beginning of the breeding season, there is a good deal of territorial rivalry between males, culminating in the 'dance of the adders'. Two males face each other with head erect and the forepart of the body held off the ground. They sway from side to side, then with bodies entwined each attempts to force the other to the ground by pushing and thrusting. They do not attempt to bite each other.

Finally one gives up and departs. The female, who is frequently waiting close at hand, will accept any victorious male, if she is ready, and a male will mate with any female. He crawls up behind her and loops his coils over her body, rubbing his chin (which has especially sensitive skin) on her back until he reaches the back of her neck, and mating takes place.

Adders are ovoviviparous: that is, the eggs remain inside the mother's body until they are fully developed, and the young are born coiled up in a membrane which is ruptured by their convulsive movements. They have an egg tooth, which in other animals is used to rupture the egg membranes, but in adders it is degenerate as they have no need of it, and the tooth is so situated that it is of no use for this purpose. It is shed a few days after birth.

The young are born in August or September and the number ranges from five to 20: 10-14 are most common, each measuring 6-8 inches in length. They are immediately capable of independent existence, but often they appear to stay with the mother. Young adders disappear so quickly when disturbed that there is an ancient legend, an account of which appears in Holinshed's Chronicle of 1577, that in times of danger the mother adder swallows her offspring. This legend could be due to early observers cutting up an ovoviviparous mother and finding unborn adders inside. Not knowing that adders hatch from the egg inside the parent they would think she had swallowed them.

△ *Male (left) and female adders are always differently coloured.*

▽ *Adder with day-old young.*

The adder has no external ear or ear drum, but picks up vibrations from the ground through its lower jaw. The vertical slit pupil gives quick perception of horizontal movement.

Enemies although poisonous

Like most animals—even those well capable of defending themselves—adders are most likely to flee if confronted with danger, and they usually bite only if suddenly frightened. But, despite not having the excuse of self-defence, man is their chief enemy. However, the killing of adders on sight has not led to their decline, although nowadays increased urbanisation is destroying their habitat.

Undoubtedly many carnivores will take adders. Foxes and badgers kill them, and they have been found in the stomachs of pike and eels. Surprisingly, perhaps, the hedgehog is a great adversary of adders: one reason is that it can tolerate large doses of venom without harm. Its method of killing is to bite the adder, then curl up leaving nothing but a palisade of spines for the snake to strike at. It repeats the process of biting and curling until the snake is dead, after which the hedgehog eats it.

A confusion of names

The Anglo-Saxon name for the adder was *naedre*, which became 'a nadder' or 'a nedder' in Middle English. Later the *n* was transposed, so that we now have 'an adder'. The alternative name viper comes from the Anglo-Saxon *vipere* or *vipre*, itself derived from the Latin *vipera*. This was a contraction of *vivipara*, from *vivus* (alive) and *parere* (to bring forth)—alluding to the animal's method of reproduction. In general 'viper' was used to mean any venomous snake. There being only one such snake in England, viper and adder became synonymous for the one species (viper also being used to describe a venomous or spiteful person).

These two words have spread with the English language all over the world, being used not only for snakes of the genus *Vipera*. There are the near relatives such as the gaboon viper, more distant, like the pit vipers and mole vipers, and the death adder, which is not even in the viper family.

class	**Reptilia**
order	**Squamata**
suborder	**Serpentes**
family	**Viperidae**
genus & species	***Vipera berus***

Puff adder

There are 8 species of puff adder in Africa and they range in size from the Peringuey's desert adder, 1 ft long, to the Gaboon viper, 6 ft or more long. They are stout bodied snakes with short tails. The head is very broad compared with the neck, and is covered with small overlapping scales. There is a deep pit of unknown function above the nostrils, and in many species one or more erectile scales on the snout form 'horns', as in the rhinoceros viper. Not all puff adders are given this name, although they all belong to the same genus, and they fall into two groups. These are the highly coloured Gaboon viper and rhinoceros viper, of the tropical African forests, and the sombrely coloured brown and grey puff adders of the savannah and deserts. One of this second group, the common puff adder, is yellow to brown with darker bars or chevrons on the back. It ranges from Morocco southwards across the Sahara to the Cape and is also found in Arabia. The others have less extensive ranges, the Cape puff adder, for example, being found only in the mountains of Cape Province, South Africa.

Melting into the background

Savannah and desert puff adders, with their duller colourings, tend to harmonize with the differently coloured soils on which they are living. So also do the Gaboon and rhinoceros vipers in spite of their bright colours, for their colour patterns are disruptive. The Gaboon viper has a gaudy pattern of yellow, purple and brown arranged in geometric forms. The rhinoceros viper, even more brilliantly coloured with more purple, and blue as well, has green triangles margined with black and blue on its sides. But both snakes are virtually invisible on the carpet of dead and green leaves on the forest floor. The smaller species of puff adder live on sandy soils. Several of these smaller adders are able to climb into bushes, but generally puff adders keep to the ground, hunting mainly during the night.

Inoffensive yet deadly

The broad head of the puff adder houses the large venom glands and although the effect of this snake's bite is less rapid than that of a mamba or a cobra it is just as deadly. Fortunately, these snakes strike only to disable prey or in self-defence, and need a fair amount of provocation to make them hit back. Africans are said to be more afraid of harmless geckos than of the Gaboon viper, and Herbert Lang tells of a small boy dragging a 5 ft live specimen into his camp to sell it to him. If their venom is slow-acting it is nonetheless potent. R Marlin Perkins, curator of reptiles in the St Louis Zoological Gardens, nearly died from the bite of a Gaboon viper. Some years

◁ *The attractive 'horned' head of the rhinoceros viper is deceptive; it houses the venom glands.*

later, in 1964, the Director of the Salt Lake City Zoo died from a puff adder bite received while handling the snake. Puff adders can give out as much as 15 drops of venom at a time—4 drops are enough to kill a man. But usually snakes give a first warning by hissing. The hissing sound is produced by forcing air from the lungs and windpipe through the glottis. Puff adders have an especially loud hiss. Their puff makes a sound more like the noise of a horse when it forces air through its lips.

Beckoning their food

The food of puff adders varies widely between the species. Small prey, such as a frog, is grabbed and swallowed without being poisoned. Larger prey is struck with the fangs and allowed to run away to die. The snake later follows its trail to eat it. The carcase is dragged into the snake's mouth by the teeth in the lower jaw. Once part of the victim has reached the throat, muscular swallowing movements carry it down, the snake holding its head up to assist this. Some scientists claim that the long fangs, which may be 2 in. long in a 5ft Gaboon viper, are used to drag the victim into the snake's mouth. South African herpetologists do not support this, but suggest the long fangs make it possible to inject the venom deeply.

The common puff adder and the Gaboon viper eat rats and mice, ground-living birds, frogs, toads and lizards. The Cape Mountain adder feeds on the same but is known to eat other snakes. The many-horned adder and the horned puff adder bury themselves in the sand, except for the eyes and snout, to catch lizards. The horned puff adder leaves the tip of its tail sticking out of the sand and waggles it to attract its victims within striking distance.

An enemy to many small animals, the puff adder has few adversaries itself, mainly birds of prey, mongooses and warthogs, and man. Puff adders can store large quantities of fat and this is sold by African herbalists as a cure for rheumatism.

Large families

Puff adders are ovoviviparous. That is, the eggs are hatched inside the mother so the young are born alive or else they wriggle out of the egg capsule soon after it is laid. Mating is usually from October to December, the young being born in March and April. The young from a mother 3 ft long, are about 8 in. at birth. There are 8—15 in the litter of the smallest species, 70—80 or more in the large puff adders.

Fasting to grow

The paradoxical frog is named because of the paradox that the tadpole is much greater than the froglet into which it changes. The puzzle is, where does all the spare flesh go? The situation is reversed in the baby puff adder. As soon as it is born it can kill and eat small mice although it moults first before looking for food. It can, however, happily go without food for as much as 3 months. The ability to fast is not unusual. What is extraordinary is that the baby puff adder still grows 25% in length and increases its girth by a quarter while doing so.

△ Sedate mating, two love-locked common puff
adders, the male is on the right. Mating
usually takes place from October to December.
Fertilisation is internal and sperm may
survive inside the female for long periods.
Most reptiles lay their eggs but puff adders
are ovoviviparous, the female retains the eggs
until the young are ready or nearly ready to
hatch 5—6 months later.

◁ Submerged for the day, a small Peringuey's
puff adder spends the day well hidden.
Alerted by the photographer the snake raises
its head so giving its position away. But its
sandy colouring blends well with the soil
making the snake very inconspicuous.

class	**Reptilia**
order	**Squamata**
suborder	**Serpentes**
family	**Viperidae**
genus & species	**Bitis arietans** *common puff adder*
	B. atropos *Cape Mountain adder*
	B. caudalis *horned puff adder*
	B. cornuta *manyhorned adder*
	B. gabonica *Gaboon viper*
	B. inornata *Cape puff adder*
	B. nasicornis *rhinoceros viper*
	B. peringueyi
	Peringuey's puff adder

Pit viper

Some of the most-feared snakes are to be found among the 60 species of pit vipers (family Crotalidae) including well known forms like the fer de lance, (named so because of its lance-shaped head and body), and the sidewinder and the rattlesnakes, which we shall come to later. Here we shall consider others, such as the American water moccasin, copperhead and bushmaster, as well as the Asiatic pit vipers. Pit vipers are a diverse group with several interesting specializations, which is why we have given them three entries. Here, while dealing with the family in general terms, we pay special attention to what has been called their sixth sense, the two pits on the head that give them their name.

Pit vipers are solenoglyph. That is, they have fangs which fold back and are erected when about to be used. Most pit vipers are land-living, some are tree-dwellers, a few have taken to water and others lead a partially burrowing life. Water moccasins are heavy-bodied, up to 5 ft long, and while living on land they readily take to water when disturbed and they hunt in water. They are slate black to olive or tan with indistinct brown bands. The copperhead, a brown snake with hourglass markings along the back, is up to 3 ft long. It lives in rocky outcrops and quarries and among piles of rotting logs. The bushmaster is the longest of the American pit vipers, up to 12 ft, mainly grey and brown with large diamond blotches along the back. It has large venom glands and unusually long fangs. Its generic name **Lachesis** is from one of the Fates that influenced the length of life of people – a grim pun by the scientist who named it, for the bushmaster is one of the most dangerous of snakes. The Asiatic pit vipers are of two kinds, tree-dwelling and ground-living, the first having prehensile tails that assist their climbing. The Himalayan pit viper lives at altitudes of 7 000–16 000 ft, sometimes being found even at the foot of glaciers.

The Asiatic pit vipers are found mainly in eastern and southeast Asia with one species extending as far west as the mouth of the River Volga. Wagler's pit viper is kept in large numbers in the Snake Temple in Penang. The water moccasin and the copperhead are widespread over the eastern and middle United States, the bushmaster ranges from Costa Rica and Panama to northern South America.

Warm-blooded food

The warning posture of the water moccasin, mouth open showing its white lining, gives it the alternative name of cottonmouth. It also vibrates its tail at the same time, like its relatives the rattlesnakes, although it has no rattle to make a warning sound. Pit vipers, apart from their pits, are very

△ *Trimeresurus gramineus.*

ordinary snakes. Some take a wide range of foods, like the water moccasin which eats rabbits, muskrats, ducks, fish, frogs, other snakes, birds' eggs, and nestlings. The copperhead eats small rodents, especially the woodmouse, other snakes, frogs, toads, and insects, including caterpillars and cicadas. The bushmaster, by contrast, takes mainly mammals, and pit vipers generally tend to hunt warm-blooded animals more than cold-blooded, as one would expect from snakes with heat-detector pits. They have one on each side of the head between the eye and the nostril. Using these a pit viper can pick up the trail of a warm-blooded animal.

'Seeing' heat

Each pit is $\frac{1}{5}$ in. across and $\frac{1}{4}$ in. deep. A thin membrane is stretched near the bottom and temperature receptors, 500–1 500 per sq mm, are packed within this membrane. These receptors are so sensitive they can respond to changes as small as 0·002 of a C°, and they allow a snake to locate objects 0·1 of a C° warmer or cooler than the surroundings. In more understandable terms a pit viper could detect the warmth of the human hand held a foot from its head. The membrane with its receptors can be compared to an eye with its retina. The overhanging lip of the pit casts 'heat shadows' onto it, so the snake is aware of direction, and since the 'fields of view' of the two pits overlap there is the equivalent of stereoscopic vision, giving a rangefinder. A pit viper hunting by day has the advantage of being able to follow an animal's heat trail through low vegetation after the animal has passed out of sight. It could, of course, do this equally well by scent. The facial pits come into their own in night hunting, when prey can be tracked by scent with the facial pits guiding the final strike. At first it was thought they had something to do with an accessory aid to smell or as an organ of hearing—snakes have no ears. Another suggestion was that they might be organs for picking up low-frequency air vibrations. Then, as late as 1892, it was noticed that a rattlesnake, one

of the pit vipers, was attracted to a lighted match. Then came the discovery that pythons have pits on their lips that are sensitive to heat. The first experiments on pit vipers were made in 1937, and left no doubt that the pits are heat detectors and further studies since have shown just how delicate they are.

Snakes in cold climates

Pit vipers usually bear living young. There are a few exceptions, the bushmaster being one, and that lives in the tropics. Pit vipers extend from the Volga across Asia and across America. There may be a direct connection between these two facts. One of the advantages of bearing living young, as against laying eggs, is that the offspring are protected not only against enemies but also against low temperatures until they are at an advanced stage of development. At some time pit vipers must have crossed the land bridge that used to exist where the Bering Straits are now. This is well north, and it would have been far easier for snakes able to bear live young to survive in these latitudes and so make the crossing. It probably explains also why the Himalayan pit viper can live so near glaciers, and why the most southerly of all snakes is a pit viper named *Bothrops ammodytoides*, living in the Santa Cruz province of Argentina.

class	**Reptilia**
order	**Squamata**
suborder	**Serpentes**
family	**Crotalidae**
genera & species	***Ancistrodon contortrix*** copperhead ***A. himalayanus*** *Himalayan pit viper* ***A. piscivorus*** *water moccasin* ***Trimeresurus wagleri*** *Wagler's pit viper*

Rattlesnake

These are heavy-bodied and usually highly venomous snakes, best known for the rattle, sometimes called a bell, cloche, buzzer or whirrer, on the tail. When disturbed the rattlesnake vibrates its tail, or rattle, as if giving warning that it is about to strike. Rattlesnakes are found almost entirely in North America, from southern Canada to Mexico, where there are 30 species and over 60 subspecies, with one species in South America.

There are two groups of rattlesnakes, each represented by one genus: the pygmy rattlesnakes **Sistrurus** *have short slender tails and very tiny rattles, and they never exceed 2 ft in length; and the rattlesnakes proper* **Crotalus,** *which are usually around 3½–5 ft but exceptionally grow to 8 ft or more. The timber or banded rattlesnake of the eastern States is marked with dark chevrons on the back. In the prairie rattlesnake the markings are irregularly oblong. Most others have diamond markings. Rattlesnakes share with other pit vipers (page 99) a tolerance of low temperatures. The Mexican dusky rattlesnake lives at altitudes of up to 14 500 ft.*

Sound varies with size

The rattle is made up of a number of loosely interlocked shells each of which was the scale originally covering the tip of the tail. Usually in snakes this scale is a simple hollow cone which is shed with the rest of the skin at each moult. In rattlesnakes it is larger than usual, much thicker and has one or two constrictions. Except at the first moult, the scale is not shed but remains loosely attached to the new scale, and at each moult a new one is added. The rattle does not grow in length indefinitely. The end scales tend to wear out, so there can be a different number of segments to the rattle in different individuals of the same age, depending on how much the end of the rattle is abraded. It seldom exceeds 14 segments in wild rattlesnakes no matter how old they may be, but snakes in zoos, leading a more untroubled life, and not rubbing the rattle on hard objects, may have as many as 29 pieces in a rattle. The longer the rattle the more the sound is deadened, 8 being the most effective number to give the loudest noise. The volume of sound not only varies with the size of the snake and the length of the rattle, but it also varies from species to species. At best it can be heard only a few feet away.

◁ *Threatening tiger rattlesnake. Between its coils is a large rattle, a unique organ composed of horny segments of unshed skin. The fact that rattlesnakes shed their skin three or four times a year during the first years of their lives disposes of the popular idea that the number of rattles corresponds to the years of the snake's age. The best reason to be found for the evolution of the rattle in an animal that is deaf is that it acts as a warning device to large animals that may molest or tread on the snake.*

101

Rattlers not all black

It is hard to generalize on the size and effectiveness of the rattle as it is on any other feature of rattlesnakes. For example, these snakes have a reputation for attacking people, and of being bad tempered. It applies only to some of them. Unless provoked or roughly treated the red diamond rattlesnake may make no attempt to strike when handled. It may not even sound its rattle. The eastern and western diamond backs, by contrast, not only rattle a warning but they will also pursue an intruder, lunging at it again and again. How poisonous a snake is also depends on several things, such as its age – the younger it is the less the amount of poison it can inject – and whether it has recently struck at another victim, when the amount of venom it can use will be reduced. Cases are known in which a snake has taken nearly two months to replenish its venom to full capacity. Rattlesnakes of the same species from one part of the range may be more venomous than those from another part. Prairie rattlesnakes of the plains are about three times as venomous as those of California, and half as poisonous again as those of the Grand Canyon.

Waterproof skin

Rattlesnakes feed on much the same prey as other pit vipers (page 99), mainly small warm-blooded animals and especially rodents, cottontail rabbits and young jack rabbits. Young rattlesnakes, including the pygmy rattlesnakes, take a larger proportion of coldblooded animals, such as frogs, salamanders and lizards. Studies have also been made on how much rattlesnakes drink, and the remarks that follow probably apply to all snakes. Their needs are not as great as those of active and warm-blooded animals because the water loss from the body is not high. They need about one-tenth as much water as a mammal of similar size. In one test it was found that twice as much water is lost from a rattlesnake's head, and this mainly in its breath, as from the whole of the rest of its body, which suggests that its skin is almost waterproof. When it does drink it sucks up water from a pond or stream. There is no evidence that it laps it with the tongue, as is sometimes stated, or that it drinks dew.

Two years to be born

All rattlesnakes give birth to live young. Whether they have one litter a year or less depends on the climate. The prairie rattlesnake has one litter a year in the southern part of its range, but in the northern part it may be two years before the young are ready to be born. Mating is in spring and the number in a litter may vary from 1 to 60 according to the size of the mother, the usual number being between 10 and 20.

Slaughter of infants

Their venom does not spare rattlesnakes from being killed and eaten. Hawks of all kinds kill them, so do skunks and snake-eating snakes. Pigs, deer and other hoofed animals trample them, especially the young ones, and many die of cold or excessive heat, or from starvation. Indeed few from a litter survive their first year.

Sensitive eyes

Snakes are known to be deaf yet they often seem to be reacting to sounds. In fact, they seem at first glance to be able to hear but there is more to it than this, as Laurence Klauber found in his celebrated tests on rattlesnakes. First, having placed a rattlesnake under a table, he clapped two sticks together making sure his hands and the sticks could not be seen by the snake. It reacted, apparently to the sound. Puzzled at first, Klauber finally found the reason. He was sitting on a stool, his feet dangling, and every time he clapped the sticks together his feet moved and the snake reacted to sight of them. So he put a screen between the snake and his feet, and still the snake reacted when he clapped the sticks – it was seeing a reflection of Klauber's feet in a nearby window.

He found his red diamond rattler highly sensitive to footsteps on a concrete floor 15 ft away, and it still reacted to footsteps that distance away after he had placed it on a blanket. He decided to test this further. He put the snake in a fibreboard box, suspended this by a rubber band from a stick held each end on a pillow, to insulate it from vibrations through the ground. It still reacted to clapped sticks and to the radio. It was, in fact, as Klauber finally found, picking up the beat from the valves of the radio as these warmed up, and it was reacting to vibrations in the floor and sides of the fibreboard box, against which its body rested. So the box was changed for a Chinese woven bamboo basket hung from the same stick. Still the snake appeared to react to sound, but further tests showed it was reacting to Klauber's hand movements seen through the very tiny cracks between the bamboo withies. Apart from anything else, these experiments show how hard it can sometimes be to test a particular animal sense. They also show, among other things, how sensitive a snake's eyes are to small movements.

class	**Reptilia**
order	**Squamata**
suborder	**Serpentes**
family	**Crotalidae**
genus & species	***Crotalus adamanteus*** *eastern diamond back*
	C. atrox *western diamond back*
	C. horridus *timber or banded rattlesnake*
	C. pusillus *Mexican dusky rattlesnake*
	C. ruber *red diamond back*
	C. tigris *tiger rattlesnake*
	C. viridis *prairie rattlesnake*

◁ *Sparring partners – two western diamond back rattlesnakes engage in combat. Although it is difficult to observe both snakes simultaneously during the fight it seems that the twining of the necks is a manoeuvre for an advantageous position from which one snake may forcefully throw his opponent.*

Sidewinder

Also known as the horned rattlesnake, the sidewinder is named after its peculiar form of locomotion which allows it to move over soft sand. Sidewinders are small rattlesnakes, the adults being only 1½–2 ft long. The females are usually larger than the males, whereas in other rattlesnakes it is the reverse. The body is stout, tapering to a narrow neck with a broad head like an arrowhead. Above each eye there is a scale that projects as a small horn. There is a dark stripe running backwards from each eye. The body is pale grey or light brown with a row of large dark brown spots running down the back and smaller ones on each side. The tail is marked with alternate light and dark bands and the underparts of the body and tail are white.

The single species of sidewinder lives in the deserts of the southwest United States, including Nevada, Utah, California, Arizona and in the northern part of the state of Baja California in Mexico.

The sidewinder is a small squat rattlesnake that is perfectly adapted for living in deserts.

Sand snake

Sidewinders are most common in areas of loose, windblown sand and although they can be found among rocks or on compacted sand there is usually loose sand nearby. Although other rattlesnakes live in deserts and can be found on loose sand, the sidewinder is the most characteristic of this type of habitat. It is likely that in this habitat the sidewinder has an advantage over the other snakes. By adapting to life in moving sand the sidewinder does not compete with other snakes. These can move over sand by the usual eel-like wriggling. The sidewinder's unusual looping movement enables it to get a good grip on loose sand and so move faster.

Sidewinders are most active in the early part of the night when air temperatures are not dangerously high and when their prey is also active. They spend the day in mouse-holes or buried in sand, usually under the shelter of a creosote bush or a yucca. They bury themselves by shovelling sand over themselves with looping movements of the body until they are coiled like springs, flush with the surface of the sand. Their mottled brown colour makes them very difficult to see as they lie there half buried.

Desert prey

The shallow saucers in the sand where sidewinders have been resting are often found near mouse and rat burrows as the sidewinders are probably attracted to these areas where they will find prey plentiful. Their main food is small rodents, such as deer mice, kangaroo rats and spiny pocket mice, and lizards such as the tree-climbing utas and other sand-dwelling iguanids. Sidewinders also eat a few snakes, such as the glossy snake and even other sidewinders, and a few small birds.

The breeding habits of sidewinders are the same as those of other rattlesnakes (page *101*). Mating takes place when they emerge from hibernation in spring and the young are born alive.

How snakes move

Sidewinding is like a coiled wire rolled along the sand making a series of oblique parallel tracks. Only the white areas touch the ground.

In serpentine movement the body literally skates along in a series of shallow curves which get a grip on any projecting object.

Concertina movement: with the tail anchored the head and neck dart forward, the neck grips the ground and the rest of the body is then pulled up.

Sidewinding

Many snakes will perform 'sidewinding' movements if placed on a sheet of glass, throwing their bodies into loops to get a grip on the smooth surface. The sidewinder, and the horned viper and puff adder of African deserts, make a habit of sidewinding, leaving characteristic tracks in the sand. These are a series of parallel, wavering lines each with a hook at one end made by the sidewinder's tail.

It is very difficult to see how the track is made without seeing a sidewinder in action. In normal, or rectilinear, movement, a series of waves passes down a snake's body, pushing against the ground and driving the snake in the opposite direction to the waves. Sidewinding is very different; it is more like a coil spring being rolled or the movement of the tracks of a caterpillar tractor. The snake throws its body into curves and, when moving, only two points of the body touch the ground. These two points remain stationary while the raised parts move at an angle to the direction of the waves that pass along its body. As the snake progresses the part of the body immediately behind is raised, so that the body is laid down and taken up like a caterpillar track. When the point of contact reaches the tip of the tail, a new point is started at the head end and the snake moves along a series of parallel tracks.

class	**Reptilia**
order	**Sauria**
suborder	**Serpentes**
family	**Crotalidae**
genus & species	***Crotalus cerastes***

103

Birds

There is no doubt that among non-scientists birds are the most favoured of all animals, largely because they are the most obvious, because of their colours and their songs. They have also received more than their fair share of attention from scientists and one result of this is that it is unlikely that new species will be discovered in the future.

Another consequence of this attention is that the classification of birds has reached a stable form. In this classification 27 orders of living birds are enumerated, with two more for the recently extinct moas of New Zealand and elephant-birds of Madagascar. This is a higher proportion of orders to a single class of animals than in any other area of the animal kingdom.

Side by side with this, it has to be recognized that there are few, if any, other major groups of animals so poorly represented by fossils, as are birds. Fortunately, there are the remarkably complete fossils of the earliest known bird, the Archaeopteryx, the so-called lizard-bird, that indicate very clearly the evolution of birds from reptilian ancestors. This paucity of fossils is probably to be correlated with the flying habits, so that, as has often been said by palaeontologists, "birds do not make good fossils". The situation is similar for bats – but not for the pterodactyls or flying reptiles. This absence of all but a few scattered fossils is the more remarkable when it is recalled

that birds have certainly been in existence for about 180 million years.

The class Aves used to be divided into two main divisions: the Ratitae and the Carinatae, the first including the large, flightless, running birds, such as ostrich, emu, cassowary, rhea and kiwi, the second including all the rest. Today, both names are used, if at all, merely as convenient group names, the surviving ratites being assigned to four separate orders, the Struthioniformes (ostriches), Rheiformes (rheas), Casuariiformes (emus, cassowaries) and Apterygiformes (kiwis), on the assumption that these birds are not necessarily related but look alike as a result of convergent evolution.

Of the remaining 23 orders, one is by far the largest and contains the most familiar of all birds. It is named the Passeriformes, after *Passer domesticus*, the house sparrow, the most familiar of all birds in the western world, where the main work on the early classification of birds was carried out. This order, sometimes referred to merely as Passeres, contains more than half the known species of living birds and includes 56 of the 149 families of the 'Carinatae'.

In its turn, the Passeriformes, also known as the perching birds, is divided into four suborders, the Eurylaimi (broadbills), Tyranni (woodcreepers, antbirds, antpipits, ovenbirds, tapaculos and others), Menurae (lyrebirds, scrub-birds) and Oscines

(songbirds). The first three of these account for only 15 of the 56 families and about 1040 species of the 5000 or more species of Passeriformes.

The Passeriformes therefore bear comparison with bony fishes in having been evolved, geologically speaking, in a very short space of time. They have proliferated into numerous species, are worldwide, have successfully adapted to environments most of which are man-made, nesting or roosting on buildings and making use very often of 'unnatural' foods. Like the bony fishes, they have exploited a wide variety of habitats. Since they use agricultural land and buildings so much they are brought into close contact with people, whether in rural or urban districts, so that the Passeriformes can reasonably be said to have played a major role in the social phenomenon of the 20th century known as bird-watching.

It has been said, doubtless with a fair degree of truth, that we hold as favourites those animals having characteristics similar to our own. The passerines have these in generous degree. Most birds are deficient in the sense of smell, and this is especially true of passerines. With rare exceptions, birds are 'eyesight animals', like humans, meaning that sight is the most important sense. Above all, the Passeriformes are especially vocal, if not vociferous, a feature of human behaviour almost without parallel in the animal kingdom.

Ostrich

*The ostrich is the largest living bird and
one of the most familiar because of its
bizarre appearance. A large male may
stand 8 ft high of which nearly half is
neck. The plumage of the male is black
except for the white plumes on the wings
and tail. It is these plumes that first led
to the numbers of ostriches being greatly
reduced in many places and later to
ostriches being raised on farms. The
plumage of the females is brown with
pale edging to the feathers. The head,
most of the neck and the legs are almost
naked, but the eyelids have long, black
eyelashes. There are two strong toes on
each foot, the longest being armed with
a large claw.*

*A few million years ago, in the Pliocene
era, there were nine species of ostriches,
but only one survives today. About 200
years ago five subspecies of this species
ranged over much of Africa, Syria and
Arabia, in desert and bush regions. They
are now extinct or very rare over most of
this area. The Asian subspecies was
last recorded in 1941. Ostriches are still
plentiful in East Africa, and they live
wild in a few places in south Australia
where they were introduced.*

Strange social life

Ostriches are extremely wary, their long
necks enabling them to detect disturbances
from quite a distance. As a result it is very
difficult to study ostriches in the wild and
until recently our knowledge has been based
mainly on observations on domesticated
ostriches. Incomplete observations in the
wild have led to many mistaken ideas about
the habits of these birds which have now
become legendary. A husband and wife
team of zoologists, the Sauers, studied
ostriches in South West Africa by the in-
genious method of disguising their hide as
a termite mound. Ostriches and several
other animals treated this hide with complete indifference with the result that the
Sauers were afforded a grandstand view of
ostrich social life, and they found that in
some respects this is almost as strange as
the legends.

Ostriches often live in very dry areas and
they move about in search of food, often
in quite large groups. During wet spells
the herds break up into family groups,
consisting of a pair with chicks and im-
matures. The herd is led by a cock or hen
that chooses grazing grounds and makes
decisions as to when to move. If the herd
leaves familiar territory or comes to a water
hole where no other animals are drinking,
the dominant ostriches push the immature
birds forward to spring any ambushes.

Eats nearly anything

Ostriches feed mainly on plants including
fruits, seeds and leaves. In deserts they get
their water from succulent plants. They
also eat small animals and are even said to
eat lizards and tortoises. Their reputation

for eating almost anything including lumps
of metal and tins of paint is widespread and
perhaps exaggerated but ostriches swallow
considerable amounts of sand to aid digestion and it is said that it is possible to trace
the movements of an ostrich by examining
the kinds of sand and gravel in its stomach.

Unstable society

Until recently there was considerable doubt
as to whether ostriches were polygamous or
monogamous. Proponents of monogamy
pointed out that there was never more than
one male or one female seen at a nest or
leading a group of chicks. It is now known
that ostriches may be monogamous but
more usually they are polygamous. The
Sauers found that the social organisation
of ostriches is very flexible and that a male
accompanying a female with chicks need
not be the father of the chicks.

Breeding takes place at any time of the
year, depending on the time of the rainy
season. At first the males develop a red
pigment on their heads and feet and they
display to each other, chasing around in
groups with wings held out to show off the
white plumes. Later they establish territories away from the communal feeding
grounds, and here they are joined by the
females. A male ostrich usually has three
hens in his harem but it is not unknown for
him to have up to five.

The courtship ceremony is elaborate.
The male separates one female from the
group and the pair feed together, syn-
chronising the movements of head and
neck. The male then sits down and opens
his wings to show the white plumes. At the
same time he rocks from side to side and
twists his neck in a corkscrew. The female
walks around him and eventually drops into
the mating position.

Each female lays 6–8 eggs which are
about 6 in. long and weigh up to 2½ lb.
The members of a harem all lay in one nest,
which consists of a depression in the ground
that may be about 3 yd across. It may take
nearly 3 weeks for all the eggs to be laid,
after which the dominant hen drives the
others away and the nest is guarded by the
single hen and the cock. Incubation consists
of keeping the eggs cool by shading them
rather than keeping them warm. Towards
the end of the 6-week incubation period
some eggs are rolled into pits on the edge
of the nest. These eggs are those that are
most advanced and this is probably a
mechanism to synchronise the hatching of
the eggs as much as possible.

The chicks can run almost as soon as
they hatch and after a month can attain a
speed of 35 mph. When they leave their
parents they form large bands, breeding
when 4–5 years old.

Running to safety

Adult ostriches have little to fear from
predators. They are very wary and can run
at 40 mph, but the eggs and young ostriches may fall prey to jackals and other
predators. The adults lead their chicks
away from enemies and perform distraction
displays while the chicks scatter and crouch.

▷ *A bizarre creature with a long naked neck:
the ostrich is the largest living bird.*

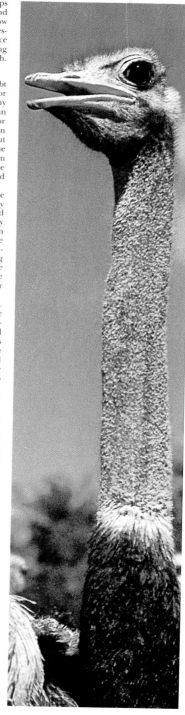

Beating their wings and calling loudly the ostriches run to and fro presenting a broadside to the enemy and occasionally dropping to the ground and setting up a cloud of dust with the wings. Sometimes the male continues the display while the female leads the chicks away.

Burying their heads

One of the popular notions about ostriches is that they bury their heads in the sand when danger threatens. The action is used to describe the behaviour of a person who thinks that a problem can be solved by ignoring it, and has been the subject of many jokes and cartoons. This idea is very old, for the Roman writer Pliny says '... the veriest fools they be of all others, for as high as the rest of their body is, yet if they thrust their head and neck once into any shrub or bush, and get it hidden, they think then

◁ *Too many eggs? At the end of the incubation period the most advanced eggs are rolled into a pit beside the nest to synchronize hatching.*
▽ *Arrival date. Ostrich chicks hatching.*

they are safe enough, and that no man seeth them.'

Like so many legends there is a basis of truth in the ostrich burying its head and the story is probably due to the difficulty in observing ostriches. When an ostrich is sitting on the nest, its reaction to disturbance is to lower its head until the neck is held horizontally a few inches above the ground. The ostrich is then very inconspicuous and the small head may well be hidden behind a small plant or hummock.

class	**Aves**
order	**Struthioniformes**
family	**Struthionidae**
genus & species	***Struthio camelus***

▷ *A handsome male ostrich gives chase to two females busy displaying.*
▽ *Ostriches on the march. Flocks of them move about in the dry season, looking for food.*

Emu

One of Australia's flightless birds, the emu is the second biggest bird in existence. It stands 5–6 ft high, 2–3 ft less than the ostrich and dwarfed by the giant moas of New Zealand that became extinct a few centuries ago. Emus are related to cassowaries and share with them the coarse, drooping plumage and small wings hidden by the feathers. The feathers are double, as in cassowaries, with the aftershaft—the small tuft at the base of the vane in many birds—the same length as the main vane. The feathers are also downy, like the feathers of chicks, for the barbs do not have hooks linking them to make the stiff vane. The downy feathers, together with other anatomical features, suggest that emus and the other flightless birds known as ratites, such as ostriches, rheas and kiwis, are neotenous—that is, that juvenile characters have been retained in the adult.

Before Europeans settled in Australia there were several species of emu, but all except one have been wiped out. At one time Tasmania, Kangaroo, Flinders and other islands, had their own emus, but they were killed off so rapidly that hardly any specimens reached museums.

Apart from the female being slightly the larger, it is difficult to tell male and female emus apart. Their voices, however, are very different. The male makes guttural cries, whereas the female has a resonant booming call made by a large air sac connected to the windpipe.

Pests in the dry season

Emus live in most parts of Australia, except where building and agriculture have driven them out. They are found in the deserts, on plains and in forests—but not in the dense rain forests of northeast Australia, where their place is taken by the cassowary. Outside the breeding season emus live in small parties, sometimes banding together into large herds. They are nomadic, moving about the country in search of food and water. In the dry season they become a pest. They move from the arid areas into agricultural land, raiding crops and using water holes that in bad years are barely enough to support domestic stock and farmers shoot on sight of them.

Like their flightless relatives, emus are strong runners. When pressed they reach 40 mph in short bursts, covering over 9 ft in one stride. Normally they run at a slower and steadier cruising speed that enables them to cover long distances. They are extremely inquisitive, investigating any new object. This may explain the habit, shared with ostriches, of swallowing all sorts of strange objects: keys, nails, bottle tops, coins and so on. One emu is reported to have drunk the contents of a tin of paint, then eaten the tin. Another chased a man for 4 miles, having been attracted to his shiny bicycle; but they will follow men apparently just to look at them.

△*The second largest of living birds—the emu. The external ear opening is visible as only downy feathers cover the head and neck.*

▽*In the nonbreeding season these huge Australian birds congregate in small flocks, moving through the outback in search of food and water.*

Keeping down harmful insects

Fruit of many plants, leaves, grass and insects are the food of emus. During the winter months insects, especially caterpillars probably make up the bulk of the diet. Wheat crops are attacked when they ripen and for this reason emus are often persecuted. Nevertheless, eating insects must repay the debt to a large extent. One emu killed in an official campaign had nearly 3 000 harmful caterpillars in its stomach.

Father guards the eggs

Emus breed when 2 years old, laying their eggs in February or March, the Australian autumn. The male builds the nest, about 3 ft across, making a shallow bowl of grass and weeds, usually under a tree or bush. After the female has laid her clutch of 8–10 dark green eggs, she leaves the nest and the male incubates them for 8 weeks. During this time he rarely leaves the nest, and when he does, he may cover it with leaves to make the already inconspicuous eggs almost impossible to find.

At the end of the 8 weeks the eggs, which were rough, have become smoother and darker. They are often collected and turned into curios or souvenirs by etching the thick shell, revealing the paler layers under the surface in a cameo-like effect.

The chicks leave the nest shortly after hatching. They are miniature versions of the adults but very pale grey with conspicuous black stripes running along the body. The father guards the chicks for up to 18 months, until they are nearly mature. The young chicks feed themselves, mainly on insects, but there is a legend that emus lay a sterile egg either for the chicks to eat or to support a colony of fly maggots for the chicks to eat after hatching.

Oil and outsize omelettes

The natural enemies are wedge-tailed eagles that take young emus; and nest robbers such as various lizards, mammals and birds raid unguarded nests. Black-breasted buzzards, however, drive male emus off their nests then drop stones on the eggs to break them.

The early destruction of emus living on islands was brought about by seal hunters and early settlers killing the emus not only for their flesh but for the oil that can be extracted from their bodies. About 4 gallons of oil can be got from one emu, and it was used for lighting and as an embrocation. Eggs were also taken, if they could be found. To make an omelette, the egg was broken into a basin and left overnight so that the oil could be skimmed off before cooking it in the morning. One emu egg, weighing 1½lb, made an omelette sufficient for the hungriest of families to go to work on and feel well-filled.

The great emu war

It is ironical that both the emu and the kangaroo, which appear on the Australian coat-of-arms, should be considered vermin. Both have had bounties on their heads, and in Queensland 121 768 emus and 109 345 eggs were destroyed in one two-year period alone. This slaughter had its lighter side, however. In 1932 some farmers persuaded the government to declare war on the emus on a large scale. On November 2 a battery of the Royal Australian Artillery engaged the emus with machine-gun fire, but the emus resorted to guerilla tactics and split into small parties, so spoiling the hopes of pouring a hail of fire into the serried ranks of birds. Next, ambushes were tried, with the emus being driven towards the guns. When the emus were at point-blank range the gunners opened fire. A dozen birds fell and the gun jammed. From then on the war got bogged down and after a month the offensive was discontinued.

The government, feeling perhaps that public money had been wasted, asked the farmers for £24 each to offset the cost of ammunition. In reply they received the following claim from one of them:

To victualling H.M.'s troops...............£ 9
To transporting of troops...................£10
To damage of transport vehicles..........£ 5
                                         _____
                                          £24

A 4 days old emu chick surveys a 1½lb emu egg. The father guards the 8–10 chicks for 18 months. The chicks feed mainly on insects, but there is a legend that emus lay a sterile egg either for the chicks to eat or to support a colony of fly maggots for the chicks to eat after hatching.

class	**Aves**
order	**Casuariiformes**
family	**Dromaiidae**
genus & species	***Dromaius novaehollandiae***

King penguin

King penguins look very much like emperor penguins, to which they are very closely related. They have the same stately walk as the emperors, with their long knife-shaped bills held up. King penguins are the smaller of the two, 3 ft long instead of 4 ft, but are otherwise similar in appearance. They both have blue-black backs and white fronts with yellow and orange patches around the neck, but in the king penguin the patches are separated into two comma-shapes on the side of the neck with a 'bib' of yellow on the breast.

King penguins live farther north than emperor penguins, in the ice-free sub-Antarctic seas between the Falkland Islands southwards to the South Sandwich Islands and Heard Island. There are very small colonies on Staten Island, near Cape Horn, and on the Falkland Islands. The largest colonies are found on islands such as South Georgia, Kerguelen, Macquarie and Marion.

Feeding at sea

Like other penguins, king penguins live at sea when they are not breeding and sometimes swim long distances, turning up on the fringes of the Antarctic pack ice. The latitudes in which the king penguins live are those of the roaring westerly gales, but these are unlikely to affect the penguins much except to drive them off course. Penguins are perfectly adapted to life at sea. Their bodies are streamlined and a layer of blubber under the skin insulates them from the cold water. The large king and emperor penguins can dive to considerable depths to hunt squid and fish which they catch in their sharp bills. The eyes of aquatic animals are designed to see underwater. Light is not bent so much as it passes from water into the eye as when it passes from air. To compensate, the lens is very strong. As a result aquatic animals are short-sighted out of water.

Prolonged childhood

The king penguin has the same problem of child care as the emperor penguin. Both are very large birds and their chicks take a long time to grow, yet the Antarctic summer is very short. The emperor penguin has solved the problem in an unexpected way by starting the 7-month nursery period in midwinter so the chicks become independent before the following winter. The king penguin has a different method. It lives farther north where the sea does not freeze and the adults are able to feed near the colony. So instead of laying their eggs in midwinter, the king penguins lay in spring or summer and when the chick hatches after 7½ weeks it is fed throughout the following winter, becoming independent the next summer.

Just before they start breeding king penguins come ashore to moult. They spend a fortnight ashore shedding their old feathers to reveal the brilliant new coat, then retire to sea to feed and build up reserves of food before breeding. Returning to land, they make their way to the colony among the tussack grass and mud where each male takes position and advertises for a mate. He stretches his neck, ruffs out his feathers and tilts his head back and calls, braying like a donkey. If an unmated female hears him, she wanders over and the two penguins introduce themselves by flagging their bills up and down. They then set off on an 'advertisement walk', strutting along on their toes, waving their heads from side to side, showing off their brilliant patches of colour. The colours are important—if they are covered with black paint a penguin stands no chance of getting a mate.

At first these partnerships do not last very long. The male displays at any female and keeps company with a succession of prospective mates. Gradually, however, he pays attention to one particular female and the bond between them strengthens and they perform another display; standing side by side they raise their beaks and stand on their toes as if stretching themselves.

The king penguin, like the emperor penguin, makes no nest but balances the single large egg on its feet, protected by a fold of skin. He does, however, defend a small territory rather than wander about with his egg. The first eggs are laid in November,

*Yetis of the Antarctic! The little sheath bill **Chionis** is dwarfed by the big brown penguin chicks.*

and more are laid until April. After laying the female goes off to feed and make up the food reserves she lost forming the egg. The male is left guarding the egg until the female's return 2 weeks later. Thereafter, there is a shuttle service, each parent taking a turn in guarding the egg or chick.

As the chicks get older they spend more time on their own and eventually form creches where they huddle together while parents go fishing. On its return a parent king penguin finds its chick by sound. It walks up to the creche and calls, and one chick out of hundreds replies. They both walk towards each other, calling, and may even walk past, until another call brings them back to each other. Several pounds of food are transferred at each feed and the chicks put on weight rapidly, but as winter sets in feeding becomes very infrequent and the chicks huddle in their creches, protected by their thick, woolly down but gradually losing weight. Then, in spring, when food becomes abundant again, the chicks put on weight, lose their down and the adult plumage emerges.

The chicks take to the sea 2 months later and learn to fish for themselves. This is well-timed because food is abundant at this season. The young king penguins stay at sea for most of their early life, spending more time ashore as they get older and begin to practise their courtship displays. At 6 years old, they come ashore and start courting in earnest.

Boiled for blubber

The enemies of king penguins are leopard seals. They lie in wait off the colonies, but the seals will find them difficult to catch as the penguins have an alarm system. When a king penguin sees a leopard seal, it panics and rushes towards the shore. Its flippers beat on the surface of the water and the clattering sound they make alerts other king penguins, and they all rush clattering to the shore. Not only are all the penguins alerted but the leopard seals are probably confused and will be able to catch only weak or unwary penguins.

At one time, man was a far greater enemy. As elephant and fur seals became scarce sealers killed king penguins for their blubber, which was used for tanning leather. Their eggs were taken and their skins sometimes used for fancy clothing.

Slow breeding

It took only a few years for the sealers to reduce the numbers in a king penguin colony to such an extent that it was not worth their while to exploit them further. The reason for this is the extremely slow rate of breeding. After the egg has been laid, a pair of king penguins spends a year incubating, guarding or collecting food. By the time they are free of their offspring it is too late in the year to begin again and they leave the colony to feed during the winter and start breeding the following spring.

Therefore, king penguins, like the larger albatrosses (page *112*) which also spend their first winter on the nest, cannot raise more than one young every two years. Furthermore, not all their offspring survive the first winter. If the egg is laid too late in the summer the chick will not have had time to accumulate enough fat with which to survive the winter. Without the attentions of the sealers, king penguins flourish; they are long-lived and generally survive to rear enough offspring to keep numbers constant.

class	**Aves**
order	**Sphenisciformes**
family	**Spheniscidae**
genus & species	***Aptenodytes patagonica***

Albatross

A family of birds in the petrel order. They are the largest members of the order and among the largest of flying birds. They have goose-sized bodies with very long, slender wings: of the 13 species, the largest is the wandering albatross, which has a wingspan sometimes exceeding 12 ft. The plumage is black and white or, in a few species, brown. In only some of the species is it possible to tell the sexes apart.

Ocean wanderers

Nine species of albatross are confined to the Southern Hemisphere, breeding mainly on the sub-Antarctic and oceanic islands. The other four are found in the North Pacific. None breed in the North Atlantic, although fossil remains have been found in England and a few have been recorded as vagrants in modern times. These vagrants include wandering, black-browed, yellow-nosed, grey-headed, and light-mantled sooty albatrosses. One black-browed albatross appeared in a Faroese gannet colony in 1860 and for 30 years—until it was shot—it accompanied the gannets on their annual migrations. Another visited the Bass Rock gannet colony off the Scottish coast in 1967 and returned in 1968.

The doldrums, the windless belt around the Equator, are possibly one of the reasons why so few albatrosses have been recorded in the North Atlantic, as albatrosses need a sustained wind for flight. They are heavy birds with comparatively small wing muscles, but they can remain airborne for long periods and cover vast distances because of the difference in the speed of the wind at the water's surface and some 50 ft above, due to friction slowing down the air at the surface. The albatross glides swiftly downwind and surfacewards, gathering speed. When just above the water it swings sharply round into the wind and soars up. As it rises it loses momentum and its ground speed (*i.e.* in relation to the water surface) decreases. Its air speed, however, does not decrease so fast, as the bird is rising and so continually meeting faster wind currents. By the time the air speed has dropped completely the albatross will have gained sufficient height to start the downward glide again. Thus it progresses in a series of zig-zags.

*1. Yellow-nosed albatross (**Diomedea chlororhyncha**) landing, showing its large wingspan. This enables it to soar for hours in the oceanic air currents.*
2. The albatross nests on cliff tops where it can easily take off. The chick is guarded by its parents for several weeks.
3. Later both parents can be away feeding for ten days at a time.
*4. Black-browed albatross (**Diomedea melanophrys**) ranges over the oceans between 30° and 60° latitude south, breeding on such islands as Tristan da Cunha, South Georgia, and the Kerguelen and Auckland Islands. It has been recorded as a vagrant to the British Isles and even to the Arctic.*

The main haunt of albatrosses is the sub-Antarctic zone where the Roaring Forties and Howling Fifties sweep around the world and there is nearly always enough wind to keep the albatrosses aloft — although they can glide in quite gentle breezes. To increase speed the albatross 'close-hauls', partly closing its wings to reduce air resistance without seriously affecting lift.

With their great wingspan and weak wing muscles albatrosses have difficulty in taking off. When there is enough wind — especially if there are thermal currents or eddies around the cliffs on which they nest — takeoff is not so difficult; but on still days they have to taxi, running along and flapping their wings until they have gained sufficient air speed to take off.

Some species are fairly confined in their range, like Buller's albatross in New Zealand; others, like the wandering, black-browed and sooty albatrosses circle the world from Tropics to Antarctic.

Marine feeders

All species of albatross feed on marine organisms living at the surface of the sea, such as fish, squid and crustaceans. They also take small sea birds on occasions, and they like refuse from ships, flopping down into the water as soon as a bucketful is tipped overboard. Sailors who have fallen overboard have reputedly been viciously attacked by albatrosses.

Cliff top breeding sites

Breeding grounds, where albatrosses gather in tens of thousands, are usually on the top of cliffs where the birds can take off easily. They are extremely faithful to their nest sites, and populations have survived such calamities as volcanic eruptions or pillage by man because the immature birds that were absent at the time later returned to breed.

Albatrosses are very long-lived birds: one recaptured 19 years after being ringed as an adult must have been at least 26 years old. They do not start breeding until at least seven years old, but young birds return to the breeding ground before then and court halfheartedly. Courtship displays, which are to be seen throughout the breeding season, are most spectacular. The two birds of a pair dance grotesquely and awkwardly with outstretched wings to the accompaniment of nasal groans and bill snapping. At the beginning of the breeding season several males may dance around one female.

A single egg is laid in a cup-shaped nest of mud and is incubated by both parents for periods ranging from 65 days in the smaller species to 81 days in the larger ones. The chick is also brooded for a short time and is guarded by the adults for several weeks. It is then left by itself and both parents can be away feeding at once. They return every 10 days to give the chick a huge meal of regurgitated squid and fish. The young of the smaller albatrosses fledge in two to three months, but larger ones may spend eight or nine months in the colony, sitting out the severe southern winter until the following summer. The parents feed them the whole time, so breeding is only possible in alternate years.

The young albatrosses leave the breeding grounds to glide away around the world, driven by the winds of the Westerly Drift. Before they return to start courting several years later they may circle the globe many times.

No natural enemies

Albatrosses have no natural enemies, living as they do on remote islands. Any introduced carnivores would, however, wreak havoc among the densely packed nests, for the sitting albatross's reaction to disturbance is just to sit tight on the nest and clack its bill. It also spits oil from digested crustaceans and fish — as does the chick — but this is hardly likely to discourage a determined predator.

The sailors' curse

Albatrosses have been known to sailors since the days of Magellan. Their inexpressive, fixed facial expression as they glide alongside a ship for miles on end without a flicker of the eye has brought them various nicknames: Mollymawk (from the Dutch Mallemok, 'stupid gull'), Gooney (English/American for a stupid person), Bakadori (Japanese for 'fowl-birds').

But they not only had a reputation for idiocy; they were considered to be harbingers of wind and storms — not, perhaps, surprising in view of their difficulty in remaining aloft in calm weather. They were also regarded as the reincarnations of seamen washed overboard, and it was thought extremely unlucky to kill them.

But, despite the chance of having an albatross hung round one's neck and suffering the far worse experience that later befell the Ancient Mariner, sailors have not always treated albatrosses kindly. Their capture on baited hooks trailed from the stern of a ship often relieved the monotony of life and diet.

More seriously, albatrosses were once favourite material for the 19th-century millinery trade, the wings sometimes being cut off the still-living birds. The North Pacific colonies bore the brunt of this fashion for plumage which, luckily, ceased before all the birds were dead.

Since the Second World War there has been another crisis for the albatross. Long-range aircraft flights have made oceanic islands necessary as staging posts, and one such is Midway Island, the home of the Laysan albatross. Not only are albatrosses using the United States Navy's runways for taking off, they also soar in the thermals above them, providing a serious danger to aircraft. Of the many methods that have been tried to reduce this danger, the most effective has been the bulldozing of dunes by the runways which cause the updraughts that the albatrosses need for flying.

class	**Aves**
order	**Procellariiformes**
family	**Diomedeidae**
genus	*Diomedea spp.*
& species	*Phoebetria spp.*

Pelicans often found their colonies in tall trees. The nests, unlined structures of dry twigs, are large and ungainly.

Pelican

The pelican is known to many people only from seeing it in zoos or on ornamental lakes where its ungainly appearance often makes it the subject of ridicule. In the wild, however, it is a superb flier and swimmer.

There are eight species, two of which occur in the New World and six in the Old, distributed over the tropical and warm temperate parts of the globe. The species differ only in the smaller details of size, colour and geographical range. Both sexes are alike and all have massive bodies, supported on short legs with strong webbed feet. They have long necks, small heads and a thick, harsh plumage. They are among the largest living birds, from 50 – 72 in. long. The most conspicuous feature is the enormous beak; the upper part is flattened and the lower part carries a pouch that can be distended to grotesque proportions. It can hold about 17 pints of water and is used, not for storing food, but as a dip net for catching fish.

Apart from the brown pelican, in the majority of the species the adult plumage is mainly white, tinged with pink in the breeding season in some species such as the pink-backed pelican of Africa. The primaries are black or dark. Some species have crests and in some there is yellow, orange or red on the bill, pouch and bare part of the face. The brown pelican, the smallest member of the family, with a wing-span of up to 6½ ft and weighing about 8 lb, has a white head with a yellow tinge. In the breeding season the neck turns a rich brown with a white stripe running down each side. The wings and underparts are dark brown. The larger white species may have a wing-span of 10 ft and weigh 24 lb.

The brown pelican, which is a sea bird that does not venture far from the shore and breeds on small islands, is found along the south Atlantic and Gulf coasts of North America through the West Indies to Venezuela. Along the Pacific it ranges from central California to Chile with one population on the Galapagos Islands. The other New World species is the American white pelican that breeds on inland lakes from western Canada to southern Texas. In the Old World there are pelicans in Africa, southern Asia, including the Philippines, and Australia and in southeast Europe there are isolated colonies of the large silvery white Dalmatian pelican which ranges eastward from there into central Asia, visiting Egypt and northern India in winter. It nested at least as far north as Hungary until the middle of the last century and according to Pliny it nested in the estuaries of the Elbe, Rhine and Scheldt.

Fishing cooperation

Pelicans feed mainly on fish but crustaceans are also taken. The white pelicans fish while floating on the surface or wading about in the shallows. They thrust their heads under the water, using their pouches as dip nets to catch the fish. Occasionally a large flock of birds will cooperate by forming a line across the water and swimming abreast, beating the surface violently with their wings to drive schools of small fish into shallow water where they can easily scoop them up.

Community breeding

Pelicans are very sociable and all the species nest in large colonies sometimes of tens of thousands. Most of the white species breed on isolated islands in large inland lakes usually making their nests on the ground but occasionally they nest in low trees. On the ground the nest is sometimes just a depression scooped out of the earth. The brown pelican which breeds on small islands on the coast, makes a loose nest of sticks in mangrove trees and low shrubs or sometimes on the ground.

In all species the breeding season varies from place to place and from year to year. In some tropical areas they may even breed throughout the year. Chalky white eggs numbering 1 – 4 are laid which both parents help to incubate for 29 – 30 days. The babies are born naked and blind but quickly grow a soft white down. Both parents feed the young, at first dribbling regurgitated food out of the ends of their beaks into the chicks' open mouths, but after a few days the chicks are strong enough to stick their heads into their parents' pouches to get the food. Before the chicks are 2 weeks old they leave the nest and form noisy juvenile groups but the parents continue to feed them for some time. The young mature slowly, only acquiring adult plumage after several years. They seldom breed until they are 4 years old. Pelicans are long lived birds. Although the accepted record is 52 years, there are less well authenticated accounts of birds living to a much greater age. The Emperor Maximilian is said to have had a pelican which lived for more than 80 years.

Many hazards for the young

Mature pelicans have few natural enemies. Sometimes they may be killed by sea lions in the Pacific or occasionally eaten by sharks but among the young mortality is very high. When the young birds congregate after leaving the nest many fall from trees or get caught in the branches or even trampled on by clumsy adults. When a baby pelican is hurt a larger fledgling is likely to eat it. The adult birds do little to protect their young and sometimes entire nesting colonies are wiped out by predatory animals. It is doubtful if even half the young birds survive. Fishermen have been known to destroy colonies of pelicans to prevent them taking so much fish. At Pelican Island, Florida, in 1911 a plague of mosquitoes caused an entire colony of breeding birds to abandon the rookery, leaving 600 nests containing nestlings. In Peru the guano diggers often damage the nests, knocking young birds out of the way and frightening away the parents, so leaving the chicks an easy prey for predators. Nowadays the pelican colonies are often in danger when marshes are drained or lakes dry up due to large water schemes.

Superb in flight

The pelican has often been described as a clumsy bird, a statement no more justified than it would be to speak of a duck or a swan as clumsy merely because they walk on

land with a waddle and because the body is heavily built. When a pelican has managed after much effort and flapping to become airborne it is a strong and graceful flier, and it is no less graceful in the water. With legs up, head well back on the shoulders and its large bill resting on the front of the neck it can sail through the air with little effort.

Pelicans seem to possess quite unnecessary powers of flight considering that all their food is taken from the water and everything about them suggests adaptation to an aquatic mode of living. They fly at about 26 mph and there is an authentic record of their having maintained this speed for 8 miles, so it seems they also have the quality of endurance in flight. There is one record of the common pelican having achieved 51 mph. They regularly fly in formation either in line astern or in V-formation, all members of the flight beating their wings in perfect unison. The sight of a flock gliding down like a squadron of flying-boats is spectacular. They also have the vulture's trick of using thermal currents, soaring in spirals to

a great height, even as much as 8 000 ft, where by alternately flapping and gliding they may circle for hours.

Symbol of piety

The principal myth concerning the pelican is that the parent bird, if unable to find food for her brood, pierced her breast with the tip of her bill and fed the youngsters on her own blood, and that is how the bird is figured in the earliest pictures of it. It was because of this belief that the pelican was chosen as an emblem of charity and piety and became a favourite heraldic emblazonment. There is a different version of the story according to Bartholomew. Writing in 1535 he says that the young pelicans smite the parents in the face, whereupon the mother retaliates, hitting them back and killing them. Then, on the third day, the mother smites herself in the side until the blood runs out onto the bodies of her youngsters, bringing them to life again.

These two stories may have arisen because in feeding its young the parent presses its

△ *Fish scoop. A yawning common white pelican shows its enormous pouch for catching fish.*

bill against its neck and breast in order to make the contents of the pouch more readily available to the young, who thrust their bills into the pouch to take the food. The red tip on the common pelican's mandible may also have made the story more plausible.

class	**Aves**
order	**Pelecaniformes**
family	**Pelecanidae**
genus & species	***Pelecanus crispus*** Dalmatian *pelican* ***P. erythrorhynchos*** American *white pelican* ***P. occidentalis*** *brown pelican* ***P. onocrotalus*** *common white pelican* ***P. rufescens*** *pink-backed pelican others*

Flamingo

Beautiful but bizarre, flamingos, like giraffes, have an appearance of unreality bordering on disbelief. Their necks and legs are proportionately longer than in any other bird; they feed with their heads upside down in foul, alkaline or saline water yet keep their delicately pink plumage immaculate.

There are four species of flamingo in both Old and New Worlds. Their plumage is tinged with pink, except for the black flight feathers. The greater flamingo, standing about 4 ft high, is found in America from the Bahamas to Tierra del Fuego, including the Galapagos Islands, and in the Old World from southern Europe to South Africa across to India. The lesser flamingo lives in eastern Africa and India. The two remaining species live in the Andes, 14 000 ft above sea level, in Bolivia, Chile, and Argentina. The Andean flamingo is common locally, but the James' flamingo is very rare and at one time was feared to be extinct.

Vast flocks of beautiful waders

Flamingos are gregarious, living in vast flocks of many thousands. One colony of the lesser flamingo in East Africa, the commonest species, numbers at least 1 million pairs. Flamingos breed, feed and travel in flocks and a flock of flamingos wading or swimming in a lake or flying in skeins, like geese, with necks and legs outstretched and wings slowly beating must be amongst the most beautiful sights in the world.

Flamingos are always found on lakes or lagoons of brackish water, where they breed and feed in shallow water. Many of them are migratory, and in recent years greater flamingos from the Camargue have been found to be flying south across the Mediterranean to spend the winter in Africa on the same lakes as the lesser flamingos.

Upside-down filter feeding

Shallow lakes and lagoons are the invariable homes of flamingos because it is here that minute plants and animals exist in the vast concentrations needed to feed the flamingo flocks. Flamingos extract their food from the water by a filtering mechanism which is very similar to that used by the blue whale. They wade through the water with necks lowered and heads upside down, sweeping from side to side. They adopt this unlikely position to sieve their food from the water. The upper and lower mandibles of the bill are fringed with bristles which trap particles as the flamingo sucks in water. The outer layer of coarse bristles keep out large particles while minute algae such as diatoms are collected on an array of bristles inside the bill. The collected algae are then worked off onto the tongue and swallowed after the water has been expelled.

The greater flamingo has a more varied diet than other species. The other flamingos sweep their heads through the surface water but the greater flamingo feeds nearer the bottom. Its bill has fewer filtering bristles

and has a flatter upper mandible. With it the greater flamingo sweeps up small snails and shrimps, as well as quantities of mud from which it extracts the organic matter, rejecting the inedible silt. The greater and lesser flamingos feed together in mixed flocks in the lakes of eastern Africa as the slight difference in feeding ground and feeding habits is sufficient to prevent them from competing for food.

They nest on hummocks

Flamingos breed in colonies. In East Africa where they are most abundant the colonies may be enormous. Several with over 900 000 pairs are known and at one time it was estimated that one had over 1 million pairs. Sometimes a particular colony may be deserted for several years in succession. Then the flamingos may perhaps rear two broods in very quick succession.

The erratic nature of the breeding is most likely due to changes in the water level of the breeding lake. The nests are towers of mud some 6 – 14 in. high with a depression in the top for the eggs. The water level has only to rise a foot or so for the colony to be

▷ *Rarity in captivity: the James' flamingo, which lives in the Andes, 14 000 ft above sea level. Very scarce, it was once believed extinct.*

▽ *A stilt-legged trio of greater flamingos, showing off their balance on dry land.*

A single egg is laid in the saucer-shaped depression in the nest and is incubated for a month by both parents in turn. After the chicks hatch they stay on the nest for 2–3 days then they join the other chicks in bands which can run readily, and swim when 10 days old. The chicks look very much like goslings. They are covered in grey down and their bills are straight, not sickle-shaped like their parents'. Because of the resemblance of young flamingos to goslings and the goose-like flight of the adults, flamingos have been thought to be related to geese, but most ornithologists now think that the flamingos are related to storks and ibises.

Until its bill has developed the characteristic shape, a young flamingo is unable to feed itself and has to rely on its parents. To feed a chick a parent stands behind it and lowers its neck so the chick may take the tip of its bill in its own. The adult regurgitates liquefied food which runs down into the chick's mouth. The parents seem to be able to recognise their own chicks even when they are among a dense crowd of other chicks which may be running or swimming together. The crowds of chicks are always accompanied by adults that lead them away from danger.

Many enemies

The main enemies of flamingos are the fish eagles that can pick the young flamingos out of the rafts and carry them off. Hyaenas, cheetahs and jackals also kill any stragglers they find. In Roman times flamingo tongues were a delicacy and flamingos are still eaten by local hunters. At one time they were prized for their plumage but now the main human menace to them is disturbance of the breeding colonies, especially by low flying aircraft.

How do they sit down?

While idly looking at the more grotesque animals at the zoo, one is often led to wonder how they carry out simple everyday functions. How, for instance, does a heron or a flamingo sit down on its nest? Strangely, this was long in dispute, perhaps because the ornithologists writing about flamingos had never seen them at their nests and could only theorise. In 1697 William Dampier thought that the flamingo leaned back on its nest as if sitting on a shooting-stick. Even a century ago there were still some strange ideas on this point. One was that it sat astride its nest, another that it sat with the legs sticking straight out behind. The correct answer is that it sits like any other bird. The legs are doubled up beneath it, the 'knees' (actually the ankles) hinge backwards, so the folded legs stick out behind the sitting bird.

Aftermath of disaster: smashed and deserted eggs in the potash-ridden waters of Lake Magadi, Kenya.

inundated. On the other hand, if the water level of an alkaline lake drops, thick deposits may form and become caked on the legs of flamingo chicks when they leave their nests. In 1962 Lake Natron in Kenya was flooded and the flamingos moved to Lake Magadi to breed. Thousands of chicks perished, caked with soda that formed heavy anklets round their legs. A rescue operation was launched and many chicks were saved. A flamingo is long lived, however, and produces many chicks in its lifetime, so it is very unlikely that such a catastrophe would have a serious long term effect on the population.

At the beginning of the breeding season the flamingos indulge in spectacular courtship displays. Banding together in tightly-bunched flocks the male flamingos run to and fro with the necks held straight up and bills pointed skyward. At the same time there is a continual guttural uproar while the flock appears to be shimmering because the flamingos are jerking their heads sideways, fitfully and never in unison. At other times they bend their necks, sweeping their bills across their backs. Within the colony of thousands of flamingos these tightly-knit flocks of males flow and eddy.

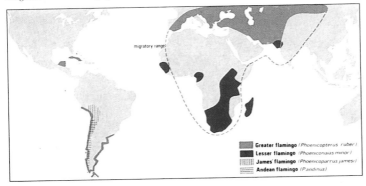

migratory range

Greater flamingo (Phoenicopterus ruber)
Lesser flamingo (Phoeniconaias minor)
James' flamingo (Phoenicoparrus jamesi)
Andean flamingo (P.andinus)

class	**Aves**
order	**Ciconiiformes**
family	**Phoenicopteridae**
genera & species	***Phoenicopterus ruber*** *greater flamingo* ***Phoeniconaias minor*** *lesser flamingo* ***Phoenicoparrus jamesi*** *James' flamingo* ***P. andinus*** *Andean flamingo*

Mallard

Although there are many species of wild duck the mallard is the one that most people think of as the 'wild duck'. It is the ancestor of most of the domesticated ducks. It is about 2 ft long and weighs 2½ lb. The male, or drake, is brightly coloured from September to June. His belly and most of his back are grey. His head and neck are a dark glossy green and a white ring at the base of the neck separates the green from the brown of the breast. He has small curled feathers on the tail and his voice is a low hoarse call. The female, or duck, is a mottled brown, her voice is a loud quack and she has no curly tail feathers. From July to August the drake is in eclipse plumage, and is unable to fly. That is, he moults his colourful feathers at the end of June, is clothed in a mottling similar to that of the duck, and resumes his coloured plumage at the end of August. Both sexes have wing patches (specula), which are dark or purplish-blue with white edges.

Mallard breed in Europe and Asia from the Arctic Circle southwards to the Mediterranean, Iran, Tibet and Central China, and in northern and central North America. Throughout the range there is a movement south in autumn to Africa, southern Asia and, in America, to Mexico and Florida.

Make your own duck pond

Wild duck are attracted to any water: from a small pond in woodland to large lakes, to rivers, streams and marshes, although they often live on dry land well away from water. This habit is taken advantage of by wild-fowlers and bird-lovers alike as they can be encouraged to breed quite easily by digging a pond with small islands or floating basket nests. Mallard spend much time on land even when water is available, but whether on water or on land, and apart from feeding, they do little more than stand or sit about, preening from time to time. Indeed, ducks spend a large part of their time simply doing nothing. On land they waddle apparently awkwardly; on water they swim easily and dive only when alarmed. In the air they fly with rapid wingbeats and with neck outstretched, taking off in a steep ascent.

Wide choice of food

Mallard feed by day or by night, mainly on leaves and seeds, grain, berries, acorns, as well as much small animal life such as insects and their larvae, worms, tadpoles, frogs' spawn, small frogs and small fishes. They dabble in mud on land and at the edge of water and upend in deeper water to feed from the mud at the bottom.

Ritual courtship

Mallard form pairs in autumn and begin breeding in spring. Pairing is preceded by a ritualized courtship. This is initiated by a duck swimming rapidly among a group of drakes with an action that has been called nod-swimming or coquette-swimming. She swims with the neck outstretched and just above water and head nodding. This makes the drakes come together in a tighter group and they begin their communal displays. These are made up of stereotyped actions known as mock drinking, false preening, shaking, grunt-whistling, head-up-tail-up and up-and-down movements. These same movements are seen more easily when the drake and duck are courting.

The duck chooses a drake, who follows her away from the group. She symbolically looks back by turning her head, inciting him to drive away other drakes that may be following. The 'inciting' has become ritualized and is carried out even if no other drakes are there. Mock drinking is a formalized gesture of peace and two drakes meeting head on will 'pretend' to drink. It is a sign they have no intention of attacking each other. In false preening a drake lifts one wing slightly, reaches behind it with his bill as if to preen. Instead, he rubs the bill over the heel of the wing making a rattling sound. In shaking the drake draws his head back between his shoulders so the white ring disappears. The feathers on the underside of the body are fluffed out, so the drake appears to ride high on the water. The head feathers are raised so the green sheen disappears and the head rises high so he is almost sitting on his tail on the water, and then he shakes his head up and down.

When a drake grunt-whistles he thrusts his bill almost vertically into the water then throws his head back, scattering a shower of water drops, and as he does this he grunts. Head-up-tail-up is fully descriptive of the

▽ *Tired of just dabbling in things, a pair of mallard take to deeper water. The male will lose his lovely plumage once the breeding season is over.*

next movement, and in the up-and-down movement the bill is quickly thrust into the water and jerked up again with the breast held low in the water. Another movement is known as gasping; one drake utters a low whistle and the rest give a kind of grunt.

These actions may be made in sequence by a group of drakes facing into the centre or by one or two drakes, or between drake and duck. Also, one or other may be seen as isolated actions. Together they form a ritual pattern of courtship carried out in the autumn but actual mating does not take place until spring. More remarkable, in spite of the complicated courtship, there is a high degree of promiscuity in mallard; a drake will mate with a duck while the drake with whom she is paired looks on.

High-diving ducklings

The nest, built by the duck, is a shallow saucer of grass, dry leaves and feathers lined with down. It may be on the ground, usually under cover of bushes or in a pollarded willow, in the disused nest of a large bird such as a crow, or in a hollow in a tree up to 40 ft from the ground. Up to 16, usually 10 – 12, greyish, green or greenish-buff eggs are laid, from March to October, incubated by the duck alone, for 22 – 28 days. When the ducklings have dried, soon after hatching, the duck calls them off the nest and leads them to water, or if far from water to a feeding ground. Sometimes the drake

is in attendance but takes no part in the care of the ducklings. Even when the nest is 40 ft up in a hollow tree the ducklings leave the nest when the duck calls, each in turn tumbling to the ground without injury. The ducklings are covered with yellowish down broken with large patches of brown. They take nearly 2 months to fledge.

Mother is one enemy

The natural enemies of mallard are birds of prey and ground predators such as foxes. These probably have little effect on mallard populations. The main losses are at the duckling stage. A duck may hatch a brood of 12 and in a fortnight be left with only one duckling. Crows, rooks, magpies, rats and other ducks attack the ducklings. The duck herself may tread on one or more or sit on them in the water, drowning one or two. By contrast, the same duck may then lay a second clutch of 12 and rear all the ducklings to fledgling.

Tongue acts as a piston

When a duck dabbles its bill in mud it is doing much the same as when a large whale-bone whale opens its huge mouth and swims through a mass of krill. Both are using a highly efficient filter in which transverse plates on the inner edges of the duck's bill play the part of the baleen plates of the whale. As the duck dabbles its tongue acts as a piston sucking water or mud into the

mouth and driving it out again. Only the edible particles are left behind on the transverse plates, but how the sorting out is done nobody knows. It used to be thought birds had no taste buds, the groups of cells on the tongue that give a sense of taste. Mallard have, however, 200 arranged in rows along the sides of the tongue. It may be these that tell the duck how to sort out edible from inedible particles.

class	**Aves**
order	**Anseriformes**
family	**Anatidae**
genus & species	***Anas platyrhynchos***

▽ *These obedient children always follow when their mother calls them to water very soon after they have dried out from hatching.*

Swan

The six species of swan are very closely related to the geese. Together they make up a tribe of the order Anseriformes separate from the various tribes of ducks. One possible exception is the Coscoroba swan of South America, which is the smallest swan and has a comparatively short neck; it is thought to be in some way related to the whistling or tree ducks.

The most familiar swan is the mute swan that originally bred in parts of Europe and Asia, but has been domesticated and introduced to many parts of the world such as North America and Australia where it has gone wild. It is thought that it was introduced to Britain by the Romans. The mute swan is 5 ft long and weights about 35 lb. The plumage is all white and the bill is orange with a prominent black knob at the base. The Bewick's swan and the whooper swan are two other species that breed in Eurasia. Bewick's swan breeds in the tundra of northern Russia and Siberia and visits Europe in the winter. The whooper swan breeds farther south, including northern Scandinavia and Iceland, with a few pairs nesting sporadically in Scotland. Both have black bills with a yellow base, the pattern differing slihgtly between the two, and Bewick's swan is rather smaller than the whooper with a shorter neck. There are two swans in North America; the whistling swan has a black bill, sometimes with a yellow spot at the base, and is smaller than the trumpeter with a completely black bill. The whistling swan breeds mainly north of the Arctic Circle and migrates to the southern coast of the United States. The trumpeter used to breed over much of North America but is now confined to the northwest United States and southwest Canada where there are now about 1500 individuals under protection. The only swans in the southern hemisphere, aprt from the Coscoroba swan, are the black swan of Australia, and the black-necked swan of South America, from Brazil to Tierra del Fuego and the Falkland Islands. The black swan is all black but with white primary wing feathers, and a red bill. It has been introduced to New Zealand. The black-necked swan has a black head and neck, a white eyestripe and a red bill.

▽DMute swan takeoff. Their heavy bodies clear the water of the pond with difficulty.

Not so mute

Compared with other swans the mute swan is quiet, but its name is a misnomer for it has a variety of calls. A flock of mute swans can be heard quietly grunting to each other as they swim along a river. When disturbed or in defence of the nest mute swans hiss violently. The sighing noise during flight is caused by the wings. The whooper swan has a bugle-like call when flying and a variety of quiet calls when grounded. Bewick's swan has a pleasant variety of honks and other sounds and the trumpeter is named after the trombone-like calls produced in the long, coiled windpipe. It is said that the swan-song, the legendary song of a dying swan, is based on a final slow expiration producing a wailing noise as it passes through the long windpipe.

A danger to cables

Despite their great weight swans are strong fliers. They have four times the wing loading (the body weight divided by the surface area of the wings) of a herring gull or crow and they have to beat their wings rapidly

1 Profile: head of a whooper swan.
2 Swan song? A black swan stretches up its neck and wails through its long windpipe.
3 Reflecting swan: the Coscoroba swan has features of both ducks and swans.
4 Black-necked swans guard their young.
5 A pair of Bewick's swans sit upright on the water while their young paddle around.

to remain airborne. A high wing loading makes take-off and landing difficult and swans require a long stretch of water over which they can run to gain flying speed or surge to a halt when landing. Swans are also unable to manoeuvre in flight and the chief cause of mortality in built-up parts of the world is collision with overhead cables.

Shallow water feeders

Swans feed mainly on plants but they also feed on water animals such as small fish, tadpoles, insects and molluscs. They often feed on land, grazing on grass like geese, but more often they feed on water plants, which they may collect from the bottom by lowering their long necks underwater, sometimes upending like ducks. This limits the swans' distribution to shallow water because they very rarely dive and are only occasionally seen on deep water.

Centuries-old colonies

Swans nest near water. Male mute swans set up territories, each defending a stretch of river from which they drive other males and young swans. Intruders are threatened

△ *A pair of nesting mute swans, seen through the reeds, renovate their nest.*

by an aggressive display in which the neck is drawn back, the wings arched over the back and the swan propels itself in jerks with the webbed feet thrusting powerfully in unison, instead of alternately as in normal walking. There are a variety of displays between the male, the cob, and the female, the pen, involving tossing and swinging the head and dipping it into the water.

Mute swans mate for life and nest in the same territory each year, some violent fights taking place if a new pair tries to usurp the territory. The nest is a mass of water plants and twigs, roughly circular and cone-shaped with a depression in the centre. Wild mute swans nest among reeds on small islands in pools but semi-domesticated ones may nest in the banks of ponds in parks or in other inhabited places. Occasionally, mute swans nest in colonies rather than spaced out territories.

There are usually 5–7 eggs, sometimes twice as many, and they are incubated mainly by the female, the male taking over only when she leaves to feed. In the smaller swans incubation lasts 4 weeks, but it is 5 weeks in the larger species and 5½ weeks in the black swan. While the last eggs are being brooded by the female the male takes the cygnets to the water. The family stays together until the cygnets fledge at 4–5 months. When young they swim together in a tight bunch with the female leading and rooting up plants for them to eat.

class	**Aves**
order	**Anseriformes**
family	**Anatidae**
genera & species	***Coscoroba coscoroba*** *Coscoroba swan* ***Cygnus atratus*** *black swan* ***C. columbianus bewickii*** *Bewick's swan* ***C. c. columbianus*** *whistling swan* ***C. cygnus buccinator*** *trumpeter swan* ***C. c. cygnus*** *whooper swan* ***C. melanocoryphus*** *black-necked swan* ***C. olor*** *mute swan*

Swan (Breeding grounds)

Mute *(Cygnus olor)*
Bewick's *(C. columbianus bewickii)*
Whistling *(C. columbianus)*
Trumpeter *(C. cygnus buccinator)*
Whooper *(C. c. cygnus)*

Martial eagle

The martial eagle is the largest of the African eagles. Like many other eagles it bears a crest. It has long wings and a relatively short tail and in flight can be confused with only one other eagle, the serpent eagle. The upperparts are dark grey with light grey bars on wings and tail. The underparts, including the feather 'leggings', are white, barred and spotted with black. The bill is black and the legs and toes, which are armed with long curved talons, are blue-grey. The total wingspan may be as much as 8 ft. The females have larger spans than the males and are more powerfully built. They are easily distinguished, being more spotted on the underparts than the males.

The martial eagle lives in Africa from the southern borders of the Sahara to the Cape, but not in the thickly forested regions such as Zaire.

Shy eagle

A pair of martial eagles inhabits a range of as much as 50 sq miles, soaring over the countryside for hours at a time, often at great heights where they are almost invisible to the naked eye. Martial eagles are shy birds as compared with other eagles, and shun human settlements, which is to their advantage as they are often persecuted for taking farm stock. Because of persecution and their dislike of inhabited areas, martial eagles are much rarer than they once were. They are found in savannah, semi-desert and other

▷ *A martial eagle discourages intruders on its reptile repast – monitor lizard.*
▽ *A golden glower from Africa's largest eagle.*
▽▷ *Grounded: sub-adult martial eagle showing its white chest and abdomen.*

open country, and breed only in forested regions when there is open country nearby.

Swoops down on prey

Martial eagles spot their prey from a great height, swooping down on it in a well-controlled glide. The speed of the descent is regulated by the angle at which the wings are held over the back. When they are held almost horizontal the glide is shallow and the descent slow, but if the wings are raised in a 'V' they get less lift and the eagle drops at a steep angle.

They usually prey on small mammals and birds that live in the open, but the species vary from place to place. Their favourite foods seem to be game birds such as francolin, bustard and guinea fowl and mammals, like hyraxes. They will even eat impala calves. Jackals, snakes and lizards are sometimes taken but martial eagles rarely eat carrion. Domestic poultry, lambs and young goats are often eaten, but Leslie Brown, the authority on African eagles, has suggested that on the whole martial eagles are beneficial to man and that their destruction of livestock has been exaggerated.

Choice of nests

Martial eagles build large nests of sticks in tall trees, often on hillsides so there is a clear run-in to the nest. The female builds the nest, which may be 4 ft across and 4 ft deep, while the male collects sticks, or even small branches. The nests are used year after year and usually the female has to do no more than repair the nest and add a lining of fresh green leaves. Some pairs of martial eagles have two nests, each being used in alternate years.

Nest repair may take several weeks and when complete a single white or pale greenish-blue egg with brown markings is laid. The laying date varies between November in Sudan to July in South Africa. The female alone incubates and broods the chick

when it hatches out after about 45 days. For about 2 months the male brings food to the female who then gives it to the chick. Later, the female also hunts for food for the chick. The chick makes its first flight when it is about 100 days old. For some days it returns to the nest to roost and thereafter it stays fairly near the nest. Young martial eagles have been seen near their parents' nest when 3 years old. Unlike the crowned eagle that breeds in alternate years, the martial eagle may breed several years in succession, then fail to do so for several years.

Separate interests

In the course of his remarkable studies on African eagles, Leslie Brown found a hill on which five, and in one year six, species of eagles nested. The hill was appropriately named 'Eagle Hill'. There seemed to be no reason for this gathering except a natural gregariousness; there was no special abundance of food and there were plenty of other suitable nesting places nearby.

While on 'Eagle Hill' the different species did not interfere or compete with each other. The martial eagles fed on game birds caught in open country whereas African hawk-eagles hunted those in bush country. Brown snake-eagles caught snakes. Verreaux's eagles ate hyraxes that they hunted among rocks; the crowned eagles preyed on duikers and monkeys in the forests and Ayres' hawk-eagles took small birds from the trees. So, although crowded, the eagles did not have to compete for food.

class	**Aves**
order	**Falconiformes**
family	**Accipitridae**
genus & species	***Polemaetus bellicosus***

A scintillating moment of breathtaking beauty as greater flamingos take to the air.

Vulture

The name 'vulture' was originally applied
to only the large, scavenging birds of prey
of the Old World, but after the discovery
of America the term was extended to the
condors, turkey vultures and other
members of the New World family of birds
of prey. They resemble the Old World
vultures in appearance, presumably
through convergent evolution, both groups
having similar habits.

Vultures have naked or nearly naked
heads, and sometimes naked necks, which
is an asset to birds that regularly thrust
their heads into carcases. Unlike other
birds of prey, which kill their food, they
have relatively weak feet which are adapted
for running rather than holding prey.
Both groups of vultures have heavy
bodies but they soar effortlessly for hours
on their long, broad wings.

There are 15 species of Old World
vultures, with dark brown or black
plumage, except in a few cases. The bare
skin of the head and neck may, however,
be orange, pink or white. The European
black vulture is the largest bird in the
Old World. It has a wingspan of over 8 ft
and weighs over 15 lb. The plumage
is almost wholly dark brown or black,
with pale skin on the head and neck.
It ranges from Spain to Korea and Japan.
At the other end of the scale there is the
lammergeier, or bearded vulture, and
the Egyptian vulture. The latter has a
wingspan of over 5 ft and is almost pure
white except for black on the wings. The
Egyptian vulture ranges through Africa,
southern Europe, the Middle East and
India. Only a little larger is the hooded
vulture which is dark brown with a
pinkish head and neck. It is very common
in Africa south of the Sahara. The seven
species of griffon and white-backed
vultures are, perhaps, the 'typical'
vultures. They are found throughout
southern Europe, Africa and Asia, often
in large groups, and they nest in colonies.
They are medium-sized and have a ruff
of long feathers around the naked neck.
The remaining vultures are the palm-nut
vulture, which has a feathered neck and
black and white plumage, the white-
headed vulture with blue at the base of the
bill and the lappet-faced vulture. All of
these live in Africa and have wattle-like
folds of skin on the head and neck. There
is also the Asian black vulture, which has
a bright red head and neck.

◁ Gregarious griffons. Cape vultures gorge
on a common zebra carcase. Most vultures
are not strong enough to rip the hide so have
to wait for it to decompose.

△ *White-backed vultures:* **Gyps africanus**.

where there is likely to be an abundance of carcases of large animals easily visible from the air. Vultures are rarely found in forests, except for the hooded vulture. This is the most widespread, although not the commonest vulture in Africa. It regularly scavenges around towns and villages, providing a valuable garbage disposal service, and even follows people as they till the soil, to feed on insects that are turned up. Because of its exploitation of man it is able to penetrate forests where there are human settlements.

To be able to soar at great heights, the heavy-bodied vultures make use of thermals, the 'bubbles' of hot air that rise from the ground as it heats up. A thermal is like a smoke-ring with a stream of air rising through the centre of the ring, which is spinning rapidly. The vultures glide around inside the ring, using the rising air to hold them aloft. This is the same principle as is used by glider pilots. The dependence of vultures on thermals is shown by their daily habits. They do not take off in the morning until the ground has warmed up and thermals begin to form. The lighter species of vulture take off before the heavier vultures, which need more lift.

Tool-users

There are very few animals that use tools – the Galapagos woodpecker finch, the chimpanzee and the sea otter are probably the best known examples – but in 1966 another was added to the list. This is the Egyptian vulture, which throws stones at eggs. The habit is so well developed in a population in Tanzania studied by Jane Goodall that it is surprising that there are no previous records. These vultures smash the tough shells of ostrich eggs either by throwing them against a rock or another egg, or by throwing a stone at them. If there is no stone nearby a vulture may search for one up to 50 yards away, fly back with it in its bill then sling it with a violent downward movement of the head. The action is repeated until the shell cracks. One vulture managed to throw a 2lb rock, and continued to do so for some time, no mean feat for a raven-sized bird.

Ripe food only

Vultures hunt by sight, detecting carrion from vast distances by watching the behaviour of other vultures and other carrion-eating animals. Large carcases may attract large flocks of vultures but despite their heavy bills most vultures have difficulty in breaking through the skins of large animals. Therefore they have to wait for the carcase to decompose or for another animal to attack it. The large vultures, such as the lappet-faced vulture, are powerful enough to rip through hide and, although solitary in habits, they take precedence over the gregarious griffon and white-backed vultures at a carcase. These, in turn, keep away the small vultures which have to be content with scraps.

The rasp-like tongues of vultures enable them to pull flesh into the mouth and their long necks allow them to probe deep into a large carcase, while the lack of feathers means that they have no problems about preening blood-stained feathers. Vultures do not feed on carrion exclusively, however. The largest vultures sometimes prey on the chicks of flamingos or on small rodents and the palm-nut vulture feeds on oil-palm nuts as well as shellfish from the seashore and sometimes hunts in shallow water for small fish.

Huge nests

Unlike the condors and many other birds of prey, the Old World vultures build their own nests instead of laying their eggs on the ground or in the abandoned nests of other birds. The lammergeier and the Egyptian vulture nest in caves or rock crevices, as do the griffon vultures which nest in colonies of over 100 on cliffs. The Indian griffon and the white-backed vultures often nest in trees, with up to a dozen nests in one large tree. The large vultures, the hooded vulture and the palm-nut vulture, nest singly in trees. The nests are huge cups of sticks and twigs lined with leaves, pieces of hide and refuse.

There is usually a single egg, two in smaller species, which is incubated by the female. Incubation ranges from 46 to 53 days, depending on the size of the vulture, and the chicks stay in the nest for up to 4½ months. The male feeds the female while she is incubating, then both parents feed the chicks by regurgitation.

Decreasing scavengers

Vulture numbers are decreasing wherever modern agricultural methods and methods of hygiene are being introduced; there are fewer carcases left lying about, and those that remain have often been poisoned. Although the vultures are not so useful nowadays as scavengers around human settlements they still help to clear up the carcases of stock, which are a potential source of infection. Unfortunately they are not always seen in this light and are persecuted for allegedly killing livestock, although only the largest vultures could possibly attempt to do so.

Riding the thermals

Vultures are most common in dry, open country where they can soar effortlessly in ascending air currents. They are also found in mountain country, up to 20 000 feet. Apart from supplying the air currents necessary for flight, these areas are also those

class	Aves
order	**Falconiformes**
family	**Accipitridae**
genera & species	**Aegypius monachus** European black vulture **Gypohierax angolensis** palm-nut vulture **Gyps africanus** white-backed vulture **G. coprotheres** Cape vulture **G. indicus** Indian griffon **Necrosyrtes monachus** hooded vulture **Neophron percnopterus** Egyptian vulture **Sarcogyps calvus** Indian black vulture **Torgos tracheliotus** lappet-faced vulture **Trigonoceps occipitalis** white-headed vulture, others

Chicken

When we say somebody 'keeps chickens' in his backyard, we mean that the person owns domesticated fowls of the kind known scientifically as **Gallus gallus.** This is also the name of the red jungle fowl of southern and south west Asia, from the foothills of the Himalayas to Java. It is from this the domestic fowl is believed to have been bred, although some scientists believe that other wild fowl of the same region may have been involved, and they prefer to call the domestic fowl **Gallus domesticus.** The red jungle fowl lives in forests from sea level to 5 000 ft.

The cock of the wild fowl is mainly red and black, the black feathers having a greenish iridescence. The hen is russet and brown. The cock has a high arched tail, twin wattles on the throat and a saw-edge comb. The beak is short and strong, the legs powerful, the toes on each foot are armed with strong claws used in scratching the earth. Of the four toes one is directed backwards, set at a higher level than the rest and, in the cock,

armed with a long spur. The wings are small and rounded, capable of strong but not sustained flight, consisting of bursts of wing beats alternating with glides. Their food is leaves, roots, bulbs, seeds and berries, earthworms and insects. The nest is on the ground. The chicks, able to run about soon after hatching, feed mainly on insects.

The cock's voice is a loud crowing, used to advertise his possession of a territory. He is polygamous and defends his territory if necessary by fighting with beak and spurs.

Early domestication

The date of domestication of the jungle fowl is uncertain. It may have been as early as 3 200 BC but had certainly taken place by 2 000 BC in India. There were domestic chickens in China by 1 400 BC as well as in Egypt and Crete, and they reached south-eastern Europe by 700 BC.

The evidence from archaeological relics, such as pottery, figurines, coins and mosaics, suggests that the birds were kept primarily for religious and sacrificial purposes, as well as for the sport of cockfighting. They were later valued for their egg-laying. According to Aristophanes (about 400 BC)

every Athenian, even the poorest, kept his hen for laying eggs. The Greeks also invented the capon, or castrated cock, for fattening, but the eating of chicken flesh was the least of the economic uses until the 19th century. Another use for the bird was as an 'alarm clock' for the farmer.

From Ancient Greece to Ancient Rome was but a short step, and with the Roman conquest of much of Europe the domestic chicken was taken farther afield, although it seems also to have been taken along the trade routes in advance of the Roman legions. The Celts of northern Europe, for example, had it before Caesar invaded Britain.

▽ Barnyard family. Cockerels are polygamous and defend their territories, if necessary, by fighting with beak and spurs. There are more than 100 breeds or varieties of chickens, but the number kept for egg or meat production is limited. Modern farming is so specialised that hens are now rarely found scratching around for a living. They tend to be kept in large flocks under standard conditions by poultry farmers only, either in deep litter houses or in batteries of cages. Separate units are maintained with some breeds kept as table birds and others as layers.

Ornamental and commercial breeds

The modern breeds are divided into Mediterranean and Asiatic types. Of the former there are now 37 breeds used commercially, as well as 24 ornamental breeds. In addition to show birds and fighting cockerels, the breeds tend to be grouped into prolific layers and table birds. The names of some are almost household words: the white leghorn, the best egg-layer, closely followed by the Rhode Island red and the Plymouth. Among the ornamental breeds the most spectacular is the long-tailed Yokohama, bred for the long tail, which in the cock may reach 20 ft.

The peck order

In the scientific field chickens have been responsible for one of the biggest advances in our knowledge of animal behaviour. In 1922 the idea of a peck order was first published. It was discovered by observation of the common or farmyard domestic hen. Briefly, it amounts to this: if a dozen hens new to each other are put into an enclosure, they will separate into couples and start to fight. One of each couple will triumph over the other, either because she is stronger than her opponent or because her opponent refuses to fight. She will be dominant, the other will be subordinate.

Then the dominants will face each other in couples, from which half will emerge once more as dominants, the other half as subordinates. In the end a hierarchy will have been established which can be expressed as follows. If we identify the hens by the letters A to L there will be the boss hen (A) which can peck all the others and they will not peck back. The next in succession (B) will be able to peck all except A, C can peck D−L, but not A and B, and so it will go down the line, until the lowest in the hierarchy (L) will be subordinate to all the rest, the one which gets pecked by all the others.

Any hen can change her position in the hierarchy by winning a fight with a superior hen, but without such a challenge the positions in the hierarchy are accepted by all.

This is a simplified version but the principle is there, and subsequent research in a large number of animal species has confirmed it. In most animal communities (including our own) there is a social order of dominance and subordinance, among males as well as females. It is generally referred to as a peck order, because the first discovery was with domestic hens. And the discovery has revolutionized our study of the social behaviour of animals as well as human beings.

Chicken fortune tellers

The behaviour of chickens in their peck order has become almost a symbol in the philosophy of the modern scientist. Chickens have served as symbols in other ways in earlier civilizations. Hens were symbols of fertility, because of their egg-laying, and this was later transferred to the cock, largely from the elaborate display he uses in wooing the hen. He became an erotic symbol as well as a symbol of health.

The Romans went further and used chickens for prophecy, the *oraculum ex tripudio*. Hens were put in a cage with food. If they

△△ Wild relative — the jungle fowl, which lives in forests from sea level to 5 000 feet. It is characterised by the iridescence of its feathers.

△ One of the more exotic breeds: the long-tailed Yokohama. Many varieties have been specially bred for their attractive plumage patterns.

ate greedily, the omens were good. Should they show little taste for food, the omens were unfavourable. The method was open to abuse. One had only to starve the hens beforehand to obtain a good omen.

In the first Punic War a consul, angry with his hens because they refused to eat when he needed a good omen, cast them into the sea saying: 'Let them drink if they won't eat.' He was subsequently defeated in a battle at sea, a fate which the people of

Rome attributed to his lack of respect for the hens.

class	**Aves**
order	**Galliformes**
family	**Phasianidae**
genus & species	*Gallus gallus*

Sunbittern

The sunbittern is a large and little-known inhabitant of tropical American forests. It is related to the coots, cranes and bustards rather than the true bitterns of the heron family. It is, however, heron-like in appearance, about 18 in. long, with a long slender neck, small head and long bill. The bright orange legs are also long and slender and the toes are unwebbed. The wings and tail are broad. The plumage is soft like that of an owl and is mainly brown and grey with black bars and spots. The crown of the head is black and two white streaks run across the face. There are two broad black bands across the tail. The bill is black on the upper mandible, yellow on the lower. When a sunbittern opens its wings a pattern of chestnut and orange becomes visible on the back with white and black patches on the wings.

Sunbitterns are found from southern Mexico to Bolivia and central Brazil.

Sunset display

Sunbitterns, like herons, live singly or in pairs along the banks of rivers or in swampy woodland and wade slowly through the shallows in search of food. Captive sunbitterns have been described as standing with their bodies swaying from side to side in the same manner as bitterns, reputedly to make them less conspicuous among the waving reeds. They also spend a considerable time motionless with the neck withdrawn as herons do. Sunbitterns are reluctant to fly preferring to walk and to swim across streams. When disturbed, however, they fly into trees. Their flight is very quiet, presumably because of the soft plumage, and their broad wings give them the appearance of gigantic fluttering moths. Sunbitterns are usually silent but sometimes they utter quiet whistles or rattles.

The display of the sunbittern is most spectacular. The forepart of the body is lowered while the head is raised and the wings are spread with the rear edges raised and the tail fanned and brought up, so that the whole of the beautifully patterned plumage is displayed in a semi-circle. The bright chestnut and orange of the back and wings have been described by Alexander Skutch as looking like 'a sun darkly glowing in a sunset-tinted sky'. During the display a harsh rattle is given. This display is used during courtship and also as a threat.

Sunbitterns feed on insects, crustaceans, small fish and other small animals found in shallow water along the banks. Their feeding behaviour is very much like that of herons; they stalk slowly or stand motionless then suddenly shoot out their necks and grab their prey in the dagger-like bill.

Nests rarely seen

Very few sunbittern nests have been found in the wild. Alexander Skutch describes one which consisted of a 12in. mass of decaying leaves, twigs, moss and mud, lined with green

△ *Out on a limb: an unusual photograph of a brooding sunbittern on its nest of moss and mud.*

leaves and perched on a 2in. branch. A tree is the usual place for a sunbittern to build its nest but they may build on the ground.

The first record of the nesting behaviour of the sunbittern was the description given of a pair that nested in London Zoo in 1865, and a century later it is still the most detailed account, although sunbitterns have since nested in other zoos. The pair built their nest of straw, grass, mud and clay on a specially provided platform, 10 ft up. The first egg was found broken under the nest but a second was laid shortly afterwards and was incubated by both parents for 27 days. The chick was like that of a snipe and was fed by both parents on food carried in their bills until its wing feathers had grown enough for it to fly to the ground, at the age of 21 days. The parents continued to feed it and 2 months after it had hatched another egg was laid and incubated mainly by the male while the female continued to feed the original chick. In the wild the normal clutch seems to be 2 eggs.

Mixed crowd

The order Gruiformes, to which the sunbittern belongs, contains some unusual birds. There is the large family of rails,

some of which are flightless, the button-quails in which the female plays the leading role in courtship, the mesites of Madagascar which are probably flightless, the cranes, finfoots and the bustards. Some of the Gruiformes resemble birds outside the order, such as the stork-like kagu, the ibis-like limpkin and the heron-like sunbittern. Despite a variety of external form and habit the gruiform birds have many similarities in the form of their skeletons and muscles. One habit which is, however, very common in the group is that of nesting on the ground and producing chicks that can walk soon after hatching. The sunbittern is an exception because it nests in trees and although its chicks are hatched with a coat of down and appear well-developed, they are fed in the nest for some time.

class	Aves
order	Gruiformes
family	Eurypygidae
genus & species	*Eurypyga helias*

Oystercatcher

*The oystercatchers are large waders that are found in many parts of the world. Some species have black and white plumage, hence the old name of 'sea-pie' but others are all black. The most widespread oystercatcher Haematopus ostralagus is found in Europe, the Canaries, South Africa, Asia, Australia, New Zealand and North and South America. It is largely black above with white underparts and has a long red bill and pink legs. Another pied oystercatcher is the American oystercatcher **H. palliatus** that ranges from New Jersey and California to Argentina and Chile, while a third **H. leucopodus** lives in southern South America. The sooty oystercatcher **H. fuliginosus** lives on the coast of Australia and other black oystercatchers **H. bachmani** and **H. ater** live in western North America, southern South America and Australia. In some places the common oystercatcher is all black, as in the Canaries, Africa and America.*

Moving inland

Oystercatchers are usually seen on rocky shores or sandy beaches, on mudflats, or in sand dune areas just behind the shore but they sometimes breed inland. They have nested inland in Scotland for centuries and they are now breeding inland in northern England. In New Zealand, oystercatchers are found by the snow rivers of South Island. Outside the breeding season oystercatchers gather in large flocks, and those that breed in high latitudes migrate to warmer regions in the winter. The Burry Inlet in South Wales, for instance, is the winter home of oystercatchers from Scotland, Iceland, the Faeroes and Norway.

The pied plumage and red bill of the oystercatcher are unmistakable, yet, surprisingly, they are sometimes difficult to see if they are motionless. They often give away their presence by their loud shrill calls of 'kleep-kleep' or a shorter, rapid 'kic-kic'. Oystercatchers are wary and run rapidly or take flight when approached.

Musselcatchers

It is difficult to see how the oystercatcher got its name. The authoritative *Handbook of British Birds* does not include oysters in the diet of the oystercatcher, and it would be surprising if it did because oysters live below the lowtide mark and oystercatchers feed between the tides or on land. A better name would be the old local name of musselpecker. Mussels, together with limpets, cockles, winkles, crabs and worms, make up a large part of the oystercatchers' diet. Cockles and worms are found by probing the sand with their bills. They also eat insects, especially their larvae, some plant food and occasionally eggs of other birds. The composition of the diet depends on the animal life living in the oystercatchers' habitat; whether sandy or rocky shores, farmland and so on.

The methods by which oystercatchers eat molluscs that are protected by strong shells, have been studied in detail. Limpets are dealt a sharp blow with the tip of the bill. Small ones are dislodged and large ones are shifted so they can be levered off or holed. The oystercatcher can then insert its bill and tear the strong muscles that hold the limpet down. Two different ways are used for opening bivalve molluscs such as mussels and cockles. If the shellfish is covered with water and its valves, or shells, are agape, the oystercatcher stabs downward then levers and twists to sever the adductor muscle that closes the valves. These fall open and the flesh is rapidly pecked out. If the shellfish are exposed to the air and firmly closed the oystercatcher has to smash its way in. Examination of mussel shells that were the remains of oystercatcher meals, shows that they are regularly smashed on the bottom edge and tests have shown that this side of the shell is much weaker than the top edge even in large mussels. The oystercatcher carries a mussel or cockle to a patch of firm sand, places it with its ventral margin upwards, and starts to hammer it. If the shell falls over it is righted or if it sinks it is carried to a firmer patch. On average, five blows of the bill are needed to penetrate a mussel shell and the bill is then inserted to cut the adductor muscle and prise the two halves apart. Cockle shells are not attacked in any particular position as their shells are weaker than those of mussels. Small crabs are flipped onto their backs and killed with a stab through the brain. The shell is then prised off and the flesh cut out with the same scissoring movements that are used for eating other shellfish.

In some places, such as the Burry Inlet

Posed on a cliff top beside a clump of thrift before flying down to feed at the mussel beds between the tide lines below. The strong red bill for prising open mussels and the thick red legs add flashes of colour to the oystercatcher's stark black and white plumage.

*S. African black oystercatcher **Haematopus moquini**.*

in Britain, oystercatchers are considered a pest because of the damage they do to the cockle beds. Each oystercatcher eats about one cockle every minute and consumes on average 336 cockles per tide. As flocks number several thousands, they eat many millions of cockles each winter; but oystercatchers are only one of several enemies of cockles and it is debatable whether they seriously affect the cockle industry. In the Faeroes, they are considered beneficial as most of their food is insects and other invertebrates in grassland.

Piping display

Oystercatchers arrive at their breeding grounds in flocks but then split up into pairs. Each pair forms a territory which it defends against the other oystercatchers. Among their several displays there is the quite spectacular piping display in which a group of birds, or sometimes just a pair, run rapidly to and fro with necks outstretched and open bills pointing at the ground. At the same time they utter a

piping call that varies from a clear 'kleep-kleep' to a quavering trill.

The nest is a shallow depression in shingle, sand or turf, sometimes with no lining but at other times lined with stones, shells, or dead plants. There are usually three eggs, yellowish or light brown with spots or streaks of dark brown. Both parents incubate the eggs which hatch in 24–27 days. The chicks leave the nest after a day or two and are fed by both parents. They fly in about 5 weeks and are fed by their parents for another 5 weeks.

Family traits

The careful study of the way oystercatchers open mussels was made by M Norton-Griffiths of Oxford University. He found that some oystercatchers regularly stabbed open mussels while others hammered the shells. Furthermore, young oystercatchers developed the same feeding habits as their parents. This is, perhaps, not so surprising as the chicks were learning to feed on only those animals which their parents brought

to them. First the chicks practise pecking empty shells and picking up pieces of flesh left in them, learning the scissoring movements of the adults. Later they take opened shellfish from their parents and remove the flesh by themselves. Eventually they open the shells themselves, starting on small ones and graduating to large ones as they become more proficient. Norton-Griffiths never saw a 'crab-eating' chick attack a mussel and when a 'mussel-eating' chick found a crab it was frightened of it. The differences in feeding habits are so marked that a population of oystercatchers is distinctly divided by them and 'mussel-eaters' mate only with 'mussel-eaters' and 'cockle-eaters' with 'cockle-eaters'.

class	**Aves**
order	**Charadriiformes**
family	**Haematopodidae**
genus & species	*Haematopus ostralagus* oystercatcher, others

Puffin

The puffin, a small auk about 12 in. long, with a massive, brilliantly coloured and decidedly bizarre bill, is perhaps the most popular and well known of sea birds. The comical effect of the bill is enhanced by coloured horny patches above and below the eyes. The plumage is basically the same as that of other auks; black above and white underneath, with the black extending around the neck as a collar. The legs are bright orange and the sides of the face ashy grey. The triangular bill has red, yellow and blue stripes with a thick yellow skin in the corners of the mouth. Outside the breeding season the basal part of the horny covering of the bill, including the blue parts and the yellow skin, are shed, leaving the base of the bill narrower and horn-coloured. At the same time the red tip becomes yellow. The bill of young puffins is more conventional, narrower and plainly coloured, the inner half greyish brown, the outer half reddish brown.

The puffin breeds along the coasts of the North Atlantic from Greenland to the Gulf of the St Lawrence in the west and from Spitzbergen and Novaya Zemlya to the British Isles and northern France in the east. Some spread as far south as the Canaries and into the Mediterranean as far as the Adriatic. British puffins have been found wintering in American waters but not all puffins migrate away from their breeding places. Puffins regularly spend the winter in Baffin Bay and in mild winters they stay near Amsterdam Island, north of Spitzbergen, despite the low temperatures and continual darkness of the Arctic winter. The horned puffin, which lives in the North Pacific and is a close relative of the Atlantic puffin, has fleshy growths over the eyes and differs in the colouring of the bill. It breeds on either side of the Bering Sea. Another Pacific puffin is the tufted puffin, all black but for a white face and long tufted feathers sprouting from above the eyes. The bill is red and green.

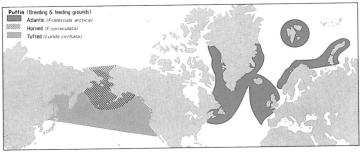

Puffin (Breeding & feeding grounds)
- Atlantic (*Fratercula arctica*)
- Horned (*F. corniculata*)
- Tufted (*Lunda cirrhata*)

▽ *These two puffins are engaged in a ritualised courtship ceremony known as billing.*

Cliff nester

From spring until the end of the breeding season puffins contribute to the masses of auks that fly continually to and from the nesting cliffs. Instead of shuffling on their haunches like other auks such as the guillemots, puffins walk quite easily with a waddling gait. When they take off from the cliffs their wings appear to be too small to support them and they plunge steeply until their rapidly whirring wings become effective. When cornering in flight or coming in to land the orange feet are spread out to help in steering or braking.

Mysterious fish stackers

Puffins feed on small fish, such as sand eels and cod fry, together with crustaceans, floating molluscs and other planktonic animals. Outside the breeding season they go far out to sea, usually out of sight of land. Food is caught by diving, the puffins swimming underwater with their wings. If puffins have chicks to feed they carry their catch back in the bill. Puffins are quite tame on their breeding cliffs and can be watched from close quarters landing with fish draped crossways in the bill. They can carry up to 30 fish in this way, but this is exceptional. How they arrange the fish in the bill is still

a mystery. Presumably each fish is killed by a nip with the bill but how it is then placed alongside ones caught previously without dropping them is difficult to visualize. The tongue and the serrated floor of the upper mandible may be used to manoeuvre and hold them. Pictures of puffins with fish arranged in the bill head-to-head or alternating head-to-tail are based on either imagination or coincidence. Working the fish into a pattern would be very difficult and would serve no useful purpose.

Slow development

When puffins arrive at the breeding ground they start digging burrows or clearing out old ones. They dig with their heavy bills and scrape the loosened soil out with their feet. In large colonies burrowing can be so extensive as to cause a landslide. Sometimes they take over shearwater or rabbit burrows.

Puffins arrive at the breeding grounds already paired but there is a considerable amount of displaying around the burrows. The large colourful bill is used as a signal, being thrust forward in threat or shaken in appeasement. Mating takes place on the water after the male has chased the female.

A single egg, white with faint markings, is incubated for 40–43 days. The parents

share the task, but at intervals they leave the egg and parade together outside the burrow. The chick is fed on fish by both parents, but when 6 weeks old it is deserted by the parents who go out to sea to moult, during which time they become flightless. The chick stays in the burrow for another week then flutters down from the cliffs and paddles out to sea. The young puffins leave the burrows at night when there is less danger from gulls and skuas. Until they can fly they avoid danger by diving. Seven weeks is a very long fledging period for an auk, but puffins are reared in the safety of a burrow, whereas guillemots, razorbills and other auks breed on cliff ledges where their chicks are vulnerable to predation by gulls. These auks also leave the nest before they can fly, but unlike puffins are not independent and remain in the care of the adults.

Rat and oil problems

A certain number of puffins fall prey to gulls and skuas; on the island of Foula in the Shetlands, for instance, the cliffs are sometimes littered with the remains of puffins eaten by skuas, but their numbers are more severely reduced when rats are introduced to their breeding grounds. At one time the puffin population of Ailsa Craig was described as phenomenal, but in 1889, rats got ashore from a wreck and the population has since declined almost to extinction. A similar decrease has also occurred on Lundy, the name of this island being Norse for Puffin Island.

Recently there has been another threat to puffins, and other auks. Oil pollution is particularly serious to auks, because of their gregariousness and their habit of diving out of trouble and resurfacing in the oil patch. They are also particularly vulnerable when flightless during the moult.

Cliff crop

Man is another predator of puffins. The islanders of Faeroe, Shetland, St Kilda and other places have for a long time relied on sea birds for food, although the practice has declined in recent years. On St Kilda where sea birds formed the mainstay of the islanders, more puffins were killed than any other bird, including gannets and fulmars. They were the main food during the summer, eaten roasted, and their feathers were collected and sold. Catching puffins was usually the women's work, assisted by dogs who helped locate nests. They were hauled out of their burrows, snared or caught in nets as they flew in. On Foula, the sheer cliffs where many of the puffins nested were divided so that each man had a section where he could hazardously collect his crop.

class	**Aves**
order	**Charadriiformes**
family	**Alcidae**
genera & species	***Fratercula arctica*** *Atlantic puffin* ***F. corniculata*** *horned puffin* ***Lunda cirrhata*** *tufted puffin*

Wood pigeon

From being a harmless rarity up to the end of the 18th century, the wood pigeon, or ring dove, has become one of the most common and most destructive pests of agricultural land, especially in certain parts of Europe. It is a handsome, rather heavily built bird, about 16 in. long with a wing span of about 18 in. The upper parts are bluish-grey with darker grey on the upper wings and black on the upper tail and wing quills. The breast is vinous shading to pale grey or lavender on the belly, flanks and under the tail. The rump and head are a bluer grey than the rest and the sides of the neck are a metallic purple and green. The base of the bill is pink, the rest yellow shading to pale brown on the tip. The base of the bill expands into a soft fleshy lump over the nostrils. The legs and feet are pink with a mauve tinge. The straw colour of the eye and its unusual pear-shaped iris give the bird a very alert expression. The wood pigeon can always be distinguished from other doves by the white patch on the sides of the neck, which is absent in young birds, and the broad white band across the wing. The male and female are alike except that the males tend to be slightly larger and their plumage brighter.

The typical race of the wood pigeon is found throughout Europe, except in the extreme north. It ranges eastwards to Russia and in the south extends to the north coast of the Mediterranean and to the various Mediterranean islands from the Balearics to Cyprus, and around the Black Sea. It is replaced by allied races in northwest Africa, the Azores, Madeira, Turkestan and Transcaspia to Iran, Baluchistan, Kashmir and Sikkim.

Wary in the country

The wood pigeon is primarily a bird of the woods but since the spread of agriculture it has taken to feeding on cultivated land. It is also a familiar bird in town parks and suburban gardens and is often found on downs and on coasts, some way from woods.

From autumn to spring and sometimes also in summer it congregates in large flocks to feed, although single birds and small groups may also be seen. In the towns and parks it may become quite tame but in the open country it is wary of humans and will

△ *Just beginning to lose their sparse yellow down, a pair of large young wood pigeons wait for the arrival of one or other of their parents with some food. After their first three days, when they are fed with pigeon's milk, their main diet is ripe cereal grain.*
◁ *One of the greatest enemies of farmers in Europe, the gentle-looking wood pigeon is easily distinguishable from other doves by the white patch on the sides of its neck. In order to reduce their numbers, the most effective method has proved to be nest destruction.*

137

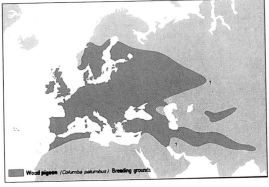

Wood pigeon (*Columba palumbus*) Breeding grounds

△ *Two greedy young wood pigeons eagerly reach out of the nest trying to get more food from their ever-patient parent.*

take off with a loud clatter of wings at the slightest disturbance. Its normal flight is fast and strong with quick regular wing-beats and occasional glides. On the ground it struts about, restlessly moving its head to and fro. It roosts in trees, sometimes in large numbers.

The wood pigeon's voice, which is heard at all times of the year but more frequently in March and April, is often said to be a series of coos but the phrase 'two coos, Taffy take' repeated several times gives a better idea. The alarm note is a short, sharp 'roo' sound.

Agricultural menace

Originally the wood pigeon fed on acorns and beech mast as well as seeds, nuts, berries and the young leaves of many trees. Since the spread of agriculture and the dis-appearance of many woods it has turned, to a large extent, in many areas to cultivated crops and found them just as palatable and in greater abundance. Cereal grains are the most important food for both adults and young in late summer and autumn and in some areas peas and beans are taken in large quantities. In winter the birds depend mainly on clover, turnip tops and young greens. The pronounced hook at the end of the bill makes it easy for the pigeon to tear off the leaves of these plants. Some animal food is taken including caterpillars, earth-worms, slugs, snails and insects.

The wood pigeon needs quite a large quantity of water and drinks greedily, not in sips like most other birds.

Billing and cooing

The courtship of a pair of wood pigeons begins while they are still in flocks. A pair separate from the main body and on the ground or a perch in a tree they bow to each other, their breasts touching the ground or perch, with their tails raised and spread, all the time cooing to each other. This bowing and cooing is often interrupted by a nuptial display flight in which the bird rises steeply with strong wingbeats then glides down and rises again with stiff set wings in an undulating course. At the top of its rising flight it usually makes several

claps with its wings, caused by a strong downbeat of the wings and not, as so often supposed, by the wings clapping together. Also at this time pairs of birds start to establish territories in the trees, the males driving away any intruders with aggressive posturing or actual attacks.

Young fed on milk

The breeding season is long, usually from April to September, but there are records of nests in every month of the year for the southern parts of the wood pigeon's range. The peak of breeding activity seems to be July, August and September in the British Isles when there is plenty of ripe corn for feeding the young. There are usually three broods a year. The nest is built in almost any kind of tree or in tall hedgerows, sometimes on top of the old nest of crows or sparrowhawks or on a squirrel's drey. Very occasionally it is built close to the ground or on ledges of rocks. In towns, buildings are used. The nest is a flimsy structure of intertwined sticks, often used for several years in succession. The male brings the material but only the female builds. Usually two, occasionally one or three, white, fairly glossy eggs are laid and are incubated for about 18 days, by both parents.

When the young birds hatch they are covered in sparse yellow down and for the first three days are fed at frequent intervals on a fluid from the parents' crops known as 'pigeon's milk'. After this, ripe cereal grain is the main food with some green food and weed seeds supplemented with animal foods. They stay in the nest for about 22 days, and afterwards are still fed by one or both parents for at least another week.

The average age attained by a wood pigeon in the wild in the British Isles is only 38 months but the oldest one recorded was in its 14th year.

Large numbers shot

Apart from man the adult wood pigeon has few enemies, but many of their eggs are taken by jays and magpies. The losses among young birds are due mainly to starvation, especially when they leave the nests and compete for food with the adult birds. In really severe winters the mortality among wood pigeons is very high but their numbers soon seem to increase again.

Owing to the widespread destruction of crops by wood pigeons a great deal of re-search has been done into methods of keeping down their numbers. Shooting the birds is still the most widely used method although some sportsmen contend that wood pigeons are difficult to shoot as the shot glances off their feathers. There is no evidence to show that widescale shooting makes any impression on their numbers.

Migrant or not?

The subject of migration of wood pigeons to and from the British Isles has provided a constant source of argument amongst countrymen, sportsmen and bird-watchers for many years. Apparently the wood pigeons in the British Isles are mainly sedentary but with a tendency to move south in the winter. Only a small proportion of the population undertakes long flights and these are usually young birds. There is probably a latent urge, inherited from migratory ancestors, which shows itself in only a few individuals. The only birds recovered abroad reached no farther than France. In continental Europe the migra-tory behaviour is rather different. Wood pigeons in Scandinavia and the Baltic are forced to migrate south in winter to escape the snow and some of these do arrive on the east coast of Britain, but the numbers vary considerably from year to year. Obser-vers have told of hordes of wood pigeons arriving from the Continent and although large numbers may arrive in some years, confusion very often arises because of the flocks of wood pigeons that seem to fly out to sea from the British Isles and then fly back again!

class	**Aves**
order	**Columbiformes**
family	**Columbidae**
genus & species	***Columba palumbus***

Macaw

The 18 species of macaw include the largest and most colourful members of the parrot family. They live in tropical America, from southern Mexico through Central America to Paraguay. They have large beaks, the upper mandible being long and strongly hooked. The skin on the cheeks and around the eyes is naked except for a scattering of very small feathers.

The largest is the scarlet or red and blue macaw, of Mexico to Bolivia, 3 ft long, of which 2 ft is tail. It is mainly scarlet except for the yellow wing coverts and the blue of the flight feathers, the lower back feathers and outer tail feathers. The blue and yellow macaw, ranging from Panama to Paraguay, is only slightly smaller. It is a rich blue on the crown, nape, back, wings and upperside of tail, golden yellow on the underside, including the underside of the tail. There is a large black patch on the throat, the bill is black and the white sides of the face are marked with black wavy lines. The military or great green macaw, 30 in. long and ranging from Mexico to Brazil, is green, shading to blue on flight feathers, rump and tail coverts, with a crimson band on the forehead and red on the upperside of the tail. Less gaudy but probably more beautiful, certainly more prized by fanciers, is the hyacinthine macaw, 34 in. long, a cobalt blue throughout its plumage. Its range is limited to the interior jungles of the Amazon basin. The smaller species are usually green.

Commuting parrots

Macaws move about in screeching flocks except when breeding. Their day starts with a screeching chorus as individual birds leave their roosts to gather in a tree. There they bask in the early morning sun before setting off to feed. As the midday heat builds up they seek the shade, but when the sun's rays begin to weaken they come out again to feed. At dusk they return to their assembly point, usually a bare tree, before dispersing to roost.

Steamhammer beaks

Most macaws feed on seeds, nuts and fruits, the larger of them cracking even hard-shelled nuts such as Brazil nuts with their beaks and extracting the kernels with the

▽ *Rendezvous at Felipe Benavides Fountain — red and blue and blue and yellow macaws.*

beak helped by the fleshy tongue. Precise details of their feeding in the wild are hard to come by, but in captivity, although these form their basic foods, they seem to show a liking for such things as bread and butter and cake, and tame macaws have been known to take meat readily. It may be, therefore, that they take some insect food in the wild. This possibly explains, at least in part, their readiness to pull wooden structures to pieces, such as the edges of nesting boxes or woodwork frames in the aviary. In the wild the same activities would expose insect grubs.

Bashful male

Except for the hyacinthine macaw, which is said to nest in holes in earth banks, macaws nest in hollows in trees, sometimes high up from the ground. Once the eggs are laid macaws are aggressive towards anyone approaching their nest. Even tame macaws will defy their owners trying to see what is happening. A fairly clear account can, however, be given of the breeding behaviour of the blue and yellow macaw, based mainly on observations published by Mr Donald Risdon, in the *Avicultural Magazine* for 1965. He found little distinction between male and female except that the male blushes when excited, the bare skin of his face going a deep pink. The female seldom blushes and when she does the colour hardly shows. At the same time as he blushes the male nods his head up and down and contracts the pupils of his eyes. When Risdon's pair showed signs of breeding he gave them rotten wood, which they chewed up in typical macaw fashion. The eggs are slightly larger than pigeon's eggs. The nestling is still naked and blind at a week old. The wing quills begin to erupt at 4 weeks, the bill darkens and the eyes open. The back then begins to grow feathers followed by the tail and later the rest of the body and head, the young macaw becoming fully feathered by 10 weeks of age. It does not leave the nest for another 3 weeks, except to sit at the entrance. The parents feed it during this time by regurgitation. At 6 months the young macaw is as large as its parents and looks like them.

Vulnerability

With so formidable a beak a macaw could be a match for most small predators. Its main enemy is the harpy eagle. Their habit of feeding in flocks combined with their garish colours have made macaws vulnerable to the South American Indians with their blow-pipes and arrows.

class	**Aves**
order	**Psittaciformes**
family	**Psittacidae**
genera & species	***Anodorhynchus hyacinthinus*** *hyacinthine macaw* ***Ara ararauna*** *blue and yellow macaw* ***A. macao*** *scarlet macaw* ***A. militaris*** *military macaw, others*

Cuckoo

The cuckoo is regarded in sharply contrasting ways; it is to some the harbinger of spring, to others, a base parasite. Of the many species, only the common cuckoo of Europe and Asia gives the loud insistent call that has given rise to the name. It is called **coucou** in French, **Kuckuck** in German, **Kukushka** in Russian and **Kak-ko** in Japanese.

The common cuckoo has distinctive black and white barring on the underparts and a grey head and neck. The tail is long and the wings narrow, so in flight the cuckoo looks very much like a hawk. It can be distinguished, however, by its longer neck, the shape of the head and a pale streak under the wing.

Other cuckoos are gaudy by comparison with the common cuckoo. The red-winged Indian cuckoo has a magpie-like tail and a black head, back and tail. Related to it is the great spotted cuckoo, similar in shape but with white spots on the wings and back. The emerald cuckoo of South Africa is a brilliant golden green, except for a yellow belly.

Cuckoos belong to two subfamilies, with their relatives the anis, roadrunners, couas and coucals in other subfamilies. One subfamily, to which the common cuckoo belongs, ranges across the Old World from western Europe to Polynesia, while the other belongs to both Old and New Worlds. The former are all parasitic; the female lays her eggs in other birds' nests. It is for this habit that the cuckoos are best known, but it is by no means widespread in the family as a whole.

The lodger awaits acceptance in hedge sparrow's nest. When the foster parent is away the cuckoo flies down, lifts an egg out, swallows it or drops it and lays one of her own in its place.

Long migrations

Many cuckoos migrate over thousands of miles, from the tropics to the temperate regions. The common cuckoos begin to arrive in the British Isles in the last few days of March and leave during July to early September, each bird flying on its own bound for tropical Africa although exactly where is not known. The shining cuckoo of New Zealand makes an even more impressive migration, across 2 000 miles of ocean to the Solomon Islands. How they find their way over vast distances is especially puzzling as the young birds migrate from the breeding grounds several weeks after the adults have gone. This is sure proof that the urge to migrate, the ability to navigate, and the knowledge of the route are inherited, for there is absolutely no chance of the young cuckoos learning from their elders.

Feeds on many pests

Cuckoos eat insects, especially the larvae, but they will also eat worms, spiders, and centipedes. The beetles, flies, dragonflies, butterflies and moths eaten often include those harmful to agriculture; for instance, cockchafers, cabbage white butterflies and wireworms. In particular they eat hairy or toxic caterpillars including those of the cinnabar moth which are usually left alone by other birds. The yellow-billed and black-billed cuckoos of North America are useful because they eat the tent caterpillars that weave large communal shelters, from which they sally forth to strip trees of their leaves. Fruit is sometimes eaten, especially by the koel, a cuckoo of Asia and Australia.

Boarding out the children

It has been well-known since ancient times that the common cuckoo does not build a nest of its own, but lays its eggs in those of other birds. Other members of the cuckoo family do the same, as do other kinds of birds; for example, the cowbird and the honeyguide. It is far from easy to watch the cuckoo lay an egg in the host nest as so much depends on being in the right place at the right time. Nevertheless, the amazing ways in which she ensures that her offspring have a good chance of surviving until independent are now well-known.

The female cuckoo keeps a watch for small birds building their nests. When the nest is complete and the unwitting foster parent has laid an egg, the cuckoo flies down. Choosing a time when the foster parent is away, she lifts an egg out of the nest, swallows or drops it, and very quickly lays one of her own in its place and departs before the foster parent returns.

Cuckoo eggs are sometimes found in domed nests of willow warblers and it was once thought that the cuckoo laid her egg on the ground then carried it to the nest in her bill, but it is now known that she presses her body against the nest and ejects the egg through the entrance. In Australia and New Zealand the shining cuckoo lays in domed nests of wrens by forcing its head in through the entrance then out through the far wall. The egg is laid while it straddles the nest, then it scrambles out through the hole it has made. The foster parent, when it returns, merely repairs the gap in the nest.

Observations have shown that clutches with a cuckoo egg are more likely to be deserted than normal clutches, but usually the cuckoo egg is accepted. It hatches in 12½ days and often the chick emerges before its nestmates. This advantage is used by the baby cuckoo to evict the other eggs and any newly hatched young. It is perhaps this part of the parasitic habit, more than any other, that has earned the cuckoo its bad name. The baby cuckoo manoeuvres itself in the bottom of the nest so that an egg or chick becomes balanced on its back, between the wings. It then hoists the unfortunate creature out of the nest, to be followed by the others. Occasionally two cuckoo eggs may be laid in one nest, when two female cuckoos are keeping watch in one area. After a few days jostling, the urge to empty the nest of competitors dies away and both young cuckoos grow together.

If the cuckoo did not evict its nestmates they would surely die in any case, for the young cuckoo grows rapidly, and its foster parents are hard put to feed it. After 3 weeks it leaves the nest which it has outgrown, and the foster parents keep feeding it, often having to perch on its back to drop insects in the gaping beak.

The African emerald cuckoo is a brilliant golden green.

Almost ready to moult at the end of the season, hedge sparrow feeds its giant foster child.

The common cuckoo arrives in Britain in late March leaving between July and September.

The baby cuckoo usually hatches first and begins to evict the other eggs.

The second egg does not survive long, being ejected from the nest in the same manner.

A newly-hatched tree pipit receives the same treatment being unable to defend itself.

Matching egg colours

Surveys of clutches containing cuckoo eggs show that the cuckoo egg is often very similar to the foster parents' eggs, and it has also been found that in any area cuckoos use certain host nests more than others. In Hungary, the chief dupe of the common cuckoo is the great reed warbler, and the cuckoo lays greenish eggs blotched with brown and black, like those of the warbler. In Finland, cuckoos' eggs are blue like those of its hosts the whinchat and redstart. Nearly all over its range, there are these preferences for certain hosts with a mimicking of their eggs. It seems that this reduces the chance of the foster parent abandoning the nest.

In the British Isles, however, cuckoo eggs differ surprisingly from their hosts' – yet they all tend to be of one pattern. The explanation for this seems to be that a cuckoo may lay in nests of another host if it cannot find the right one, and in Britain, where the countryside is divided into many small habitats with a large variety of possible host species, the cuckoo has not been able to form any set preferences for any particular host.

The final deception

Before the mysteries of bird migration were revealed it was thought the cuckoos turned into sparrowhawks in the winter and, even now, it is not unusual for a cuckoo to be mistaken for a sparrowhawk because of the similarity of shape and plumage. Bird watchers are not the only ones to be deceived as, when the cuckoo returns in spring, small birds will gather to mob it as if it were a hawk. There is some evidence that the cuckoos make use of this mistake. Cuckoos have been seen flying in an even more hawk-like fashion than usual, flapping and gliding in a soaring flight very much like a bird of prey. When they settle they are sometimes mobbed by meadow pipits and other small birds. On a few occasions this behaviour has been followed by the cuckoo alighting near a meadow pipit's nest, and one was seen flying away with a pipit's egg which it swallowed. It seems then that the cuckoo indulges in this hawk-like flight just before egg-laying, to lure the owners of the nest away by false pretences so that it can sneak in and lay its own egg.

Evidence for this is not conclusive but similar behaviour has been seen in other cuckoos. An Indian hawk-cuckoo that imitates sparrowhawks has been seen to lure birds from their nests in a more positive fashion, and the koel mimics a crow which is its main host in India. The male koel is black and it flies up to the host nest, calling, and is promptly chased away by the crows. Apparently they do this not so much to ward off a parasitic bird but for the same reason of ownership for which they would drive away another crow. Meanwhile the brown female koel slips in to lay her egg. The baby koel, moreover, does not eject its nestmates but it looks so like a young crow that it is hardly distinguishable from its fellow nestlings.

Of all the parasitic birds, however, the cuckoos, by reducing egg size and incubation time, and by mimicry of host birds' eggs, have applied the greatest resource to their underhand art.

class	**Aves**
order	**Cuculiformes**
family	**Cuculidae**
genera & species	**Cuculus canorus** *common cuckoo* **C. varius** *hawk-cuckoo* **Clamator coromandus** *red-winged Indian cuckoo* **C. glandarius** *greater spotted cuckoo* **Chrysococcyx cupreus** *emerald cuckoo* **Chalcites lucidus** *shining cuckoo* **Coccyzus erythrophthalmus** *black-billed cuckoo* **C. americanus** *yellow-billed cuckoo* **Eudynamys scolopacea** *koel others*

Barn owl

The barn owl's body is not as white as it appears when it is seen flying about at dusk. The upper parts are orange-buff, often speckled with grey and white. The underparts and face are pure white.

Although widespread, barn owls are not common throughout the British Isles, and are absent from the North of Scotland. In North America they do not breed north of Massachusetts, southern Ontario and Michigan, Iowa, Nebraska and northern California but they are regularly recorded as visitors farther north.

There are ten species of barn owl in various parts of the world. They differ from other owls in small details of the skeleton and proportionately smaller eyes set in a heart-shaped facial disc.

The typical barn owl is widespread, found in most parts of Europe, America, Africa, India, South-east Asia and Australia. There are about 32 races.

Ghost-like habits

The barn owl has probably given rise to many ghost stories. It often lives in churches or empty houses and is likely to give anyone not expecting it a bad shock, when it flies silently past them, a ghostly white in the gloom of night, or when they hear its eerie, long drawn out shrieks.

In Britain barn owls were formerly subject to unnecessary persecution, especially by gamekeepers. In the early 20th century, however, they made some recovery, but in the late 1940's a general decrease became apparent and by 1955 they had disappeared from many areas, especially in eastern Britain. The decrease is largely the the result of the owls' dependence on man. Old buildings and hollow trees provided roosts and nest sites and the barn owls' main prey were the rats, voles and mice that fed on man's crops. Since the Second World War, agriculture in Britain has been changing. Derelict stables and rotten trees are no longer tolerated and intensive agriculture has changed those parts of the countryside that barn owls used to frequent. The most rapid decrease in numbers over the last decade or so has, without much doubt, been due to the increased use of pesticides sprayed onto crops. These poisons accumulate in the bodies of the small animals that eat the crops and are then accumulated even further when they are eaten by owls, with the result that the barn owls often become sterile and their eggs fail to hatch.

Sometimes barn owls may be seen in broad daylight, but more usually they come out at twilight. With their white plumage, they are easy to see, flying about 15—20 ft above the ground, with fairly rapid but long wing-beats. They have regular routes which they patrol night after night, circling about and occasionally dropping to the ground to catch their prey.

Prey is taken to the nest or to a regular roost, which is identifiable by the pellets of indigestible bones, insect bodies and fur

△ *Barn owl having just swallowed its prey, indicated by the blood on the ground.*
▽ *Parent barn owls with 3-month-old chicks. At 4 months the young fly off to find their own territories.*

that are regurgitated and dropped, littering the ground about the roost. The barn owl's pellets are blackish with a varnished appearance, easily distinguishable from the greyish, soft pellets of tawny owls.

Owl pellets identify prey

It is from their pellets that the food of barn owls, and other predatory birds, can be identified. As the owls regurgitate their pellets in set places and the pellets accumulate, it is possible to get a very good idea of the diet by collecting them at intervals and pulling them apart to find the bones and other remains of the owls' prey.

A few years ago a large number of pellets were analysed in Poland. The remains of nearly 16 000 vertebrates (back-boned animals) were found and identified. Of these, 95.5% were of small mammals, 4.2% birds and the small remainder, amphibians. In Britain, similar proportions have been found. Mammal remains appear in the following order of frequency: common shrew, long-tailed field mouse, field vole and bank vole. Others, such as brown rats, house mice, even moles, bats and rabbits are taken, while several species of bird, night-flying beetles and moths, and occasional frogs and fish are found in the pellets. It is this kind of analysis which exposes the folly of persecution. Barn owls, as we now see, rarely take birds and are not a significant menace to poultry or pheasants.

Rodent control

The large number of small mammals included in the barn owls' diet shows the

useful role they play, for these mammals feed on man's crops. The numbers that a barn owl can catch are shown by the observation made on an American barn owl. In only 20 minutes it had caught 16 mice, three gophers, one rat and one squirrel. It must be added that this impressive number of animals was captured for the owl's babies.

A nest of pellets

In April or May, and again in July, piles of prey can be found at a barn owl's nest site. This is a sign that they are about to breed, for the male collects extra food to feed to the female. There is no nest made, the eggs are merely laid on an accumulation of pellets. Usually four to seven white eggs are laid, but there may be as few as three or as many as eleven. They are incubated for nearly 5 weeks by the female alone, who remains on the nest, being fed by the male.

The young hatch out at different times because the female begins incubating the first egg as soon as it is laid, so each egg begins its development before the next is laid. It has been suggested that the staggered hatching of barn owls' eggs helps to reduce the strain of providing enough food for them, because they will not all be requiring large quantities of food at once. The chicks leave the nest after 9–12 weeks to find territories of their own, where they stay for the rest of their lives.

At one time it was thought that barn owls hunted by sight. But experiments have shown that they can catch their prey in total darkness, where it is absolutely impossible to see anything. A tame barn owl was put in a pitch black room and a mouse was allowed to scuffle through leaf litter on the floor. After a short pause the owl would swoop at the ground and when the lights were put on it was back on its perch with the mouse. The experiment was repeated 17 times, and the only four misses were near misses.

A detailed examination of a barn owl's ears shows them to be very well developed, and there are flaps of skin forming 'outer ears', hidden under the feathers. These flaps are not placed symmetrically about the head, so sound coming to one ear follows a slightly different path from that going to the other ear. Thus a sound is picked up by one ear slightly before or after the other. It is this slight difference that enables an owl to judge the prey's position.

To make life even more hazardous for a small animal, the long, flight feathers of an owl's wings are tipped with down on the leading, trailing and upper surfaces. This deadens the noise of the owl's wingbeats so the intended prey has no warning of attack, unless they, too, have specially sensitive ears.

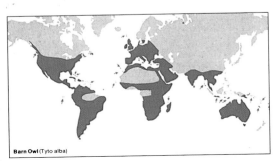

The barn owl has the distinction of being the most widely spread land bird in the world; varieties are found in every continent except Antarctica.
△ Barn owl returning to its nest after a successful foray.
▷ Barn owl with captured prey.

Barn Owl (Tyto alba)

class	**Aves**
order	**Strigiformes**
family	**Tytonidae**
genus & species	*Tyto alba*

144

Hummingbird

There are over 300 species of these minute, beautiful birds living in the New World. The largest is the giant humming-bird, an 8½ in. monster compared with the bee hummingbird of Cuba which is little more than 2 in. long; half this length is bill and tail, the body being the same size as a bumblebee. Hummingbirds are very diverse in form, although all of them are small and have the characteristic rapid wingbeats producing the hum that gives them their name. They have brilliant, often iridescent, plumage which has led to their being given names like 'ruby' and 'topaz'—and also to their being killed in thousands and their skins exported to Europe for use in ornaments. A feature of many hummingbirds is the long narrow bill, often straight but sometimes curved, as in the sicklebill. The sword-billed humming-bird has a straight bill as long as the head, body and tail put together.

Hummingbirds are most common in the forests of South America, but they range from southern Alaska to Tierra del Fuego. Some species are so rare that they are known only from collections of humming-birds' skin exported to Europe. Loddige's racket-tail was known from a single skin found in 1840 and was not found alive for another 40 years, when it was dis-covered in a small valley high in the Andes.

Hummingbird stamina . . .

Considering the diversity of habitats and food in the South American forests it is not surprising that there should be so many kinds of hummingbirds living there. It is rather surprising, however, to learn that humming-birds breed as far north as southeast Alaska, or in the heights of the Andes. The rufous hummingbird breeds in Alaska, migrating to South America for the winter, an incredible journey for so small a bird. The ruby-throated hummingbird also migrates to and from North America, crossing the Gulf of Mexico on each trip. Unlike non-migratory hummingbirds, it stores a layer of fat equal to half its body weight before setting off. At a normal rate of use, however, this would not last through a non-stop crossing of the Gulf. Yet the hummingbirds complete this marathon, so we must presume that they have some method of economising on food reserves.

. . . and speed

Even ignoring the mystery of their migra-tion, the flight of hummingbirds is truly re-markable. Their wings beat so fast they appear as a blur. Small species have wing-beats of 50–80 per second and in court-ship displays even higher rates have been recorded. The fast wingbeats enable the hummingbirds to dart to and fro, jerking to a halt to hover steadily. They are also extremely fast in straight flight—speeds of 71 mph have been recorded. Specialised filming has shown that hummingbirds do not take off by leaping into the air like other birds but lift off with rapid wingbeats. The photographs showed that a hummingbird on a thin twig actually pulls the twig up as it rises before letting go.

Flying with such rapid wingbeats requires a large amount of energy, so hummingbirds must either feed constantly or have plentiful reserves. Even at rest their metabolism—the rate at which they produce energy—is 25 times faster than a chicken's. At night when they cannot feed they conserve their food reserves by becoming torpid—going into a form of nightly hibernation. In the Andes a hummingbird's temperature drops from 38°C/100°F to 14°C/57°F, about the temperature of the surrounding air—and their metabolism is reduced six times.

Nectar seekers

Hummingbirds feed on nectar and small soft-bodied animals. To sip nectar they hover in front of flowers and insert their pointed bills down the corolla or, if that is too long, pierce it near the base. The nectar is sucked through a tubular tongue that is very similar to those of flowerpeckers. Pollen is often brushed onto the humming-birds' heads and transferred to other flowers, so pollinating them. To the flowers of the South American jungle, humming-birds are as important as pollinators as bees are in a clover field. Hummingbirds can readily be attracted to tubes containing sugar-water and they become so tame they will feed at a tube held in the hand.

Small insects are caught on the wing and spiders are taken from their webs. Most hummingbirds are unable to manipulate insects in their bills and have to rush at them so they are forced into the mouth. Some pick insects and spiders from flowers.

Tiny babies

Courtship antics of hummingbirds are difficult to watch as they flit about among dense vegetation too fast for accurate ob-servation. The males fly about in arcs, singing songs that are almost too high-pitched for humans to hear. They are usually promiscuous, mating in the air with several females, but in a few species such as the violet-eared hummingbirds (which have similar plumage for males and females) the male helps rear the family. The nest is a delicate cup of moss, lichen and spiders' webs placed on a twig or amongst foliage. The two eggs are incubated for 2–3 weeks and minute naked chicks hatch out. They are fed by the parent hovering alongside, putting its bill into theirs and pumping out nectar. The chicks grow very rapidly and leave the nest when 3 weeks old.

Hovering skill

When feeding, hummingbirds can be seen hovering steadily and even flying back-wards. They can do this because their wings can swivel in all directions from the shoulder. When hovering the body hangs at an angle of about 45 degrees so the wings are beating backwards and forwards instead of up and down. In each complete beat the wing describes a figure of eight. As it moves for-wards (the downstroke) the wings are tilted so they force air downwards and the bird upwards. At the end of the stroke they flip over so that the back of the wing is facing downwards and on the upstroke air is again forced downwards. To fly back-wards the wings are tilted slightly so air is forced forwards as well, and the humming-bird is driven back.

The flight of a hummingbird can be com-pared with that of a helicopter with its blades moving in a circle to achieve the same effect of driving air downwards as the hummingbird's wings do by moving back and forth. In the flight of most birds the power is in the downstroke, the up-stroke being merely a recovery phase, but in hummingbirds both strokes are powerful. The breast muscles of a hummingbird weigh a third of its total weight and the muscles drawing the wings upward are half as powerful as those driving the wings down. Non-hovering species have comparatively much smaller muscles for the upstroke.

class	Aves
order	**Apodiformes**
family	**Trochilidae**
genera & species	***Archilochus colubris*** *ruby-throated hummingbird* ***Ensifera ensifera*** *sword-billed hummingbird* ***Eutoxeres aquila*** *sickle-billed hummingbird* ***Loddigesia mirabilis*** *Loddige's racket-tail* ***Mellisuga helenae*** *bee hummingbird* ***Patagona gigas*** *giant hummingbird* ***Selasphorus rufus*** *rufous hummingbird, others*

■ **Hummingbirds**
(family Trochilidae)

The form of individual species of hummingbird is very varied. This male black-throated train-bearer *Lesbia victoriae,* from Ecuador, has long ornamental feathers that do not appear to hinder its aerial acrobatics. Its body is only 2 in. long but the tail is 6 in. with widely forked feathers which help make a marvellous picture when it turns sharply doing its fast manoeuvres in the air. The iridescent throat is absent in the female.

Top: Banana-boat feeder. A male velvet-purple coronet *Boissonneaua jardini* greedily sips nectar from *Heliconia jaquinii,* a relative of the bananas. Centre: The white-lipped sicklebill is perfectly adapted for sucking nectar from flowers. Bottom: The tiny ruby-topaz hummingbird *Chrysolampis mosquitus,* a beautiful Brazilian species, vibrates its wings at about 100 beats per second, fast even for the hummingbirds.

Kingfisher

There are over 80 species of kingfisher living mainly in the tropics. They are stockily built with long bills, quite short tails and often brilliant plumage, of which the common kingfisher of Europe and Asia is a good example. The common kingfisher is found throughout much of Europe and Asia, south into North Africa and east to the Solomon Islands and Japan. It is one of the most beautiful of birds, $6\frac{1}{2}$ in. long with a $1\frac{1}{2}$ in. dagger-like bill, its upperparts a shining iridescent blue or green.

▷ *Psychedelic forest kingfisher of Malaya.*
▽ *A giant kingfisher **Megaceryle maxima** glares from a vantage point over a stream.*

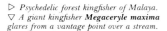

▷ *King of the world: perched aloft, a grey-headed kingfisher **Halcyon leucocephala** watches carefully for passing insects. It also feeds on beetles, grasshoppers and small reptiles.*

The underparts are chestnut, the legs red and there are patches of white on the neck. The pied kingfisher of Africa south of the Sahara and southwest Asia is dull-coloured for a kingfisher but is nevertheless striking with its black and white plumage. Like many kingfishers it has a crest. The Amazon kingfisher, also crested, has brilliant green upperparts and white underparts, with a chestnut breast in the male. The Texas kingfisher, ranging into the southern USA, is very similar.
In some species where the sexes differ in plumage, the female is the more brilliant. On the other side of the Pacific the yellow sacred kingfisher is found in many parts of Australia and is the only kingfisher in New Zealand.

A blur of colour

Kingfishers are usually seen as little more than a blur of colour as they fly low over the water on whirring wings to disappear into waterside undergrowth. If lucky one sees it perched on a branch, rock or post on the bank and its true colours can then be appreciated. Kingfishers are very much alike in habit as well as form; their feeding and breeding behaviour follow a pattern although some kingfishers rarely, if ever, go near water. Even the common kingfisher, associated so much with streams and rivers, sometimes nests some distance from water.

When thousands of exotic birds were being slaughtered and their carcases and feathers sent to Europe and North America as decorations and ornaments, it is not surprising that the dazzling kingfisher did not escape persecution. It was used for decorating hats and stuffed kingfishers in glass cases were a common household ornament. Later kingfishers were shot because they were alleged to eat enough trout fry to damage breeding stocks. The pollution of rivers and streams now threatens their wellbeing. Hard winters have a very severe effect on kingfisher populations.

Fishing over land and water

The method of catching prey is similar in nearly all species. The kingfisher waits on a perch, then darts out, catches its prey and carries it back to its perch. The common kingfisher flies out, hovers momentarily just over the water then dives in. Having caught a small fish or water insect it uses its wings to 'fly' through the water then up into the air without pausing. Larger prey are beaten against the perch to subdue them and may be tossed and caught again to get them into a suitable position for swallowing. Common kingfishers take mainly fish such as minnows, sticklebacks and gudgeon, also small perch and small trout. These last two are the reason for the persecution of kingfishers, but they also feed on water beetles, dragonfly larvae and waterboatmen which also kill small fish. Small frogs, tadpoles and pond snails are also taken.

The majority of kingfishers, however, take mainly land animals, although they hunt from a perch like the common kingfisher. They dart down from their perches like shrikes or they hawk passing insects like flycatchers. The racquet-tailed kingfisher, living in the area from the Moluccas to northeast Australia, hunts for lizards, centipedes and insects in the leaf litter of humid forests, swooping on them and sometimes driving its bill into the soft earth. The stork-billed kingfisher of India, 14 in. long with a large scarlet bill, catches fish as well as frogs, lizards, crabs and insects. It also robs other birds' nests, taking nestlings even from nests in holes in trees, but, true to its kind, it returns to its perch to swallow its prey. An exception to this is the shoe-billed kingfisher of the forests of New Guinea. It digs for earthworms with its flattened bill.

◁ *Malachite kingfisher **Corythornis cristata**, a very common African species. It feeds on fish, water invertebrates and flies.*

Common kingfisher with a prospective meal.

Hole nesting

Kingfishers nest in holes, those that hunt fish usually nesting in holes in banks near water while the more land-living kingfishers nest in holes in trees or abandoned termite nests. The striped kingfisher of Africa uses ready-made holes and may even dispossess swallows from their nests under eaves.

The nest hole is dug by the kingfishers repeatedly flying at one spot on the bank, loosening a bit of soil with their bills each time. When they have formed a ledge they can perch and dig more rapidly until the tunnel is 1½–3 ft long. The 6 or 7 spherical white eggs are laid on the floor of the tunnel and incubated for 3 weeks. During this time a revolting pile of fish bones and

droppings piles up around the eggs, a squalid contrast with the magnificent plumage of the adult birds. Until Ron and Rose Eastman made their prizewinning film 'The Private Life of a Kingfisher' in 1966 it was thought that pieces of fish were fed to the young. Their remarkable patience and technique, however, showed the young inside the nest burrow swallowing whole fish almost as big as themselves, the bones being later regurgitated. The chicks, which live in the tunnel for 3–4 weeks, are hatched naked but soon acquire a covering of bristle-like wax sheaths which are shed to reveal a plumage like that of the parents just before they leave the nest.

class	**Aves**
order	**Coraciiformes**
family	**Alcedinidae**
genera & species	**Alcedo atthis** common kingfisher **Ceryle rudis** pied kingfisher **Chloroceryle amazona** Amazon kingfisher **C. americana** Texas kingfisher **Clytoceyx rex** shoe-billed kingfisher **Halcyon chelicuti** striped kingfisher **H. sancta** sacred kingfisher **Pelargopsis capensis** stork-billed kingfisher **Tanysiptera galatea** racquet-tailed kingfisher

Woodpecker

No birds are better adapted for a life on the branches and trunks of trees than the woodpecker.

There are about 200 species of woodpecker which are spread over the wooded parts of the world, except Madagascar, Australia and oceanic islands. They are up to nearly 2 ft long and are usually brightly-coloured with patterns of black, white, green or red. A few woodpeckers have crests. The bill is straight and pointed, the legs short with two toes facing backwards and the tail is made up of pointed feathers with stiff shafts.

The 15 species of green woodpeckers inhabit the woods and forests of Europe and Asia from the British Isles to Borneo and Java. The familiar green woodpecker of Europe is 12 in. long, and has a green plumage, which is brighter below, a bright yellowish rump and a red crown. The male has a red and black stripe under the eye, while the female has a plain black stripe. The pied or spotted woodpeckers form a widespread group, the 30-odd species being distributed across North America, Europe and Asia. They are black or grey with white patches, bars or mottling. The males often have red crowns. The three-toed woodpeckers are unusual in having one toe missing from each foot. They too have a circumpolar distribution. The ivorybills of America are the largest woodpeckers and inhabit forests of large trees. As a result of these forests being cut down these species are in danger of extinction. The ivory-billed woodpecker of North America and Cuba was thought to be extinct but in 1966 a few pairs were found in Texas.

Expert tree climbers

Woodpeckers are usually seen as just a flash of colour disappearing through the trees. They live solitarily in woods and can be identified by their characteristic undulating flight: 3–4 rapid wingbeats carrying them up, followed by a downward glide. They are more likely to be given away by their harsh or ringing calls, such as the loud laugh of the green woodpecker, or by their drumming, a rapid tattoo which they make with their bills on dead branches, or even on metal roofs.

Woodpeckers spend most of their time hopping up tree trunks in spirals, searching for insects. When a woodpecker has searched one tree it flies to the base of the next and repeats the operation. In climbing vertical trunks, woodpeckers are assisted by having two backward-facing toes, sharp claws, and stiff tail feathers, which are used as a prop while climbing, rather like a shooting stick.

*Above: Female African **Campethera abingoni**. Below: Great spotted woodpecker **Dendrocopos major**.*

Boring for insects

The woodpecker's food is largely insects and their larvae. The green woodpeckers often hunt on the ground for ants and sometimes attack bee hives. The red-headed woodpecker of North America catches insects on the wing. Otherwise woodpeckers feed on insects which are prised out of crevices in the bark or drilled out of the wood. The pointed bill is an excellent chisel and the skull is toughened to withstand the shock of hammering. When drilling, a woodpecker aims its blows alternately from one side then the other, like a woodman felling a tree. Insects are removed from the hole by using the woodpecker's second useful tool – an extremely long tongue; it can protrude up to 6 in. from the tip of the bill in the green woodpecker. The tongue is protruded by muscles running round the back and top of the skulls. It is often tipped with barbs or bristles or coated with mucus for brushing up the insects.

Some woodpeckers eat fruit and seeds or drink sap. Red-headed woodpeckers and acorn woodpeckers store acorns, drilling separate holes in trees for each acorn or else using a natural cavity. There is a story of an acorn woodpecker that spent an autumn feeding acorns into a knothole in the wall of a cabin. As the hole never filled, the woodpecker 'posted' several hundred acorns in it.

Nesting in holes

With the exception of the African ground woodpecker, which burrows in the ground, woodpeckers nest in holes that they excavate in trees. They drill into a trunk then tunnel downwards to make a cavity up to 1 ft deep. There is no nest lining and the 2–8 white eggs rest on the bottom of the cavity. The eggs hatch in 11–17 days and the chicks fledge in 2–3 weeks, depending on the size of the woodpecker. Both sexes bore the nest hole, and takes turns at incubating and feeding the chicks.

Evacuating the home

Boring a nest hole several inches across does considerable damage to a tree and may weaken it sufficiently for it to fall. This happened at a nest of a pileated woodpecker observed by FK Truslow in the Everglades National Park. The tree split off at the level of the entrance to the nest, revealing that the trunk had been hollowed to leave a shell only $\frac{1}{4}-\frac{1}{2}$ in. thick. Truslow stayed in his hide hoping to watch the reactions of the woodpeckers – the female was incubating at the time. About 10 minutes later the female woodpecker did a most remarkable thing. She returned to the tree, disappeared into the nest cavity and reappeared with an egg in her bill. She then flew off with it and did not drop it for the 75 yd she was in sight. All three eggs were removed in this manner. Unfortunately this extraordinary story has no satisfactory ending as he never found out what became of the eggs. It is, however, one of the few positive records we have of birds rescuing their eggs by carrying them away.

▷ *The lesser spotted woodpecker is widespread in the woods of Europe; but, although numerous, it is seldom seen.*

class	**Aves**	
order	**Piciformes**	
family	**Picidae**	
genera & species	**Campephilus principalis** *ivory-billed woodpecker* **Dendrocopos major** *great spotted woodpecker* **D. minor** *lesser spotted woodpecker* **Dryocopus pileatus**	*pileated woodpecker* **Geocolaptes olivaceus** *ground woodpecker* **Melanerpes erythrocephalus** *red-headed woodpecker* **M. formicivorus** *acorn woodpecker* **Picoides tridactylus** *three-toed woodpecker* **Picus viridis** *green woodpecker*

Goldfinch

The goldfinch is a very handsome bird, 5¼ in. long, named for the golden-yellow bar on each wing. Its back is a tawny brown, its underparts paler. The head is boldly marked with red, white and black. The wings are black with a gold bar and white tips to the flight feathers. The forked tail is black with white tips. The beak is short and conical: a seed-eater's beak.

The young goldfinch lacks the red, white and black of the adult's head. Instead it has lines of spots or streaks on head, back and breast and, except for the golden bar on the wing, looks very like several other closely related finches. One of these is the siskin **Carduelis spinus***, which is about the same size and belongs to the same genus but has more yellow in its plumage. It spends the summer in pine-woods and the winter among the alders along the riverside. Another is the twite* **Carduelis flavirostris***, a finch of Scandinavia and northern Britain. The serin* **Serinus dermus** *is very like the siskin in appearance and habits. It is a European bird that occasionally visits Britain, which also has the lines of dark streaks. In an evolutionary sense all three are less 'grown up' than the gold-finch and show their immaturity in the streaked plumage of the adult.*

The goldfinch ranges across Europe into western and southwestern Asia, also North Africa.

A charm of goldfinches

The goldfinch is a showy bird that appears to come from nowhere at certain seasons, especially late summer, when it feeds on the seed heads of herbaceous plants. Except in the breeding season, it goes about in small flocks and attracts attention by its musical twittering and its bold and conspicuous colours seen at close range. When not feeding it perches high up in trees, on the outer twigs, and seen then in silhouette so that its coloured head is obscured, it passes for any one of a half-a-dozen small finches. At night the flocks roost in trees and in winter use oak and beech, especially those in hedges, that are late in shedding their dead leaves. As with other small finches the flight is bounding or undulating.

A flock is usually spoken of as a charm of goldfinches. Originally this was spelled 'chirm', and meant a chorus of sounds and was applied to the chatter of any birds. In recent years it has become restricted to goldfinches. It was this musical twittering that made goldfinches, as well as the re-lated linnets, popular as cage birds.

Diet of seeds

Goldfinches seldom feed on the ground although they may take insects, especially in summer. Their feeding is traditionally associated with the seeding thistle heads but they will visit the seeding heads of other

An agility at performing tricks with string made the goldfinch a popular cage bird in the past.

members of the daisy family Compositae. They also take seeds of pine and birch and may visit alders to feed from their catkins, in company with siskins, serins and red-polls. One goldfinch was seen to climb a dandelion stem until it bent over, then nip it, the stem folding at the weakened point. Then she held the top of the stem, as well as the part she was standing on, in her feet and ate the seeds. She did this repeatedly.

Away from the comparative safety of the nest, a young goldfinch faces the world.

Resourceful goldfinch hen

The breeding season begins early in May. The male flashes his golden wing bars at the female, as part of his courtship display, while swaying from side to side. The nest of interwoven roots, bents, wool, moss and lichens, lined with thistledown and wool, is built by the hen, usually well out on a branch but sometimes in a hedge. There have been a number of instances of goldfinches unty-ing the strings of labels used on fruit bushes and weaving the strings into the nests. The 5–6 eggs are bluish white with red spots and streaks, each nearly ¾ in. by ½ in. The hen alone incubates for 12–13 days, fed by the cock, but both parents feed the chicks by regurgitation for another 12–13 days. There are sometimes 3 broods a year.

Hauling in the lines

The note included above under breeding behaviour, about goldfinches untying the strings of labels, may appear remarkable, but this is not beyond their known abilities. We are used to stories of tits pulling up strings of nuts to a perch in order to eat but for centuries, according to Dr WH Thorpe, the eminent authority on animal behaviour, goldfinches have been kept in special cages so people could watch what they do. In the 16th century the gold-finch was called the draw-water or its equivalent in several European languages. These captive goldfinches were in cages so designed that to survive they had to do precisely this. On one side was a little cart con-taining seed and this was held by a string. The goldfinch had to pull the string with its beak, hold the loop with one foot, then pull in another loop with the beak, hold that, and so on until it could take the seeds. Another string held a thimble of water. To drink, the bird had to draw this up in the same way.

Canaries and other captive birds have been seen to do similar things, and the performances are not confined to cage birds. In 1957 it was reported from Norway and Sweden that hooded crows were stealing fish and bait from fishermen's lines set through holes in the ice. A crow would take the line in its beak and walk backwards away from the hole. Then it would walk forward again, carefully treading on the line to stop it slipping back. It would repeat this until the fish or the bait was drawn to the edge of the ice, when it would seize it.

class	**Aves**
order	**Passeriformes**
family	**Fringillidae**
genus & species	***Carduelis carduelis***

152

Waxbill

The waxbills are a group of small, colourful, seed-eating birds, that are popular cage birds. Waxbills are related to the sparrows and weavers and the waxbill subfamily includes the mannikins, munias, cordon-bleus, silvereyes and many others well known to bird fanciers. Unfortunately, several have different common names which makes the term waxbill open to confusion. The cordon-bleus, for instance, are also called blue waxbills. The waxbills proper belong to the genus **Estrilda** which also includes the striking avadavat.

Waxbills are small, usually about 4 in. long and many have finely barred upperparts. The species, known as the Waxbill, the common waxbill or sometimes the St Helena waxbill, is brown with fine barring. There is a scarlet patch around the eye, the cheeks and throat are white and in the male there is a pink tinge to the underparts. It is found in many parts of Africa and has been introduced to St Helena and Brazil. Other waxbills have a similar confusion of names. The grey or red-eared waxbill is also called the common waxbill. The upperparts are grey-brown with a pink tinge and the underparts light grey with a pink tinge turning to crimson on the belly. There is a crimson stripe through the eye and the rump is black. The grey waxbill has recently become established in Portugal from aviary escapes. One of the smallest is the 3½in. locust finch that flies in dense swarms. Its plumage is almost black with red on the face and throat. The smallest waxbill of all is the zebra or orange-breasted waxbill with a crimson streak through the eye and a crimson rump. The throat is yellow becoming scarlet underneath and the sides are barred with yellow. Waxbills live in Africa south of the Sahara apart from the avadavat in Asia and the Sydney waxbill that lives in eastern Australia.

Grain eaters

Outside the breeding season waxbills are gregarious, living in parties, sometimes of only a few birds, but others, such as the locust bird, in large flocks. The members of a party continually call to each other with shrill or soft monosyllables designed to inform each waxbill of its fellow's position and to keep the party together. Waxbills are mainly found near rivers or in swampy country where they feed on seeds, particularly those of grasses, and are particularly abundant in grassland and in crops of cereals, in association with other seedeaters such as mannikins and whydahs. In Sierra Leone the flocks are followed by rats which feed on the seeds they spill. In general, waxbills occur in too few numbers to be pests. They also eat some insects and catch flying termites.

△ The distinctive southern grey waxbill of western Africa.

Husband's annexe or decoy?

The typical waxbills differ from their near relatives by building nests with tubular entrances projecting from a ball of grass that are very much like the nests of sparrows and weavers. The nest is built of grass stems or flowering heads woven into an untidy mass and fastened to vertical stems or placed on the ground among grass or herbage. Some waxbills decorate the nest with paper, damp earth, feathers and other materials and a peculiar feature of the nests of true waxbills is that there is a so-called 'cock nest' incorporated into the top or side of the nest or built a short distance away. It has been said that the cock nest is used as a roost by the member of the pair that is not incubating the eggs. There is, however, no proof of this and Derek Goodwin has suggested that the cock nests may mislead predatory birds into overlooking the real nest.

The nest is built by the female waxbill but the male helps with the decoration and with lining the nest with feathers. Both sexes incubate the 4–6 white eggs, which hatch in 2 weeks. They feed the chicks by regurgitating seeds when chicks solicit by gripping their parents' bills with their own. The young waxbills are able to fly in 16–17 days.

Getting their own back?

Many waxbills are parasitised by some of the related whydahs, also known as widow birds. The whydahs lay their eggs in the waxbills' nests and their young are brought up with the young waxbills. Not all the whydahs are, however, parasites and one waxbill, the zebra waxbill, has to a certain extent reversed the situation: it lays its eggs in the nests of whydahs and bishops, but only when they have been abandoned. Bishops and whydahs finish nesting in March and the waxbills then start their nesting season taking over the nests of the bishops and whydahs and relining them.

class	**Aves**
order	**Passeriformes**
family	**Ploceidae**
genus & species	***Estrilda astrild*** common waxbill *E. locustella* locust finch *E. melpoda* orange cheeked waxbill *E. perreini* southern grey waxbill *E. subflava* zebra waxbill *E. temporalis* Sydney waxbill *E. troglodytes* northern grey waxbill others

153

Mammals

Although mammals, like birds, are descended from reptiles, the two groups are sharply contrasted in form and behaviour. They share a warm-blooded (homoiothermic) physiology and are air-breathing. But whereas all birds lay eggs, the characteristic feature of mammals is that the females bear their young alive. The bodies of birds, moreover, are clothed in feathers, those of mammals bear hair. Birds use sight as the main sense, mammals use smell except for the Primates (lemurs, monkeys, apes and man) which are mainly 'eyesight animals'. Except for man, mammals are relatively silent animals although all have voices, which mainly come into use at the breeding season.

One of the features of birds which lends credibility to the notion that they are descended from reptiles is the presence on their bodies of scales. It is true these are restricted to the legs and feet, but there they so strongly recall the corresponding structures on reptiles as to still any remaining doubts of the close relationship of birds to reptiles. When scales do occur in mammals these are of a different character and structure. Thus, the scales of the scaly-anteater or pangolin are made up of what can conveniently be called compressed hair.

When Captain James Cook visited Australia and opened the way to the settlement of that continent by Europeans, he could not have foreseen that one result would be to rescue the zoologists of those times from a dilemma. It would have been hard to convince anyone that mammals are descendants of reptilian stock without knowledge of the duckbill or platypus, of Australia, and the echidna or spiny anteater, of Australia (and also New Guinea) which

the early settlers found when they first arrived there.

Both these are undoubted mammals. They both have hair on the body and the females nourish their young in the early stages of life with milk. But both lay eggs, a feature unique among mammals. Moreover, in the shape of some of their bones, in certain other features of their skeleton, as well as in the anatomy of their reproductive, excretory and digestive systems, they bear the hallmarks of true reptiles.

Also in Australia, though not exclusively so because they occur as well in adjacent islands and in America, are the marsupials or pouch-bearers, epitomized for most people by the kangaroo. These are also undoubted mammals but they are only a degree or so removed from the egg-laying mammals in possessing some undoubted reptilian characters.

We have travelled far in this book from the point where reference was made to the phrase 'from amoeba to man'. Although in principle it is still valid and useful as a convenient catchphrase, it has been rendered outmoded, and the history of this sheds an important light on the classification of mammals.

Man has always placed his own species at the apex of the pyramid formed by the animal kingdom. Consequently, when constructing a classification of mammals, he began with the most primitive, the egg-laying mammals, and ended with the Primates, those with the most highly-organized brains, of which man is a member. This classification was accepted and used for decades.

In 1945, the eminent zoologist, Dr George Gaylord Simpson published a monograph

in which he suggested a new classification of mammals. The revolutionary idea it embodied was to give first consideration to the physical or bodily specializations, ignoring the matter of brain-development. The result can be seen in the table of classification appended here.

The classification of mammals is as follows:

Class Mammalia   3,700 species
SUBCLASS PROTOTHERIA
Order Monotremata
  (egg-laying mammals)
INFRACLASS METATHERIA
Order Marsupialia
  (marsupials or pouch-bearers)
SUBCLASS THERIA
Order Insectivora
  (shrews, moles, tenrecs)
Order Dermoptera (flying lemur)
Order Tupaioidea (tree shrews)
Order Chiroptera (bats)
Order Primates
  (lemurs, monkeys, apes, man)
Order Edentata
  (anteaters, sloths, armadillos)
Order Pholidota (pangolins)
Order Lagomorpha (pikas, rabbits, hares)
Order Rodentia (rodents)
Order Carnivora (dogs, bears, cats, etc.)
Order Pinnipedia (seals, sealions, walrus)
Order Tubulidentata (aardvark)
Order Sirenia (dugong, manatee)
Order Perissodactyla
  (horse, ass, rhinoceros, tapir)
Order Artiodactyla
  (pig, hippopotamus and other
  cloven-hoofed animals)
Order Cetacea
  (whales, dolphins, porpoises)

Platypus

Today the platypus is accepted as an unusual animal of quaint appearance, but it is not difficult to imagine its impact on the scientific world when it was first discovered. So strange did the creature appear that one scientist named it **paradoxus**, and a paradox it was with duck-like bill, furry mammalian coat and webbed feet.

Known as the duckbill, watermole or duckmole, the platypus is one of Australia's two egg-laying mammals, the other being the spiny anteater. The platypus is about 2 ft long including a 6in. beaver-like tail and weighs about 4½ lb, the males being slightly larger than the females. The 'bill' is a sensitive elongated snout and is soft, like doeskin, not horny as is popularly supposed.

Although bizarre in appearance, the platypus is well adapted to its semi-aquatic life. The legs are short with strong claws on the toes and the feet are webbed. The webbing on the forefeet extends well beyond the toes, but can be turned back when on land, leaving the claws free for walking and digging. The eye and the opening to the inner ear lie on each side of the head in a furrow which can be closed when the platypus submerges. There are no external ears, thus the platypus is blind and deaf when under water. Young have teeth, but these are replaced in the adult by horny ridges.

Thick loose skin makes the barrel-shaped body of the platypus appear larger than it is. The pelt consists of a dense woolly undercoat and long shiny guard hairs. The colour varies from sepia brown to almost black above and is silver, tinged with pink or yellow underneath; females can be identified by the more pronounced reddish tint of their fur. Adult males have hollow spurs, connected to venom glands, on the ankle of each hind limb. The poison from them can be quite harmful to a man, although not fatal.

The platypus was not discovered until 1796, nearly 200 years after the first wallaby, for instance, had been seen by a European. This is not as strange as might appear at first sight, for aquatic animals tend to be elusive particularly if, like the platypus, they are nocturnal.

Its range can be seen on the map. The western limits are the Leichhardt River in North Queensland, and the Murray, Onkaparinga and Glenelg rivers, just within the border of South Australia. It is found in all fresh water, from clear icy streams at 5 000 ft to lakes and warm coastal rivers.

▷ Out of its front door and into the river. When underwater the platypus is blind and deaf so it relies mainly on its sense of touch, highly developed in the soft rubbery bill.

Hearty appetite

Like many small energetic animals the platypus has a voracious appetite, and probably needs more food, relative to its weight, than any other mammal. It feeds mainly in the early morning and late evening, on crayfish, worms and other small water animals. It probes for these with its bill and at the same time takes in mud and sand, which are apparently necessary for breaking up the food. During the day the platypus rests in burrows dug out of the banks, coming out at night to forage for food in the mud of the river-bottom.

Egg-laying mammal

The breeding season is from August to November and mating takes place in the water, after an elaborate and unusual courtship. Among other manoeuvres, the male will grasp the female's tail and the two will then swim slowly in circles. The female digs a winding, intricate burrow in a bank 25–35 ft, sometimes as much as 60 ft, long, 12–15 in. below the surface of the ground. At the end, a nesting chamber is excavated and lined with wet grass and leaves. The female carries these by wrapping her tail around a bundle. Usually two soft-shelled white eggs are laid, each ½ in. diameter. They often stick together, which prevents them rolling, and the wet leaves and grass keep them from drying out. Before retiring to lay her eggs, 2 weeks after mating, the female blocks the tunnel at intervals with earth, up to 8 in. thick, which she tamps into position with her tail. During the incubation period of 7–10 days she rarely leaves the nest but each time she does so these earth blocks are rebuilt. Presumably this is a defensive measure, but in fact today the platypus has virtually no natural enemies, although a carpet-snake or goanna may occasionally catch one. The inference is that in past ages natural enemies did exist in some numbers and the earth-block defences were very necessary. This is an example of what is known as 'fossil behaviour' and the platypus itself is a living fossil.

Blind for 11 weeks

The young platypus is naked and blind, and its eyes do not open for 11 weeks. It is weaned when nearly 4 months old, at which age it takes to the water. The mother has no teats; milk merely oozes through slits on her abdomen where it is licked up by the babies. A platypus matures at about 2½ years and has a life span of 10 years or more.

Competing with rabbits

Formerly hunted ruthlessly for its beaver-like pelt, the platypus is now rigidly protected. Too often, however, it falls foul of wire cages set under water for fish. Should the platypus enter one it cannot escape and will drown, as it is not able to stay under water for much more than 5 minutes. The introduced rabbit of Australia threatens the platypus in a different way. Where rabbits have driven too many tunnels, the platypus cannot breed: it needs undisturbed soil for its breeding burrows. Fortunately, although reduced in numbers, it is now well protected by the Australian authorities and it is in no danger of extinction.

Creature of contrast

Fortunately for the sanity of naturalists, the paradoxical facts that the platypus, a mammal, laid eggs and suckled its young were not known when it was first discovered. In 1884, WH Caldwell, who had gone to Australia specially to study the platypus, dissected a female which had already laid one egg and was ready to lay another. Thrilled by this discovery he electrified members of the British Association for the Advancement of Science, then meeting in Montreal, with his laconic telegram – 'Monotremes oviparus, ovum meroblastic' (monotremes egg-laying, egg only partially divides). Delegates stood and cheered, for controversy over this point had raged in the scientific world for some years.

Long before this, in 1799, the first dried skin reached London and came into the hands of Dr Shaw, then assistant-keeper in the Natural History section of the British Museum. When Dr Shaw saw the skin he literally could not believe what he saw. At that time visitors to the Far East were bringing back fakes such as the 'eastern-mermaid', made from the skin of a monkey skilfully sewn to the tail of a fish. It is not surprising, therefore, that Dr Shaw should suspect someone had grafted the bill of a duck on to the body of a quadruped. He tried to prise off the bill, and today the marks of his scissors can still be seen on the original skin which is preserved in the British Museum (Natural History).

class	Mammalia
order	Monotremata
family	Ornithorhynchidae
genus & species	*Ornithorhynchus anatinus platypus*

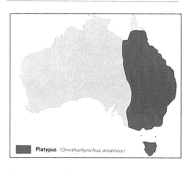

Platypus *(Ornithorhynchus anatinus)*

▽ *In the water the platypus uses its strong webbed forefeet for swimming and its hind legs as rudders. On land its forefeet are used for digging and to press the water out of its fur before it enters its burrow.*

Kangaroo

The best-known of the five kangaroos are the great grey and the red. The great grey or forester is up to 6 ft high, exceptionally 7 ft, with a weight of up to 200 lb. Its head is small with large ears, its forelimbs are very small by comparison with the powerful hindlimbs and the strong tail is 4 ft long. The colour is variable but is mainly grey with whitish underparts and white on the legs and underside of the tail. The muzzle is hairy between the nostrils. The male is known as a boomer, the female as a flyer and the young as a Joey. The great grey lives in open forest browsing the vegetation. The red kangaroo is similar to the great grey in size and build but the male has a reddish coat, the adult female is smoky blue, and the muzzle is less hairy. Unlike the great grey kangaroo it lives on open plains, is more a grazer than a browser, and lives more in herds or mobs, usually of a dozen animals.

The 55 species of kangaroo, wallaby and wallaroo make up the family Macropodidae (**macropus** = big foot). Only two are called kangaroos but there are 10 rat kangaroos and two tree kangaroos. A third species is known as the rock kangaroo or wallaroo. There is no brief way of describing the difference between a kangaroo and a wallaby except to say that the first is larger than the second. An arbitrary rule is that a kangaroo has hindfeet more than 10 in. long.

The red is found all over Australia. The great grey lives mainly in eastern Australia but there are three races of it, formerly regarded as species: the grey kangaroo or western forester of the southwest; that on Kangaroo Island off Yorke Peninsula, South Australia; and the Tasmanian kangaroo or forester. The wallaroo or euro lives among rocks especially in coastal areas. It has shorter and more stockily built hindlegs than the red or the great grey.

Leaps and bounds

When feeding, and so moving slowly, kangaroos balance themselves on their small forelegs and strong tail and swing the large hindlegs forward. They then bring their arms and tail up to complete the second stage of the movement. When travelling fast, only the two hindfeet are used with the tail held almost horizontally as a balancer. They clear obstacles in the same way, with leaps of up to 26 ft long. Usually the leap does not carry them more than 5 ft off the ground but there are reports of these large kangaroos clearing fences up to 9 ft. Their top speed is always a matter for dispute. They seem to be capable of 25 mph over a 300yd stretch but some people claim a higher speed for them.

Eating down the grass

Kangaroos feed mainly by night resting during the heat of the day. The red kangaroo, because it eats grass, has become a serious competitor with sheep, important in Australia's economy. By creating grasslands man has helped the kangaroo increase in numbers. In turn the kangaroo tends to outgraze the sheep, for which the pastures were grown, not only through its increased numbers but by its manner of feeding. Sheep have teeth (incisors) in only the lower-front jaw, with a dental pad in the upper jaw. Kangaroos have front teeth in both lower and upper jaw which means they crop grass more closely than sheep. At times, it is reported, they also dig out the grass roots. They can go without water for long periods, which suggests they were originally animals of desert or semi-desert, but where water is supplied for sheep kangaroos will, if not kept out, take the greater share.

Kangaroos set a problem

Enemies of the larger kangaroos are few now that the Tasmanian wolf has been banished. The introduced dingo still claims its victims but that is shot at sight. The loss of natural enemies, the creation of wide areas of grassland and the kangaroo being

A place in the sun: a red kangaroo group whiles away a lazy sociable afternoon. The powerful hindlegs and long tails can be clearly seen.

able to breed throughout most of the year, has created a problem, especially for sheep graziers, in Australia. Fencing in the pastures, often thousands of acres in extent, is costly – over £200 a mile – and kangaroos have a trickfo squeezing under the fence at any weak spot. So kangaroos are shot. In one year, on nine sheep properties totalling 1 540 000 acres, 140 000 kangaroos were shot and it would have needed double this number of kills to keep the properties clear of them. Another problem is that kangaroos often bound across roads at night and collide with cars causing costly damage and endangering those in the cars.

Bean-sized baby

The manner in which baby kangaroos are born and reach the pouch had been in dispute for well over a century. In 1959-60 all doubts were set at rest when the birth process of the red kangaroo was filmed at Adelaide University. About 33 days after mating the female red kangaroo begins to clean her pouch, holding it open with the forepaws and licking the inside. She then takes up the 'birth position' sitting on the base of her tail with the hindlegs extended forwards and her tail passed forward between them. She then licks the opening of her birth canal or cloaca. The newborn kangaroo, ¾in. long, appears headfirst and grasps its mother's fur with the claws on its forefeet. Its hindlegs are at this time very small. In 3 minutes it has dragged itself

to the pouch, entered it and seized one of the four teats in its mouth. The birth is the same for the great grey except that the female stands, with her tail straight out behind her. The baby kangaroo, born at an early stage of development, weighs $\frac{3}{35}$ oz at birth. It remains in the pouch for 8 months, by which time it weighs nearly 10 lb. It continues to be suckled for nearly 6 months after it has left the pouch and can run about, putting its head in to grasp a teat. Meanwhile, another baby has probably been born and is in the pouch. The red kangaroo has lived for 16 years in captivity.

Overlooking the obvious

The truth about kangaroo birth took a long time to be established. In 1629 Francois Pelsaert, a Dutch sea captain, wrecked on the Abrolhos Islands off southwest Australia, was the first to discover the baby in the pouch of a female wallaby. He thought it was born in the pouch. This is what the Aborigines also believed. In 1830 Alexander Collie, a ship's surgeon on a sloop lying in Cockburn Sound, Western Australia, investigated the birth and showed that the baby was born in the usual manner and made its way unaided into the pouch. From then on various suggestions were put forward: that the mother lifted the newborn baby with her forepaws or her lips and placed it in the pouch, or that the baby was budded off from the teat. In 1883 Sir Richard Owen, distinguished anatomist,

Full steam ahead: a shallow water sprint shows the versatility of bounding movement.

came down heavily on the side of those who said the mother placed the baby in her pouch holding it in her lips, yet in 1882 the Hon L Hope had shown Collie to be correct. In 1913 Mr A Goerling wrote a letter to the Perth *Western Mail* describing how he had watched the baby make its way to the pouch with no help from the mother. It was not until 1923, however, that this view was generally accepted, when Dr WT Hornaday, Director of the New York Zoological Gardens, watched and described the birth. Finally, in 1959-60, the whole process of birth was filmed by GB Sharman, JC Merchant, Phyllis Pilton and Meredith Clark, at Adelaide University, setting the matter at rest for all time. It seems so obvious to us now!

class	**Mammalia**
order	**Marsupialia**
family	**Macropodidae**
genus & species	***Macropus giganteus*** *great grey kangaroo* **M. robustus** *rock kangaroo or wallaroo* *Megaleia rufa red kangaroo*

Koala

The koala is probably Australia's favourite animal. It is known affectionately as the Australian teddy bear although there are a dozen names to choose from. At various times it has been called bangaroo, koolewong, narnagoon, buidelbeer, native bear, karbor, cullawine, colo, koala wombat and New Holland sloth! The last two have an especial interest. For a long time it was believed the koala was most nearly related to the wombat and was placed in a family on its own, the Phascolarctidae, near that of the wombat. Now it is placed in the Phalangeridae with the opossums. In habits the koala recalls the slow loris and the sloth, two very different animals which also move in a lethargic way.

The koala is like a small bear, 2 ft high, up to 33 lb weight, with tufted ears, small eyes with a vertical slit pupil and a prominent beak-like snout. Tailless except for a very short rounded stump, it has a thick ash-grey fur with a tinge of brown on the upper parts, yellowish white on the hindquarters and white on the under parts. It has cheek pouches for storing food and the brood pouch of the female opens backwards. All four feet are grasping. On the front feet the first two of the five toes are opposed to the rest and the first toe on the hindfoot is opposed. Also on the hindfoot the second and third toes are joined in a common skin.

Ace tree-climbers

The koala is essentially tree-living, only occasionally descending to lick earth—apparently to aid digestion—or to shuffle slowly to another tree. If forced to the ground its main concern is to reach another tree and climb it, scrambling up even smooth trunks to the swaying topmost branches where it clings with the powerful grip of all four feet. Although its legs are short they are strong and there are sharp claws on the toes. When climbing a trunk its forelegs reach out at an angle of 45° while the hindlegs are directly under the body. It climbs in a series of jumps of 4–5 in. at a time. During the day it sleeps curled up in a tree-fork. It never enters hollows in trees. Koalas are inoffensive although they have harsh grating voices, said to be like a hand-saw cutting through a thin board; it has been claimed that they have the loudest Australian voice, other than the flying phalanger.

▽ A koala squatting up a telegraph pole on Phillip Island, off eastern Australia.

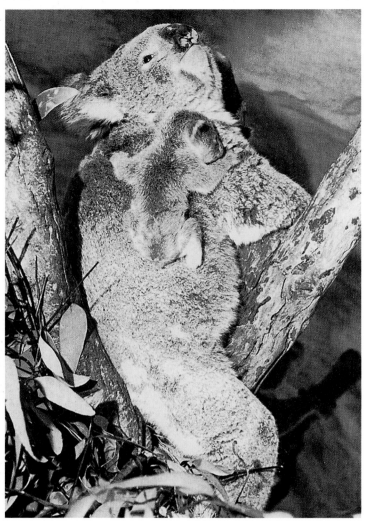

Fussy feeders

At night the koala climbs to the topmost branches to find its only food: the tender shoots of eucalyptus, 12 species of which are eaten. A koala is said to smell strongly of eucalyptus. Bernhard Grzimek, well-known German zoologist and ethologist, has spoken of koalas as smelling like cough lozenges. Their feeding is, however, more restricted than this. Different races of koala eat only certain species of gum tree. Koalas on the east coast of Australia feed only on the spotted gum and the tallow wood, in Victoria only the red gum. Even then they cannot use all the leaves on a chosen gum. At certain times the older leaves, sometimes the young leaves at the tips of the branches, release prussic acid—a deadly poison—when chewed. So, as more and more gum trees have been felled, koalas have become increasingly hemmed in, prisoners of their specialised diet. One of the difficulties of saving the koala by having special reserves is to supply enough trees for them of the right kind. Koalas are said to eat mistletoe and box leaves as well, and a koala in captivity was persuaded to eat bread and milk, but without gum leaves they cannot survive.

Get off my back!

Another drawback to preserving the koala is that it is a slow breeder. Usually the animal is solitary or lives in small groups. At breeding time a boss male forms a small harem which he guards. The gestation period is 25–35 days and there is normally only one young at a birth, ¾ in. long and ⅛ oz weight. It is fully furred at 6 months but continues to stay with the mother for another 6 months after leaving the pouch, riding pick-a-back on her, which has led to many endearing photographs. On weaning it obtains nourishment by eating partially digested food that has passed through the mother's digestive tract. The young koala is sexually mature at 4 years, and the longest lived koala was 20 years old when it died.

Pitiless persecution

Until less than a century ago there were millions of koalas, especially in eastern Australia. Now they are numbered in thousands. In 1887–89 and again in 1900–1903 epidemics swept through them, killing large numbers. This was at a time when it was a favourite 'sport' to shoot these sitting targets, often taking several shots to finish one animal which meanwhile cried piteously, like a human baby, a fact that caused Australian naturalists to condemn the sport as the most callous. At all times koalas are a prey to forest fires as well as to land clearance for human settlement. Moreover a market was developed for their pelts, their fur being thick and able to withstand hard usage. In 1908 nearly 58 000 koala pelts were marketed in Sydney alone. In 1920–21 a total of 205 679 were marketed and in 1924 over two million were exported. By this time public opinion was being aroused and before long efforts were being made to protect the surviving populations and to establish sanctuaries for them and ensure their future.

Koala *(Phascolarctos cinereus)*
■ Seen in 1967
▨ Last seen in past 25 years
▨ Last seen more than 25 years ago
▧ Western limit of red gum tree *(Eucalyptus tereticornis)*

QUEENSLAND

Curious cuddly: favourite of millions, the koala is the Australian teddy bear. It spends most of its time shuffling about its eucalyptus tree-top home. The baby above has climbed onto its mother's back from a downward opening pouch. At a year it will be ready to leave its mother and find its own gum tree. Numbers have seriously decreased in the last 100 years mainly due to fires destroying their gum trees and from persecution by man. From a 1967 survey in Queensland the present-day distribution was established in that state (left).

class	**Mammalia**
order	**Marsupialia**
family	**Phalangeridae**
genus & species	*Phascolarctos cinereus koala*

Chimpanzee

One of the great apes and the nearest in intelligence to man, the chimpanzee is one of the most studied and popular of animals. Scientists have examined its mental capacities and sent it into space in anticipation of man. To the general public, the chimpanzee is the familiar clown of circus acts and tea parties at the zoo. Yet despite all our knowledge of the chimpanzee's capabilities in the laboratory, it is only recently that its habits in the wild have been studied, and these are proving to be more remarkable than its antics in captivity.

Chimpanzees need little description. Being apes and not monkeys, they have no tail. Their arms are longer than their legs and they normally run on all fours, but they can walk upright, with toes turned outwards. When erect they stand 3–5 ft high. The hair is long and coarse, black except for a white patch near the rump. The face, ears, hands and feet are naked and, except for the black face, flesh coloured.

Forest families

The single species of chimpanzee lives in the tropical rain forests of Africa, roughly from the Niger basin to Angola. They are at home in the trees, making nests of branches and vines each night to sleep in, but they often come down to the ground to search for food. Whereas their normal gait on the ground is all fours, they will run on three legs, leaving one free to hold food, or on their hind legs, in an amusing waddling gait, when carrying an armful of food.

Chimpanzees live in small parties, occasionally numbering up to 40, but the bonds between the members of a party are weak. There is no fixed social structure like that found in baboon troops. A chimpanzee party is constantly varying in size as members leave to wander off in the forests by themselves or return from such a wandering. The only constant unit of social life is a mother with her young. She may have two or three of different ages with her at any time because they stay with her for several years. The usual size of a group is from 3–6, but numbers increase as chimpanzees gather at a source of plentiful and tasty food, or if a female comes on heat when the males will gather round her for several days.

Within a party, the males are arranged in a social order, the inferior ones respecting the superior ones. Dominance is related to age; a chimpanzee gradually rises in social position from the time he is physically mature and leaves the protection of his mother. The status of a male seems to be partly determined by noisy displays, charging about waving branches or rocks or drumming the feet on the plank-like buttresses of the forest trees. This behaviour is sometimes sparked off by frustration brought on by seeing more dominant males enjoying food without sharing it. Yet the chimpanzees recognize the right of owner-

The gamut of emotions

△ *'I'm content' – relaxed and normal.*

△ *'Hello' – the greeting pout.*

△ *'I'm happy' smile, showing bottom teeth only.*
▽ *Tantrum, showing top and bottom teeth.*

ship sufficiently to prevent a dominant male from wresting food from one of his inferiors.

First aid and affection

When chimpanzees meet after having been apart they greet each other in a very human way, by touching each other or even clasping hands and kissing. The arrival of a dominant male is the signal for the rest to hurry over and pay their respects to him. The members of a party also spend a considerable amount of time grooming each other, and themselves. Mothers carefully go through the fur of their babies for any foreign particles, spending more and more time on the task as the babies grow older. Dirt, burrs, dried skin and ticks are plucked off and splinters may be removed by pinching them out with forefingers or lips. Such mutual help may lead to further first aid. A captive female was once seen to approach her male companion, whimpering. She sat down while the other chimpanzee sat opposite her and, holding her head steady with one hand, pulled the lower lid of one eye down with the other. After a short inspection he removed a speck of grit from her eye with his finger, to her evident relief.

Hunting for meat

About 7 hours a day may be spent feeding either up trees or on the ground. The chimpanzees investigate any source likely to produce food. Crevices in logs are searched for insects and nests are robbed of eggs and chicks, but their usual food consists of fruits, leaves and roots. Ripening fruit crops, of bananas, pawpaws or wild figs, are a special attraction to them and they are sometimes a nuisance when they attack plantations. A big male chimpanzee can eat over 50 bananas at one sitting.

Until recently it was thought that the only flesh eaten by chimpanzees was that of insects and occasionally birds and small rodents. They have now been found to hunt larger animals, some individuals apparently being particularly fond of meat. Young bushbucks and bushpigs have been seen caught by chimpanzees, as well as colobus monkeys and young baboons. Jane Goodall, the British naturalist who spent several years in Africa studying chimpanzees in the wild, has given a very graphic description of a chimpanzee catching a young baboon and killing it by holding its back legs and smashing its head against the ground.

Obedient children

Chimpanzees are promiscuous. When a female comes on heat the males gather round her, bounding and leaping through the branches. All of them mate with her, no matter what their social standing. She remains on heat for several days, then the males lose interest.

A single baby – twins are rare – is born after about 230 days. If it is the female's first baby, she does not at first seem to know what to do with it, but by a combination of instinct, knowledge gained from having seen other babies, and learning, she soon starts to care for it. For 2 years the baby will be completely dependent on her. At first she carries it to her breast, but as it grows larger it rides pick-a-back.

The standard of baby care shown by

Top: Young chimps, Primrose (left) and Peter.
Right: Chimpanzees are the best tool-users apart from man, using natural objects to gather food, crack nuts, and drive off enemies.

Chimpanzee *(Pan troglodytes)*

female chimpanzees varies considerably. Some are ideal mothers, caring for their babies zealously and caressing and kissing them. Others are over-attentive, and the babies are 'spoilt'; and yet others neglect their children. The standard of care and education, however, is on the whole exemplary. The babies are not usually bullied or spoiled, yet they obey the parents' orders instantly. When they leave their mother's back they have considerable freedom, and can climb over dominant males without fear.

The babies are carried for varying periods. Sometimes they are still riding on their mothers when 4 years old. By this time the mother will have another baby and the elder one has to fend more for itself, but chimpanzees have been seen hand feeding young that are 6 or 7 years old.

Tools for chimpanzees

Man is sometimes called the toolmaker to distinguish him from other animals. It is difficult to decide when our ancestors became human-like rather than ape-like,

and toolmaking is one factor used as a line of contrast. Upright gait and speech are others, but it is difficult to make rigid pronouncements about features that must have evolved gradually.

Tools can be regarded as extensions of the body used to help with certain tasks. Few animals are known to use tools, but the real difference that separates man and the rest of the animal world is that he not only uses a variety of tools, he makes them, fashioning natural objects to suit his purpose. In this way, opening a nut with a stone is tool using, but shaping the stone into an axe is toolmaking.

Chimpanzees are the best tool-users apart from man. In captivity, they have been seen to throw stones and brandish clubs when put in a cage near a leopard and they are mentally well equipped to work out how to use tools, which are used by some other animals more or less instinctively. Chimpanzees have solved such problems as fitting two sticks together or balancing boxes on top of each other to get at otherwise inaccessible bananas.

The observations by Jane Goodall and others on wild chimpanzees have shown that they also use a variety of tools. The most common use is to extract honey, ants or termites from nests. Sticks 2–3 ft long are picked off the ground or broken from branches and pushed into nests, then withdrawn, and the honey or insects licked off. Stones are used to crack nuts, or as missiles to drive humans or baboons away from the chimpanzees' food. The stones, which sometimes weigh several pounds, are thrown, overarm, not very accurately but definitely aimed. Another material used for tools is leaves. Chimpanzees have been seen plucking leaves, chewing them up, and using the resultant mass as a sponge. Water, in a natural bowl in a tree, was soaked up into the sponge and squeezed out into the chimpanzee's mouth. Whole leaves have also been used for wiping sticky lips and hands after eating bananas.

The variety of tools used by the chimpanzees is made more interesting because they actually make some of their implements. To make a suitable rod to extract insects, the chimpanzees will strip the leaves off a twig or tear shreds off a grass stem to make it narrower. These are clear signs of modifying natural material for a specific use, as is the chewing of leaves to make a sponge. So man is not the only toolmaker, merely better at it than his relatives.

A final point arises from these observations on wild chimpanzees. Babies were seen to play with tools discarded by their elders after having watched them being used. At first their efforts at imitation were clumsy but by 3 years of age they were using them competently. Here is the beginning of a culture in which individuals learn skills passed on from generation to generation.

class	**Mammalia**
order	**Primates**
family	**Pongidae**
genus & species	**Pan troglodytes**

△ △ *Chimpanzee first-aid: incredible instance of male removing grit from his mate's eye.*
△ *A mother suckles her baby. Chimpanzees show great affection to their young, and discipline is good without the need for bullying.*

Growing old. Youngsters (above) stay with their mother for 5 years but they are 10 or 12 before they are mature and they may live to 40.

Orang utan

The orang utan is one of our more inter-esting relatives. It occupies an inter-mediate place within the Hominoidea, the superfamily that comprises the apes and man, as it is less closely related to man than the gorilla or chimpanzee, but more man-like than the gibbon.

The big male orang stands 4½ ft high when upright, and may weigh as much as a man. Females stand only 3 ft 10 in. at the most, and weigh half as much as the male. The arms are 1½ times as long as the legs, both hands and feet are long and narrow and suited for grasping, and the thumb and great toe are very short since they would only 'get in the way' of the hook-like function of the hand. The skin is coarse and dark grey, and the hair, which is reddish, is sparse, so the skin can be seen through it in many places. The male develops large cheek-flanges of unknown function, and grows a beard or moustache, the rest of the face being virtually hairless. There is a great deal of variation in facial appearance; orangs are as individual and instantly recognisable as human beings. Both sexes have a laryngeal pouch, which in the male can be quite large, giving it a flabby appear-ance on the neck and chest. The forehead is high and rounded, and the jaws are prominent. Youngsters have a blue tinge to the face.

Orang utans are found on Borneo and Sumatra. There are slight differences between the two races, and these are more marked in the male. The Borneo race is maroon-tinted, and the male looks really grotesque, with enormous cheek-flanges and great dewlaps formed by the laryngeal sac. The Sumatran race is slimmer and lighter-coloured, and males can look quite startlingly human, with only small flanges and sac, a long narrow face, and a long gingery moustache.

Old man of the woods

The orang utan is strictly a tropical forest animal. It generally lives in low-lying, even swampy forests, but is also found at 6 000 ft on mountains in Borneo. Here, at any rate, most individuals are entirely arboreal. They swing from branch to branch by their arms, though they may use their feet as well, or walk upright along a branch, steady-ing themselves with their hands round the branch above. It is reported by the Dyaks of Borneo that big old males become too heavy to live in the trees, so they spend most of their time on the ground.

When they are on the ground, orangs move quadrupedally, with the feet bent in-wards and clenched, and the hands either clenched or flat on the ground. This con-trasts with the gorilla and chimpanzee, which live mainly on the ground and 'knuckle-walk', with their feet flat on the ground and their hands supported on their knuckles. In captivity, orangs easily learn—or discover for themselves—how to walk erect, but because the leg muscles are insufficiently developed to do this easily, the knee is kept locked and the leg straight.

Anti-social 'burping'

At night the orang utan makes a nest, be-tween 30 and 70 ft above the ground. There is often a kind of sheltering roof over this nest, to protect the orang from the rain—a structure which is not found in nests made by chimps or gorillas. The nest is otherwise much more sketchily made than that of chimps or gorillas. It takes only 5 minutes to make and the orang usually moves on and makes a nest at its next night's stopping place. Sometimes the same one is used again and the previous night's nest may be used for a daytime nap.

Unlike gorillas and chimpanzees, orang utans seem to have no large social group-ings. A female with her infant often travels with other such females for a while, forming something like a smaller version of the chimpanzee's 'nursery group'. A male may join this group, but adult males live alone most of the time. Adolescents of both sexes tend to travel around in groups of twos or threes. It is possible that male orangs, like gibbon families, may be territorial, spacing themselves vocally. The laryngeal sac is filled with air, making the animal swell up terrifyingly, and the air is then released to produce what has been described as a 'loud, two-tone booming burp'. They communi-cate within a group by making a smacking sound with their lips every few seconds. The most terrifying sound which an orang makes is a roar. This begins on a high note and the tone gets deeper and deeper as the laryn-geal sac fills with air. Roaring is heard at night and before dawn, and orangs are said

▽ *An aggressive orang utan burps defiantly.*

165

to make the same noise when wounded. The Dyaks report that male orangs fight and scars are quite common.

There is no special birth season, food being available all the year round in the Indonesian rain forest. Gestation lasts 9 months. The young orang weighs only $3\frac{1}{2}$–4 lb at birth, and is sparsely covered with hairs on the back and head. At first it clings to its mother's fur, usually slung on her hip, but when it is a little older, it wanders about on its own, sometimes walking along the branch behind its mother, clinging to her rump hairs. At about 5 years or so, orangs seem to leave their mothers and form adolescent bands.

Source of contention

Man is the principal enemy of the orang utan. Orangs love the juicy, evil-smelling durian fruit, and so do human beings, so this is often a source of contention. An orang will react to a human intruder by making a great deal of the smacking sound, and breaking off branches, keeping up a continuous shower of them which is often annoying enough to drive the humans away. A Dyak recently reported that he was attacked for no reason by a huge male orang

that he came upon unexpectedly on the ground. It has few other enemies. There are no tigers in Borneo – Dyaks claim to have exterminated them about 1 000 years ago – and in Sumatra there are only a few. Leopards are unknown on both islands.

Zoos are a danger

The orang's distribution has been steadily declining. Its ancestors' remains have been found in 14 million-year-old deposits in the Siwalik Hills, Punjab, India. In the Pleistocene, 500 000 years ago, the orang was found as far north as China, and as far south as Java. Today it occurs all over Borneo – the largest and least populated of the East Indian islands – and in the north of Sumatra. It seems that deforestation and heavy human populations have affected its distribution very adversely and there are now fears that it may become extinct altogether in the wild. One reason for its decline is its slow breeding rate. A female breeds every fourth year or so, and usually not until the previous young has left her. It is possible that the average female may bear only three or four young in her life.

The biggest threat, however, to the orang's survival is, sad to say, the zoo trade.

Every zoo wants a young ape to display to its visitors, and orangs are the easiest to obtain. Many unscrupulous private zoos, especially in the United States, have paid high prices for baby orangs, and there has been quite a lucrative trade in them in Southeast Asia. Baby orangs are obtained by shooting their mothers. The dealer does not make much effort to ensure the captive's welfare as he probably bought it from the hunter at a low fee, so many youngsters die. For every one orang that reaches a zoo alive, ten orangs have probably died. It is now illegal in Singapore to possess orangs, and smugglers are penalised, but other ports in Southeast Asia are still open for this trade. There is now a list of animals in danger of extinction which, under an international convention, cannot normally be imported into the countries, including the United States, which signed the convention. They can only be imported under special licence, usually for research purposes. This may have some effect on the situation. The deforestation problem, however, remains.

In 1963 Barbara Harrisson, working with her husband, Tom, then Government Ethnologist and Curator of Sarawak Museum, estimated that only 2 000 wild

◁ A mature orang utan.

▽ Brotherly love. △ The old man of the woods. A male orang with his large cheek flanges.

orangs remained in Sabah, 1 000 in Kalimantan (Indonesian Borneo), 700 in Sarawak and 1 000 in Sumatra. Of these, only the Sabah population seems to be anything like adequately protected. In 1964 another estimate put the Sumatra population at only 100. Tom and Barbara Harrisson undertook a programme in Sarawak of reintroducing into the wild, young orangs which had been illegally bought by people. This has met with a certain amount of success. There are about 300 in zoos all over the world and breeding has been achieved several times. Most zoos that breed them now keep the Bornean and Sumatran races separate, which will help to save the Sumatran race.

class	**Mammalia**
order	**Primates**
family	**Pongidae**
genus & species	***Pongo pygmaeus pygmaeus*** *Bornean orang utan* ***P. p. abeli*** *Sumatran orang utan*

Jack rabbit

The jack rabbits of the western United States are hares belonging to the genus **Lepus** — they are close relatives of the brown hare, the varying hare and the snowshoe rabbit. The white-tailed jack rabbit, also known as the plains or prairie hare, has a brownish coat in the summer which changes to white in the winter. Only the 6in. black-tipped ears and 4in. white tail remain unchanged all the year round. This jack rabbit, which weighs up to 10 lb, lives in the prairies of the northwest, but to the south lives the smaller black-tailed or jackass hare. The latter name is derived from the 8in. black-tipped ears. The coat is sandy except for the black upper surface of the tail. It does not turn white in winter. This species lives in the

arid country from Oregon to Mexico and eastwards to Texas. There is also a small population in Florida which has come from imported jack rabbits, used in training greyhounds, that have gone wild.

The remaining jack rabbits, the two species of antelope or white-sided jack rabbits, live in restricted areas of Arizona and New Mexico.

Safety in bounding leaps

Like all hares, jack rabbits live on the surface of the ground and do not burrow. The exception is the white-tailed jack rabbit which in winter burrows under the snow for warmth and also gains protection against predators such as owls. Otherwise jack rabbits escape detection by crouching among the sparse vegetation of the prairies and semi-desert countryside. They lie up in shade during the day and come out in the evening. Each jack rabbit has several forms, hollows in the ground shaded and con-

Hare of the plain and prairie: the jack rabbit of the western United States has two obvious adaptations for grassland life — very long ears, useful for detecting predators at a distance, and long hind legs with which it runs up to 45 mph in a series of bounding leaps.

cealed by plants, within its home range. If flushed, jack rabbits will run extremely fast, sometimes reaching 45 mph in a series of 20ft springing bounds like animated rubber balls. Every so often they leap up 4 or 5 ft to clear the surrounding vegetation and look out for enemies.

Water from cacti

Jack rabbits feed mainly on grass and plants such as sagebrush or snakeweed, and often become serious pests where their numbers build up. To protect crops and to save the grazing for domestic stock, hunts are organised or poisoned bait put down. In the arid parts of their range, when the grass has dried up, jack rabbits survive on mesquite and cacti. They can get all the water they need from cacti providing they do not lose too much moisture in keeping cool. To eat a prickly cactus a jack rabbit carefully chews around a spiny area and pulls out the loosened section. Then it puts its head into the hole and eats the moist, fleshy pulp which it finds inside.

Born in the open

The length of the breeding season varies according to the range of the jack rabbit, being shorter in the north. At the onset of breeding jack rabbits indulge in the typical mad antics of hares. The males chase to and fro and fight each other. They rear up, sometimes growling, and batter each other with their forepaws. They also bite each other, tearing out tufts of fur or even flesh and occasionally violent kicks are delivered with the hindlegs. A carefully-aimed kick can wound the recipient severely; otherwise the fight continues until one of the combatants turns tail and flees.

The baby jack rabbits are born in open nests concealed by brush or grass and lined with fur which the female pulls from her body. The litters are usually of three or four young but there may be as few as one or as many as eight. The babies weigh 2–6 oz and can stand and walk a few steps immediately after birth, but they do not leave the nest for about 4 weeks.

Precarious heat balance

Large ears are a characteristic of desert animals, such as bat-eared and fennec foxes, and it is usually supposed that as well as improving the animal's hearing they act as radiators for keeping the body cool. There is, however, a drawback to this idea. If heat can be lost from the ears it can also be absorbed. The problem has now been resolved because it has been realised that a clear sky has a low radiant temperature and acts as a heat sink. In the semi-arid home of the black-tailed jack rabbit a clear, blue sky may have a temperature of $10-15°C/50-59°F$ to which heat can be radiated from the jack rabbit's ears that have a temperature of $38°C/100°F$. Only a slight difference in temperature is needed for radiation to take place and the large difference between ears and sky allows efficient heat transfer.

Jack rabbits rely on radiation to keep them cool, for, as we have seen, they do not get enough water to be able to use evaporation as a means of cooling. In hot weather jack rabbits make use of every bit of shade and in their forms the ground temperature is lower than the air or body temperature and so acts as another heat sink.

The heat balance of a jack rabbit is, however, very precarious. On a hot day it is possible for two men easily to run down a jack rabbit. By continually flushing it and keeping it in the open the jack rabbit soon collapses from heat exhaustion and is soon ready for the pot!

class	**Mammalia**
order	**Lagomorpha**
family	**Leporidae**
genus & species	***Lepus californicus*** *black-tailed jack rabbit* ***L. townsendi*** *white-tailed jack rabbit others*

◁▽ *On the look-out. White-tailed jack rabbit crouches by sparse vegetation of the prairies.*
▽ *Black-tailed portrait. Named jackass hare, after its 8in. black-tipped ears, this jack rabbit does not change to white in winter as does the white-tailed jack rabbit.*

169

Beaver

The beaver is the second largest rodent, exceeded in size only by the capybara. Stout-bodied, with a dark brown fur, it is up to 3½ ft long including 1 ft of broad scaly tail, and it may weigh between 30 and 75 lb. Its muzzle is blunt, ears small, and it has five toes on each foot. Those on the front feet are strongly clawed, used for digging, manipulating food and carrying. The hind feet are webbed, with two split claws for grooming the fur and spreading waterproofing oil. The body oil, as well as the dense underfur and the heavy outer coat of guard hairs, not only act as waterproofing but also as insulation against the cold. When a beaver submerges, its nostrils and ears are closed by valves, and it can remain under-water for 15 minutes. The tail is used for steering and sometimes for propulsion through the water. It also forms a tripod with the hind legs when the beaver stands up to gnaw trees or when carrying, with the fore feet, mud or stones for building.

There are two species of beaver, both so alike in appearance and habits that we are fully justified in speaking merely of the beaver. The first, the European beaver, must at one time have been very abundant throughout Europe, even in England, where its bones may still be found. On the Continent of Europe it is still present in small numbers in Scandinavia, along rivers in European Russia, in the Elbe and Rhône valleys, and, where given protection, it shows signs of increasing numbers.

The Canadian beaver formerly enjoyed a wide range across the North American continent, from northern Canada south to beyond the US – Mexico border. Today, in severely depleted numbers, its range extends from Canada into some parts of the northern US.

Habits

Beavers live in loose colonies, each made up of a family unit of up to 12, including the parents, which mate for life. Their home may be in a burrow in a bank, with an underwater entrance or in a lodge in a 'beaver pond', a pool made by damming a river until it overflows. The lodge is built of sticks and mud, often against a clump of young trees, with underwater entrances, a central chamber which is above water level and a ventilating chimney connecting the chamber with the top of the lodge. Secondary dams are built upstream of the lodge, with usually one secondary dam downstream of the main dam. Young trees are felled, cut up and carried to the site, and, if necessary, canals are dug to float logs to the pond.

Intelligence of beavers

Many people are convinced that beavers are unusually intelligent, largely because their dams are such fine examples of engineering works. The structure of the

△ *Beaver in the Canadian autumn. Its tail makes a tripod with the back legs so it can sit up and gnaw tree tunks.*

▽ *A beaver lodge. It is made of sticks and mud, in a pond, which is made by the beavers damming a stream so it overflows.*

Beaver swimming. It can dive instantly if danger threatens, simply by depressing its rudder-like tail, here stretched out behind. When submerged its nostrils and ears are closed by valves and it can stay underwater for 15 minutes.

beaver brain, however, gives no indication of any greater mental capacity than is found in other rodents. Moreover, some of a beaver's actions which appear to be the result of a high order of reasoning can be shown to be due to instinct, the result of an inborn pattern of behaviour.

The lodge is a conical pile of branches and sticks 2−6 ft long, compacted with mud and stones, the upper half of which projects above the surface of the water. From an engineering standpoint it could hardly be improved. It has a central chamber just above water level, one or more escape tunnels leading from the chamber to below-water exits, well-insulated walls and a vertical chimney or ventilating shaft for regulating the temperature inside and to give air-conditioning. The evidence gained from dissecting a lodge suggests that it is built by laying sticks more or less horizontally to construct a pile, with an admixture of mud which stops short a foot or so from the top of the pile. Then the beavers chew their way in, to make the entrance tunnels and the central chamber. The absence of mud packing from the top of the pile means that spaces between the sticks serve for ventilation. In other words, there is no more intelligence required than any other rodent uses to dig in the ground.

The dams are text-book examples of engineering, and beaver dams give way no more frequently than do man-made dams.

One reason for this is that a beaver dam is resilient, subject to immediate repair, is under constant surveillance and is supported by subsidiary dams. All the actions used in its construction can, however, be shown to be the result of a succession of instinctive actions, just as are those that result in the building of a bird's nest.

It is often said that beavers not only show skill in felling trees but use intelligence, by dropping the trees so that they fall towards the nearest water. This is not the case. Moreover, beavers are not uncommonly killed by the trees they fell falling on them.

Beavers often do other stupid things. The classic example is of a small lake in New York that was created by an artificial barrier of stones and cement litter. This was occupied by a family of beavers who were seen to 'repair' the dam with branches and mud although it was fully effective without these. Moreover, although the level of the pond was, so far as could be seen, satisfactory for their needs, the beavers built a subsidiary dam upstream of the pond, the only result of which was to flood the adjacent land to no purpose.

Everything considered, the achievements of beavers are more a tribute to the effectiveness of evolution in developing inherited behaviour patterns than a sign of unusual intelligence. There is, however, one qualification to be made. Young beavers stay with the parents for 2 years. During that time

they must learn a great deal by following the example of the adults. It may be justifiable, therefore, to speak in terms of a cultural inheritance, and this alone would give an appearance of a greater intelligence.

Further evidence for the theory of innate behaviour can be added. Until a few years ago, beavers in the Rhone valley were hunted and they had long taken to burrowing in the river banks. Then they were protected by law, and shortly afterwards they began once more to build lodges and dams. A beaver may live for 20 years, but here they were reverting to a former pattern of behaviour after centuries of suppression due to persecution, using techniques they could not have learned. Only great intelligence, or a very strong instinct, could have brought about this behaviour.

Aspen and willow as food

Beavers eat bark, mainly of aspen and willow, from the smaller branches cut when building. Twigs and branches are stored around the base of the lodge. These have always been regarded as for the winter use of all members of the colony. Recent research has shown that the bulk of these are eaten by youngsters; older beavers live on their fat and eat little during winter.

Life history

Beavers, which are monogamous, mate in January to February. Gestation is 65−128 days and in April, May or early June two to eight kits, sometimes more, are born, with a coat of soft fur and eyes open. At birth each weighs about 1 lb and is 15 in. long including 3½ in. of tail. At one month, each will find and eat solid food, but weaning is not complete until 6 weeks old. Young remain with parents for 2 years, becoming sexually mature at 2–3 years.

Enemies

As with all rodents, beavers are preyed upon by any carnivores of approximately their own weight or more. In this instance the enemies include wolverine, lynx, coyote, wolf, bobcat, puma and bear. A beaver's alarm signal when a predator is in sight is to bring the tail over the back then smack it down with such force on the water that the sound can be heard up to ½ mile away.

Decline of the European beaver

Beavers were once common in Switzerland, as shown by the place names Biberach, Bibersee, Biberstein and Bibermukle (biber is German for beaver). Their extermination was due partly to their valuable fur, but more particularly to slaughter for their glandular secretion used to mark their territories. This, known as castoreum, enjoyed a vogue as a cure-all in the 16th and 17th centuries, with a resulting insensate slaughter of the luckless animals. Analysis has shown castoreum to contain salicylic acid, one of the ingredients of aspirin.

The former presence of beavers in the British Isles, too, is commemorated in many place-names, such as Beverley, Beverege, Bevercotes, Beverstone and Beversbrook in England, and Losleathan in Scotland and Llostlydan in Wales, both meaning broadtail. The animal seems to have still been plentiful in Britain up to the mid-16th century. The value of its fur can be gauged from prices fixed by the Welsh prince, Howel Dha, in the 10th century, at 120 pence a skin as compared with 24 pence for a marten pelt and 18 pence for otter, wolf and fox. This undoubtedly led to the animal's extermination, and in France to its almost complete elimination except in the Rhône Valley. In the 16th century, Henry IV of France, impressed by the demand for beaver pelts for hats, trimmings, fur linings and leather for shoes, sought to increase the economic strength of his country by sending men to Nova Scotia and New-

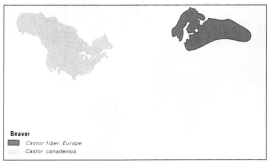

The beaver was on the way to extinction in Europe and America in the 19th century, but has since been rigorously protected and the populations are increasing. They have been so successful in some places that control is necessary.

Beaver

▪ *Castor fiber, Europe*
  Castor canadensis

foundland. In due course the British gained this resource, largely through the Hudson Bay Company, and it was the search for more and more furs, particularly beaver, that led to Canada being opened up.

Profit versus protection

In America, with the arrival of the early settlers, the beaver was recognised as a valuable source of both meat and fur. Trade was soon established with the Indians, who wisely killed only mature animals, so that their hunting could have done little to impair the number of beavers. The brisk fur trade with England that sprang up roused the old spirit of avarice, and before long white trappers joined their efforts with those of the Indians—and killed indiscriminately.

In about 150 years the beaver had been exterminated in the coastal regions of the Eastern States, and seriously reduced elsewhere. The story is, however, patchy, for in some spots their numbers remained relatively unimpaired. Also, beavers in deep rivers were less easy to catch than those in, say, mountain streams. As the North American continent was more and more opened up, so the trade continued unabated, with similar results to those seen in the Eastern States, but on a wider scale.

The Hudson Bay Trading Company was formed in 1670 and such was the growth of its beaver trade that between 1853 and 1877 it marketed nearly 3 million beaver pelts. This steady drain brought about a serious depletion which has been rectified to some extent by official conservation measures.

Beavers were not always killed for profit. At times the animal became a nuisance,

either through its inroads on timber, in settled areas, or when it took a liking to the stalks of corn. In places, too, it became a menace to river banks. Nevertheless, it was early recognised that only harm could result from its total elimination. As early as 1866, it became protected by law in the State of Maine, with the result that by the early years of the present century it had increased so much in numbers that some control had to be imposed to protect plantations.

Since that time, both in the USA and in Canada, with increasing speed to the present day, there have been many efforts made at conservation, either by individual landowners, by public bodies, or by Government action, State or Federal. In some cases the reason behind it has been no more than a desire to preserve an interesting animal. In others it is due to a realisation that the work of beavers contributes to the conservation of water in the land and to the preservation of trout streams. It has been found that it is possible, by the intelligent use of closed seasons, limiting the numbers of pelts taken and having them taken only under licence, not only to bring about increased beaver populations locally, but to derive revenue from the surplus. Consequently, there has been considerable reintroductions to re-stock areas where they had been exterminated.

The conservation of water may be summed up in the following quotation from an American water company's report: 'On almost all the mountain streams they (the beaver) should be protected and encouraged. A series of beaver ponds and dams along the headwaters of a mountain stream would hold back large quantities of mountain water during the dangerous flood season and equalise the flow of the streams so that during the driest seasons the water supply would be greatly increased in the valleys. Beaver-ponds not only hold water but distribute it through the surrounding soil for long distances, acting as enormous sponges as well as reservoirs. A series of ponds also increases the fishing capacity and furnishes a safe retreat for the smaller trout and protection from their enemies.'

Fear and flight having failed to rescue this beaver, caught away from the relative safety of its pool, it must now turn and fight for its life against the hungry hunting coyote.

class	**Mammalia**	
order	**Rodentia**	
family	**Castoridae**	
genus	***Castor fiber***	*European beaver*
& species	**C. *canadensis***	*Canadian beaver*

Meal among the toadstools: a deer mouse strikes a Disneylike pose while taking a snack.

Deer mouse

Deer mice are American, very similar to the European long-tailed fieldmouse, both in appearance and in habits, but the two belong to different families. There are about 20 species, varying in colour from sandy or grey to dark brown. Some are almost white and others nearly black, but in general those living in woods are darkish, and those living in open or arid country are pale. The underparts and feet are white, hence the alternative name of white-footed mouse. A deer mouse measures 5–15 in. from nose to tip of tail, the tail varying from 1½–8 in. in different species.

They are found over most of North America, from Alaska and Labrador southwards, and one species extends into South America, reaching the extreme north of Colombia. They inhabit many kinds of country from swamps and forests to arid, almost desert, country, but each species usually has only a limited habitat and consequently is found only in a relatively small part of the total deer mouse range.

173

Overlapping territories

Deer mice are nocturnal, coming out during the day only if they are very hungry, or if there is a cover of snow that allows them to forage under its shelter. During the evening they can be heard trilling or buzzing, a noise quite unlike the squeaks of other mice, and in some parts of the United States this has led to their being called vesper mice. They also drum with the front feet when excited.

Each deer mouse has a home range which it covers regularly in search of food. The extent of the range varies considerably and depends on the amount of food available. In the grasslands of south Michigan the average size of the ranges of male deer mice is ⅔ of an acre, while those of the females are slightly smaller. The home range of a mammal is not strictly comparable with the territory of a bird. Only a few birds keep a territory all through the year, but more important, a mammal does not defend its range so vigorously. The borders of neighbouring ranges overlap, sometimes considerably, and the ranges of two females may be almost identical, but it is only the inner parts of the territory around the nest that will be defended vigorously.

Within its range, a deer mouse may have several refuges in abandoned burrows or birds' nests, under logs or in crevices. Sometimes a deer mouse will come indoors and make its nest in an attic or storage room. Each nest is used for a short time, being abandoned when it becomes soiled, for deer mice limit hygiene to cleaning their fur.

Burrows with a bolt hole

The nest is an untidy mass of grass and leaves, lined with moss, fine grass or feathers. Sometimes the deer mice make their own burrows. The Oldfield mouse, a species of deer mouse living in Alabama and Florida, makes a burrow leading down to a nest which is 1 ft underground. Then from the other side another burrow leads up again but stops just short of the surface. This presumably serves as a bolt hole in case a snake or other narrow-bodied enemy finds its way in. A traditional way of catching these mice is to push a pliable switch or wand down the hole, twiddle it about until it can be pushed up the escape burrow, and catch the mouse as it breaks out.

Are they a pest?

Seeds and berries are the main food of deer mice but they also eat many insects such as beetles, moths and grasshoppers, which are chased and bitten or beaten to death. Insect larvae, snails and slugs are devoured, and deer mice also eat carrion such as dead birds and mammals, and they will gnaw cast antlers.

Deer mice are something of a problem in plantations or on farms, where they eat seeds of new-sown crops which they smell out and dig up. But even when abundant, they are not as much of a pest as meadow voles and other small rodents. To even the score, deer mice are helpful because they eat chafer grubs that damage the roots of young trees.

Hanging on to mother

In spring the males search for mates, per-haps finding females whose ranges overlap theirs. At first their advances are repulsed but the males eventually move into the females' nests, staying there for a few days only but sometimes, it is thought, forming permanent pairs.

The female gives birth to a litter of 1–9 young after 3 or 4 weeks. At birth the young mice are blind, deaf, and apart from their whiskers, naked. They hang firmly to their mother's teats and she can walk around with them trailing behind. If the nest is disturbed she will drag them in this manner to a new site. Any baby that does fall off is picked up and carried in its mother's mouth.

Litters of deer mice can be found from spring to autumn but more are born in spring and autumn than during the summer, and if the winter is mild, breeding will continue through it. Females begin breeding at 7 weeks, only a few weeks after leaving their mothers, and have up to 4 litters a year.

Many nocturnal enemies

Most deer mice live less than two years, and many never reach maturity but provide food for the many predators that hunt at night. Foxes, weasels, coyotes, bobcats, owls and snakes, all feed on deer mice, and even shrews will occasionally eat them.

Racial 'segregation'

Although similar, the 20 different deer mice can easily be told apart by the specialist in classification, and, one must presume, by the mice themselves. Otherwise they would mix and interbreed and their differences would disappear, especially when different kinds live in the same habitat. Experiments by an American scientist using a Rocky Mountain deer mouse and a Florida deer mouse, which are closely related, showed how the deer mice are segregated.

Special cages were made, each with two side compartments. In preparation for the experiment a Rocky Mountain mouse was put in one compartment and a Florida mouse in the other, and this was repeated for all the cages. After these had remained long enough to impart their smell to the compartments they were taken out. Now, into each cage were put either a Rocky Mountain mouse or a Florida mouse, and these naturally made full use of the available space, including wandering into each compartment. By timing the period each mouse spent in each of the two side compartments of its cage the scientist found that in all cases the test mouse was very obviously drawn to that compartment which carried the smell of its own species. This almost certainly is how mice of the same species, even when sharing a habitat with another species, would be drawn together to breed, for it was noticed that males reacted particularly strongly to the smell of females of their own species on heat. So although it may sometimes appear that there are mixed populations of deer mice, the different species are really living separately.

There was, however, one difference between the Rocky Mountain mice and the Florida mice: the latter were much more likely to spend time in compartments smelling of Rocky Mountain mice. The reason for this seems to be that in Florida there is only one species of deer mouse, and discrimination is no longer necessary; but in the west there are many species and if their strains are to be kept pure, they must be able to distinguish between their own fellows and those of closely related species.

class	**Mammalia**
order	**Rodentia**
family	**Cricetidae**
genus	***Peromyscus maniculatus***
& species	*others*

Deer mouse cleaning and drying its fur—its only hygienic habit.

Porcupine

The tree porcupines of North and South America are very different from the porcupines of the Old World. To begin with, they live mainly in trees and their hindfeet are adapted for climbing. Some species also have a prehensile tail. The best known, the Canadian or North American porcupine, is up to $3\frac{1}{2}$ ft long, of which 1 ft is tail, and has an average weight of 15 lb although large males may weigh up to 40 lb. It is heavy and clumsily built with a small head, short legs and a short, stout, spiny tail. The hindfoot has a well-developed great toe and very long, powerful claws to help the animal climb. The long fur on the upper parts is brownish-black, sprinkled with long white hairs that conceal the short, barbed spines, which are yellowish-white tipped with black.

The South American tree porcupines, of which the Brazilian tree porcupine is typical, differ from the North American species in having a long, prehensile tail, the tip of which is hairless and by having only four toes on the hindfeet with a broad fleshy pad, opposable to the toes, used rather like a thumb in gripping branches when the animal is climbing. It is of lighter build with short, closely set spines, sometimes concealed by long hairs.

The Canadian porcupine inhabits most of the timbered areas of Alaska, Canada and the United States (except the southeastern quarter), south to the extreme north of Mexico. South American porcupines extend from Mexico through Central America to Colombia, Venezuela, Brazil, Bolivia, Peru and Ecuador in South America.

△ Long fur conceals the porcupine's spines.
▽ North American porcupine revealing its arsenal of over 20 000 sharp-tipped quills.

Tree porcupine

///// Canadian or North American
     (*Erethizon dorsatum*)

▓ Brazilian (*Coendou prehensilis*)

◁ *Picking a precarious path, a South American porcupine* **Coendou** *sp. seeks its typically rodent diet of bark, stems and leaves.*

No hibernation

All the tree porcupines live in wooded areas, the North American species preferring woods of conifers, junipers and poplars. Although clumsily built they can climb well and they will also swim. They lie up during the day among rocks or in hollow trees and feed mainly at dusk and at dawn. They are usually solitary but occasionally several Canadian tree porcupines may shelter together in the same den, especially in winter. They do not hibernate but they take to dens during bad weather.

Salt addicts

The Canadian tree porcupine varies its food with the seasons. In spring it eats the flowers and catkins of the willow, maple and poplar. Later it turns to the new leaves of aspen and larch. In summer it feeds more on herbaceous plants and in winter on evergreens like the hemlock and pine. Its principal food in winter, however, is bark and the porcupines do much damage by ring-barking trees. The young red firs of the Sierra Nevada in California are occasionally destroyed by tree porcupines. When the weather is bad and the snow deep an animal may live in one tree and not leave it until all the bark above the snow-line has been stripped. Tree porcupines also have a strong liking for sweet corn and a few of these animals can completely ravage a field of it.

A more peculiar taste is the porcupine's craving for salt. Handles of farm implements which have been touched by hands moistened with sweat, leaving a trace of salt, will be gnawed. So will gloves, boots, and saddles; even the steering wheel of a car has been gnawed away. The porcupine will also gnaw bones and antlers dropped by deer. But its crowning achievement is to gnaw glass bottles thrown away by campers, presumably for the salt in the glass.

The South American tree porcupines also eat the bark and leaves of trees and tender stems but in addition they eat fruit such as bananas, and occasionally corn.

Well-developed babies

The Canadian tree porcupines mate in the fall or early winter. During courtship the male rubs noses with the female and often urinates over her. Generally a single young is born after a gestation period of 210 – 217 days. The young are very well-developed at birth; their eyes are open and they are born with long black hair and short soft quills. They weigh about 20 oz and can climb trees when 2 days old. They are weaned in 10 days, and become sexually mature in their second year.

Little is known of the breeding habits of the South American tree porcupines. There is usually a single young at a birth, born from February to May. The young of the Brazilian tree porcupine are comparatively large at birth and are covered with long, reddish hair. Their backs are covered with short spines, which are flexible at birth.

Few natural enemies

Few animals prey on the porcupine because of its spines, but the wolverine, puma and fisher marten will attack the North American species. A tree porcupine is said never to attack an enemy. If cornered, however, it will erect its quills and turn its back on its adversary, striking out repeatedly with its tail. A porcupine does not shoot its quills but they are so lightly attached that when they enter the skin of the enemy they become detached from the porcupine.

Skulls identify species

The crested porcupine is the best known species in the Old World family Hystricidae. Not all the porcupines in that family have such prominent quills as the crested porcupine. One *Trichys lipura* living in Borneo, for example, lacks true quills. It has only short, flat, weak spines and its long tail has a brush of bristles on the end. At first sight it appears not to be a porcupine at all. The same thing can be said of some of the family Erethizontidae. Since the crested and the Canadian porcupines look so alike, the question arises: What is the essential difference between the Old World porcupines and the New World porcupines? The fact that they are widely separated geographically is not important. Both families agree in having species that show a varying tendency to grow quills among the bristly coat, and both families contain a diversity of species. Therefore, those who classify these rodents have to look for something more stable upon which to separate them. They find this in the skull. Any Old World porcupine, whatever it may have in the way of quills, has a very rounded skull which has quite obviously a different shape from that of the New World porcupines.

class	**Mammalia**
order	**Rodentia**
family	**Erethizontidae**
genera & species	***Erethizon dorsatum*** *Canadian or North American porcupine* ***Coendou prehensilis*** *Brazilian tree porcupine, others*

Black bear

There are five species of black bear, each placed in a separate genus. All are smaller than the brown bears, and all are sufficiently similar for one of them, the one most studied, to serve as a type for the other four. This is the American black bear which originally inhabited practically all the wooded areas of North America from Central Mexico northwards. Its numbers are much reduced now and it has been eliminated from much of its former range, but in national parks its numbers are increasing and elsewhere it survives close to human settlement. Up to 5 ft long with a 4½ in. tail, and weighing 200 – 500 lb, it has shorter fur, shorter claws and shorter hind feet than the brown bears. The species also shows a number of colour phases: black, chocolate brown, cinnamon brown, blue-black and white with buff on the head and in the middle of the back. This last is most common in British Columbia, where it has been known as Kermode's bear. These different colour phases may occur in the same litter.

Friendly habits

Black bears are good tree climbers, powerful, quick to react, harmless to people except when provoked, cornered or injured – or through sheer friendliness. In national parks, where they are familiar with human beings and come begging food, visitors to the parks must keep to the protection of cars to avoid inadvertent injury from the bears' claws. Black bears are solitary except during the breeding season, the two partners separating after mating, to wander far in search of food. The American black bear sleeps through the winter – not hibernation in the usual sense – after laying in fat by heavy autumn feeding. It does not feed during the winter although it may leave its den, a hollow tree or similar shelter, for brief excursions during mild spells. When startled, the adult gives a 'woof', otherwise it is silent. The cubs, when distressed, utter shrill howls.

Mixed diet

Insects, berries and fruits, eggs and young of ground-nesting birds, rodents and carrion form its main foods, but young of deer and pronghorn are killed and eaten. Porcupines are killed, the bear flipping them over with its paw and attacking the soft under-belly, often to its own detriment from the quills. Black bears have been found dead with quills embedded in the mouth. Sometimes a black bear may turn cattle-killer.

Enemies

Old or sickly adults are occasionally killed by pumas and wintering bears may be attacked by wolves.

Life history

The breeding month is June and the gestation period is 100 to 210 days. Usually there are two or three cubs in a litter, exceptionally four, rarely five, born in January and

△ *Twin cubs being escorted by their mother. They stay with her until at least 6 months old.*

February. At birth the 8 in., 9 – 12 oz cubs are blind, toothless and naked except for scanty dark hair. The mother continues to sleep for two months after the birth, having roused herself sufficiently to bite through the umbilical cords. The cubs alternately suck and sleep during these two months. They stay with the mother for at least six months, and she mates only every other year.

The original Teddy Bear

In 1902, Theodore (Teddy) Roosevelt, who was a keen naturalist as well as President of the United States, captured a black bear cub on a hunting trip, which he adopted as a pet. Morris Michton, a Brooklyn doll manufacturer, used this bear as model for the first Teddy Bear, so named with the President's permission. The popularity of the Teddy Bear as a toy was immediate and world-wide. The black bear, as already stated, is such a favourite in American national parks that they take liberties with visitors. In European zoos a prime favourite with visitors is the Himalayan black bear. Such general favouritism owes much to the human-like qualities of the bears.

We tend to favour in animals, qualities which reflect our own, as with bears that talk or animals that stand erect such as penguins, owls and bears. In man the bipedal stance is habitual; in bears it is but occasional, the usual way of walking being on all-fours. That does not invalidate the comparison, and the effect of the bears' ability to stand erect at times is reinforced by the way they will sit upright, as if on a chair, and also by the characteristic way a bear will wave a fore-paw (or hand) when soliciting food. Another trait which enables us to see ourselves in bears is their way of lying prone, on their backs.

Bears also appear to be intelligent. Whether they are more intelligent than their near relatives, the cats and dogs, has never been adequately tested. At least we know that the cubs stay with the mother for six

months, often longer, and some may stay with her until her next cubs are born. A long period of parental care allows for learning by example and a longer period for experience with security. And if bears are by nature solitary they can, if circumstances compel them, as in bear-pits in zoos, live together with little discord, showing they are, like us, fundamentally friendly.

Yet in spite of the comparisons that can be drawn between bears and ourselves, and in spite of our fondness for Teddy Bears, the fact remains that the American black bear, like all other bears, has long been a target for the hunter's gun – and not only the hunter's. In 1953, 700 black bears were killed in British Columbia to provide bearskins, the ceremonial headwear, for the Brigade of Guards, for the coronation of Queen Elizabeth II. An American writer drily remarked: 'Fortunately for the black bear Great Britain's coronations are infrequent . . .'

class	**Mammalia**
order	**Carnivora**
family	**Ursidae**
genus & species	***Euarctos americanus*** *American black bear*

American black bear (*Euarctos americanus*)

Returning to their earth after a hunt: North American red fox and two cubs. Night hunting is a way of teaching the cubs how to fend for themselves.

Red fox

It is usually assumed that, but for its careful preservation by the various 'hunts', the red fox would have become extinct long ago in the British Isles except in the wildest and most remote corners. For centuries it has been persecuted outside the hunt areas because of its alleged poultry-killing habits and even today the killing of a fox is still looked on with approval. Yet, in spite of all this, the fox has survived and at times is unusually numerous.

The head and body of the red fox measure just over 2 ft with a 16in. tail, but there are records which greatly exceed these measurements, especially in Scotland. A well grown fox stands only about 14 in. at the shoulder. The dog-fox and vixen are alike except that the vixen is slightly smaller and has a narrower face as she lacks the cheek ruffs of the male. The fur is sandy russet or red-brown above and white on the underparts. The backs of the ears are black, as are the fronts of the legs, but these may be brown, and can change from one colour to the other with the moult. The colours may vary, however, not only between one individual and another, but in the same individual from season to season. The foxes (Tods) of Scotland, although of the same species, usually have greyer fur than the English fox. When fully haired the tail is known as a brush. The tip (or tag) is white but may be black. Weights vary considerably but on average a dog-fox weighs 15 lb, a vixen 12 lb.

The sharp-pointed muzzle, the erect ears and quick movements of the eye with its elliptical pupil combine to give the fox an alert, cunning appearance, so many stories

of its astuteness have been invented in the past. At the moult, in July and August, foxes lose their characteristic appearance and look thin-bodied, long-legged and slender of tail.

The red fox ranges over Europe and over Asia as far south as central India, as well as northwest Africa. It is found throughout the British Isles, except for Orkney, Shetland and all Scottish islands, but not Skye. In central Asia it lives up to 14 000 ft above sea-level. The North American red fox **Vulpes fulva** is very like the Old World red fox in build and habits. There are several mutants, the cross fox is red with a black band across the shoulders, and the silver fox has a lustrous black coat with white tips to the guard hairs.

Tree-climbing foxes

The red fox's traditional cunning is a reflection of its adaptability. It prefers wooded or bushy areas but is found in a variety of habitats. Many foxes today are even found living in urban areas or even near large towns, where they probably live off rats and mice and scavenge in dustbins. Although the fox lives mainly on the ground there are many instances of it climbing trees. Usually this occurs when a tree is leaning or when there is a trailing bough that has brokeinand is hanging down to the ground, up which the fox can clamber. There is one recorded instance, however, of a fox having its sleeping nest at the top of a bole of an elm, 14 ft from the ground, with no branches between it and the ground. Foxes are largely nocturnal, but they can often be seen during the day. Except at the breeding season the dog-fox and vixen lead solitary lives. Most of the day is spent in an 'earth' which is more of a cavity in the ground than a burrow. They may make this themselves or use a badger's set or rabbit burrow.

Foxes use a great variety of calls, the most familiar being the barking of both the dog-fox and the vixen in winter and the screaming of the vixen, generally during the breeding season. It has now been established that, contrary to common opinion, the dog-fox may also scream sometimes.

Poultry killer?

A great deal has been written about the fox prowling round farms looking for an opportunity to kill an unguarded fowl. Certainly foxes will take poultry and they will take lambs, but these habits tend to be local. A vixen that has taken to killing poultry will teach her cubs to do the same. But not all foxes are habitual poultry stealers and there have been instances of foxes repeatedly visiting poultry farms or private gardens containing a few poultry and never molesting them.

More solid information about their food comes from a Ministry of Agriculture investigation of the stomach contents of dead foxes. This showed that, now that rabbits are scarce, the chief items of food are rats, mice and bank voles. Hedgehogs, squirrels, voles, frogs, even snails and beetles are, however, also eaten, as well as a great deal of vegetable matter. Birds such as partridges and pheasants will also be taken. A fox will soon discover offal or carrion, even if buried 2 ft in the earth. Foxes also visit dustbins and a feature of the many foxes now living in towns is that they have turned scavenger. Railway marshalling yards also have their foxes, probably feeding on food thrown out from restaurant cars or on rats living on this food.

Teaching the cubs

Mating takes place from late December to February. The gestation period is 51–52 days. About April the vixen produces her single litter for the year, usually of four cubs. They are blind until 10 days old, and

remain in the earth until nearly a month old, the vixen staying close beside them, while the dog plays a large part in supplying the food. When about a month old the cubs come out in the evening and can be seen playing as a group with the parents outside the earth. This continues for several weeks.

After the cubs are weaned it has been noted, in semi-captivity, that the dog-fox continues to bring food for them and the cubs will take the food from his mouth themselves, or the vixen may take it and the cubs take it from her mouth. The cubs have to jump up to reach the parent's mouth and all the time the parent is moving its head, from side to side or up and down. In this way the cubs are being exercised so developing their limbs, and also learning to co-ordinate movements and senses. During this time the dog plays a great deal with them, more so than the vixen.

Later the vixen takes them hunting at night, so they learn from her example how to fend for themselves. The cubs leave their parents when about 2 months old, reach adult size 6 months after birth, and become sexually mature in their first winter.

'Charming'

Foxes are credited with resorting to a particular stratagem, called 'charming', to attain their end. A story is usually told of a fox which, seeing a party of rabbits feeding and knowing that they will bolt to their holes on its approach, starts rolling about at a safe distance to attract their attention. Then like a kitten it begins chasing its tail, while the rabbits gaze, apparently spell-bound, at the performance. The fox continues without a pause, as though oblivious to the presence of spectators, but all the time it is contriving to get nearer, until a sudden straightening of the body enables it to grab the nearest rabbit in its jaws.

There are too many authentic accounts of foxes charming to leave much doubt about the matter. From these, a more likely explanation evolves: foxes are naturally playful. Like some other mammals they will, without obvious cause, suddenly behave as if they have taken leave of their senses, bounding about, bucking, somersaulting, and so on. Rabbits and birds on seeing these antics are drawn to watch out of curiosity. If the fox is hungry then the spectators suffer. It is possible that a fox playing in this way and finding birds and rabbits attracted to it, might use this tactic again, deliberately. Such learning by experience would not be beyond a fox's intelligence, but there is much to be said for the view that charming, as such, is not primarily a deliberate stratagem.

class	**Mammalia**
order	**Carnivora**
family	**Canidae**
genus & species	*Vulpes vulpes* *European red fox*

▷ *With ears pricked, wary eyes glinting from its mask, the red fox with its magnificent brush is a very wily, sometimes vicious, and yet most handsome animal.*

Giant Panda

*This black and white bear-like carnivore has leapt from obscurity to worldwide fame in less than a century. Also called the panda and, by the Chinese, **beishung**, the white bear, it was first made known to the western world in 1869, by the French missionary, Père David.*

The giant panda is stockily built, with a 6 ft long body and a mere stump of a tail and weighs 300 lb. Its thick, dense fur is white except for the black legs and ears, black round the eyes and on the shoulders. There are 5 clawed toes on each foot and each forefoot has a small pad which acts as a thumb for grasping. The cheek teeth are broad and the skull is deep with prominent ridges for the attachment of strong muscles needed in chewing fibrous shoots. It lives in the cold damp bamboo forests on the hillsides of eastern Tibet and Szechwan in southwest China.

Habits unknown . . .

Giant pandas are solitary animals except in the breeding season. They live mainly on the ground but will climb trees when pursued by dogs. They are active all the year. Little more is known of the habits in the wild of this secretive animal which lives in inaccessible country. When live giant pandas were first taken to zoos it was thought they lived solely on bamboo shoots. Later it was learned that during the 10—12 hours a day they spend feeding they eat other plants, such as grasses, gentians, irises and crocuses, and also some animal food. This last includes small rodents, small birds and fishes flipped out of water with their paws.

Breeding unknown . . .

Little is known about the giant panda's breeding habits in spite of attempts to induce a mating between An-an, the male giant panda belonging to the Moscow zoo, and Chi-chi, the female in the London zoo. In 1966 Chi-chi was taken to Moscow but no mating took place, and An-an was brought to London in 1968 with no more success. It is believed that giant pandas mate in spring, and that probably one or two cubs are born in the following January, each cub weighing 3 lb at birth. Several cubs have been born in Chinese zoos. On September 9, 1963, a male cub Ming-ming was born to Li-li and Pi-pi in Peking zoo, and a female cub, Ling-ling, was born on September 4, 1964, to the same parents. A third cub Hua-hua, a male, was born to Chiao-chiao on October 10, 1965.

Bad treatment

In 1869 Père Armand David of the Lazarist Missionary Society, and an experienced naturalist, came upon the skin of an animal

Chinese mother love. Although breeding has not been achieved in the western world, despite the efforts of the Moscow zoo and London zoo to breed An-An and Chi-Chi, there are more than a dozen giant pandas in Chinese zoos, and they have been bred successfully.

in a Chinese farmhouse in Szechwan which he did not recognise. He sent it to Paris and later sent more skins. Not until 1937, however, was the first live giant panda seen outside China. Theodore and Kermit Roosevelt had shot one in the 1920's and in 1936 two other Americans, Ruth and William Harkness, with the animal collector Tangier Smith, captured several. They quarrelled, presumably over the spoils, and all the giant pandas died except one, which Ruth Harkness delivered to the Chicago zoo where it was named Su-lin. Another, given the name Mei-mei, reached the same zoo in 1938. In December the same year a young female, Ming, aged 7 months and two young males, Tang and Sung, reached the London zoo. The two males died before the female reached maturity, and she died in December 1944. In May 1946, the government of the Szechwan Province presented a male, Lien-ho, to the London zoo and he lived until 1950. By 1967 there were a score of giant pandas in various zoos, 16 or more in Chinese zoos, An-an in Moscow and Chi-chi in London.

Although the species is now protected it was formerly hunted by the local Chinese, and the history of western animal collectors does nothing to offset this. The story of Chi-chi gives point to this. In 1957, Heini Demmer, then living in Nairobi, was commissioned by an American zoo to negotiate the exchange of a collection of East African animals for a giant panda. He reached Peking zoo with his cargo, was given the choice of one of three giant pandas, chose Chi-chi, the youngest, and took charge of her on May 5 1958. Chi-chi had been captured by a Chinese team of collectors on July 5 1957, and was reckoned then to be 6 months old. She had been taken to Peking zoo and cared for night and day by a Chinese girl. By the time Demmer had taken charge of Chi-chi the United States had broken off diplomatic relations with the Chinese People's Republic, so she became automatically a banned import.

Bamboo shoots are not the sole food of giant pandas

Demmer took her on a tour of European zoos during the summer of 1958, reaching the London zoo on September 26.

After such treatment perhaps it is not surprising she refused to be mated! She died on July 21 1972.

London Zoo now has two 3 year-old pandas, Ching-Ching and Chia-Chia, which were presented to Mr Heath during his visit to Peking. Mr Nixon was similarly honoured on his visit there in 1973. In 1974 Tokyo had two pandas, and Korea and Paris owned one each.

class	**Mammalia**
order	**Carnivora**
family	**Procyonidae**
genus & species	***Ailuropoda melanoleuca***

Otter

The various species of otter are all much alike in appearance and habits. They are long-bodied, short-legged mammals, with a stout tail thickened at the root and tapering towards the tip. There is a pair of scent-glands under the tail. The head is flattened with a broad muzzle and numerous bristling whiskers. The ears are small and almost hidden in the fur. The sleek, dark brown fur consists of a close fawn underfur which is waterproof and an outer layer of long stiff guard hairs, which are grey at their bases and brown at their tips. The throat is whitish and the under-parts pale brown. Each foot has five toes, bearing claws in most species, the forefeet are small, the hindfeet large and webbed.

The common or European otter ranges across Europe and parts of Asia, to Japan and the Kurile Islands. It is 4 ft long, including the tail, but may reach 5½ ft, and weighs up to 25 lb. The bitch is smaller than the dog otter. The Canadian otter, of Canada and the United States, is very similar to the European but has an average larger size. It is sometimes spoken of as the river otter, to distinguish it from the sea otter, a markedly different animal. The small-clawed otter, of India and southeast Asia, is much smaller than the European species but the clawless otter of western and southern Africa is larger and is a marsh dweller, feeding on frogs and molluscs. The giant Brazilian otter is the largest of all the otters. It reaches 6½ ft in length, and has a tail that is flattened from side to side.

Solitary and elusive

Except during the mating season otters are solitary, extremely elusive and secretive, and always alert for any sign of disturbance. They will submerge in a flash, leaving few ripples or, when on land, they will disappear among vegetation. Their ability to merge into their background on land is helped by the 'boneless' contortions of the body and the changing shades of colour in the coat which is aided by the movements and changes in the guard hairs. For example, the coat can readily pass from looking sleek and smooth to looking, when damp, spiny and almost porcupine-like.

Otters do not hibernate. They will fish under ice with periodic visits to a breathing hole. It has been said that otters will use a trick known in aquatic insects; that is, to come up under ice and breathe out, allowing the 'bubble' to take in oxygen from the air trapped in the ice and lose carbon dioxide to the ice and water, then inhale the re-vitalised 'bubble'. This has not yet been proved, however.

▽ Prenuptial affectionate play. Usually solitary, otters are sociable in the mating season.

Master-swimmers

At the surface an otter swims characteristically showing three humps each separated by 5–8 in. of water. The humps are the head, the humped back and the end of the tail curved above the water line. When drifting with the current only the head may be in view. Occasionally an otter may swim with the forelegs held against the flanks, the hindlegs moving so rapidly as to be a blur. When this is done at the surface there is a small area of foam around the hindquarters, with a wake rising in a series of hump-like waves. It will also use this method when submerged, although more commonly it swims with all four legs drawn into the body which, with the tail, is wriggled sinuously, as in an eel. Leaping from the water and plunging in again, in the manner of a dolphin, is another way in which an otter can gain speed in pursuit of a large fish. Underwater it will often progress in a similar, but smoother undulating manner.

An otter shows its skill better in its ability to manoeuvre. It will roll at the surface, or when submerged, pivoting on its long axis, using flicks of the tail to give momentum. It can turn at speed in half its own length, using tail and hindquarters as a rudder, or it may swim round and round in tight circles, creating a vortex that brings mud up from the bottom. This last tactic is used to drag small fishes up that have taken refuge under an overhanging bank.

When an otter surfaces it stretches its neck and turns its flattened, almost reptilian head from side-to-side reconnoitring before swimming at the surface or coming out on land.

Otters are nomads, fishing a river or lake then moving on to take their next meal elsewhere. They are said at times to cover up to 16 miles overland in a night. Certainly the European and Canadian otters are met at times far from the nearest water. Overland they move by humping the back. A favourite trick is to take a couple of bounds then slide on the belly for 4–5 ft. On a steep slope the glide may take them 40–50 ft. On a muddy or snow-covered slope the slide becomes tobogganing, otters often retracing their steps to slide repeatedly down the slope in a form of play.

Otters live in rivers and lakes, especially small rivers running to the sea or to large lakes. They particularly like those free of weed and undisturbed by human beings. In times of scarcity otters will move to the coast and are then spoken of as 'sea-otters', not to be confused with the real sea otters.

Eels and crayfish favoured

The European otter has a varied diet of fish, small invertebrates, particularly crayfish and freshwater mussels, birds, small mammals, frogs and some vegetable matter. The main fish food seems to be eels and slow-moving fishes but salmon and trout are also eaten.

Otter families play sea-serpents

Mating takes place in water, at any time of the year, with a peak in spring and early summer. After a gestation of about 61 days 2 or 3 cubs, exceptionally 4 or 5, are born, blind and toothless, with a silky coat of dark hair. There is uncertainty about when the

△ *A backflip from a European otter. This photo caught an otter leaping playfully into the water for the pure joy of living.*

△ *The African clawless otter has only a small connecting web at the base of the toes.*

eyes open, the only reliable record being 35 days after birth. The cubs stay in the nest for the first 8 weeks and do not leave their mother until just before she mates again.

Young otters swim naturally, as is shown by cubs hand-reared in isolation. The indications are, however, that the mother must coax them, or push them, into the water for their first swim. In the early days of taking to water a cub will sometimes climb onto the mother's back, but normally the cubs swim behind their mother. On rare occasions two or more family parties will swim one behind the other. When this does happen a line of humps is seen, and as the leading otter periodically raises her head to take a look around the procession resembles the traditional picture of the sea-serpent.

Otters as lake monsters

It has been said that any schoolboy knows an otter when he sees one. This is so only as long as the otter runs true to form, but otters are quick-change artists and highly deceptive. Sir Herbert Maxwell has recorded how, at the turn of the century, four gentlemen crossing Loch Arkaig in a steam pinnace saw a 'monster' rise from the depths almost under the bows of their boat, create a tremendous flurry of water at the surface, then dive again out of sight. All were puzzled as to its identity, but when the stalker, a Highlander, present with them in the boat, was questioned later, he was in

no doubt that the 'monster' was an otter.

The monster of Loch Morar, near Loch Arkaig, is traditionally 'like an overturned boat towing three overturned dinghies', which could serve as a reasonable description of a bitch otter followed by her three cubs. The ogo-pogo of Canada is believed to be founded on otters swimming in line, and at least one lake monster in Kenya was proved to be a line of otters.

When President Theodore Roosevelt was big game hunting in 1911 he was out in a boat on Lake Naivasha, in Kenya, when the three humps of the local monster appeared. Roosevelt fired once, two humps disappeared, the third stayed on the surface. The skin of the otter was sent to the American Museum of Natural History in New York.

class	**Mammalia**
order	**Carnivora**
family	**Mustelidae**
genera & species	***Amblonyx cinerea*** *Indian small-clawed otter*
	Aonyx capensis *clawless otter*
	Lutra canadensis *Canadian otter*
	L. lutra *European otter*
	Pteronura brasiliensis *giant Brazilian otter*
	others

Tiger

One of the largest of the 'big cats', the tiger's sinuous grace, splendid carriage and distinctive colouring make it one of the most magnificent of all animals. A large male averages 9 ft—9 ft 3 in. in length including a 3ft tail. It stands 3 ft or more at the shoulder and weighs 400—500 lb. Females are a foot or so less in length and weigh about 100 lb less. The various races of tigers vary considerably in size from the small Bali Island tiger to the outsized tiger found in Manchuria which may reach 12 ft in total length. The ground colour of the coat is fawn to rufous red, becoming progressively darker southwards through the animal's range, the Balinese tiger being the darkest. The underparts are white. There have been rare cases of white tigers in India. The coat is overlaid with black to blackish-brown transverse stripes, and these contrasting colours provide an excellent camouflage in forest regions.

In cold climates such as Siberia and Manchuria, tigers have thick, shaggy coats which become shorter and denser in the warmer climates. The hair round the face is longer than on the rest of the body, forming a distinct ruff in adult males.

From its original home in Siberia, the tiger spread across almost the whole of Eurasia during the Ice Ages. Today it is found only in Asia where a number of geographical races are recognised, including those of Siberia, Manchuria, Iran, India, China, Sumatra, Java and Bali. The races differ only in size, colour and markings.

▷ Solitary splendour: tiger caught by flash.
▷▷ Transport solution: a helpless tiger cub is carried in the same way as a domestic kitten.

Solitary prowler

Although its original home was in the snowy wastes of Siberia the tiger's natural preference is for thick cover. It has, however, become adapted to life in rocky mountainous regions, the reed beds of the Caspian, and the dense steaming jungles of Malaya and islands such as Java and Bali. It cannot, however, tolerate excessive heat and during the heat of the day it will lie up in long grass, caves, ruined buildings, or even in swamps or shallow water.

The tiger is an excellent swimmer and in times of flood has been known to swim from one island to another in search of food. Unlike most members of the cat family it is not a good climber and seldom takes to the trees, but there is a record of a tiger taking a single leap of 18 ft from the ground to pull a man off a tree. Its hearing is very good and is the sense most used in stalking prey. It does not appear able to see unmoving animals, even at a short distance.

The tiger has a variety of calls ranging from a loud 'whoof' of surprise or resentment to a full-throated roar when disturbed or about to launch an attack.

Strength widens choice of prey

A tiger preys on deer, antelope, wild pig and smaller animals such as monkeys and porcupines. It will take fish and turtles in times of flood and locusts in a swarm. It occasionally attacks larger animals such as wild bull buffaloes, springing on their backs and breaking their necks. When food is short it may steal cattle, and an old or injured tiger too weak to hunt may attack humans. Game is, however, its natural food and it is interesting that tigers have completely deserted some forested areas of India where game animals have disappeared even though there were still plenty of wandering cattle about.

A tiger stalks using stealth for the first part of its hunt, finally attacking with a rush at its victim, grasping a shoulder with one paw and then seizing the throat. It then presses upwards, often breaking the neck in the process. After a kill it withdraws to a secluded spot, preferably under cover, taking its prey with it. If it cannot do this, or hide its kill near its lying-up place, it is forced to have a hurried meal and leave the rest of the carcase to the hyaenas and vultures and other carrion eaters.

Small striped cubs

Only while the tigress is in season do male and female tigers come together; according to some authorities, this could be for less than two weeks. During this time a tiger will not allow another male near him and will fight, sometimes to the death, over possession of the female. In India the mating season is variable, but in Malaya it is from November to March and in Manchuria it is during December. A female starts to breed at about 3 years of age and then has a litter every third year, or sometimes sooner. After a gestation of 105 – 113 days, 3 – 4 cubs are born, occasionally as many as 6. The mortality among cubs is high and usually no more than two survive to adulthood. They are born blind and helpless, weighing only 2 – 3 lb, but they have their parents' distinctive striped pattern from the beginning. The cubs grow rapidly; their eyes open after 14 days and they are weaned at 6 weeks. At 7 months they can kill for themselves, but stay with their mother until 2 years old, during which time she trains them in hunting. They are fully grown at 3 years.

Man the hunter

Although the tiger has few natural enemies it has been hunted by man from very early times, at first by the local people and later for sport. In India especially, the coming of the British and the introduction of firearms was disastrous to the tiger and it is estimated that in 1877 alone 1 579 tigers were shot in British India. Today the reduction of game animals and the reduction of its natural habitat is further diminishing its numbers, and as a result six of the eight races of tiger are listed as being in danger of extinction.

△ *Reflected glory: unlike many of the cat family, tigers often take to the water and are strong swimmers. In times of flood they have been known to feed on fish and turtles and to swim in search of stranded prey. They cannot bear excessive heat and will sometimes sit in shallow water in an attempt to keep cool.*

Not normally dangerous

Tigers have a respect and fear for man which is difficult to explain. Even if harassed by curious humans or sportsmen a tiger will not normally react until its patience is well-nigh exhausted. Normally a man can walk in a tiger's habitat without fear or hindrance and there have been several instances of a tiger approaching a man while sitting quietly near his camp and passing by, doing no harm even though it was obvious that it had seen him. Men have been followed for many miles by tigers and have come to no harm; they were probably being escorted off the territory. It is only when its normal hunting routine is disturbed that it becomes really dangerous. It may then become a man-eater, especially when shot at indiscriminately, incapacitating it rather than killing it. A wounded tiger left to its fate, without the strength to hunt, will resort to man-eating or cattle killing, out of necessity, as it will when injured by natural mishap. One of the commonest causes of injury is damage by porcupine quills. If the quills enter the paws or lower limbs the tiger cannot pull down and kill natural prey or cattle. Occasionally the quills may even penetrate the tiger's jaw and the animal starves to death. Old age may also cause a tiger to attack cattle or humans. Once a tiger has turned man-eater or cattle-killer, for whatever reason, every man's hand is against it. Whole villages will turn out and not rest until it is killed, even in areas where the tiger is protected by law.

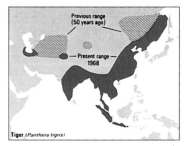

Tiger *(Panthera tigris)*

class	**Mammalia**
order	**Carnivora**
family	**Felidae**
genus & species	***Panthera tigris*** *tiger*

Lion

Lions were once common throughout southern Europe and southern Asia eastwards to northern and central India and over the whole of Africa. The last lion died in Europe between 80–100 AD. By 1884 the only lions left in India were in the Gir forest where only a dozen were left, and they were probably extinct elsewhere in southern Asia, for example, in Iran and Iraq, soon after that date. Since the beginning of this century the Gir lions have been protected and a few years ago they were estimated to number 300. A census taken in 1968, however, puts the figure at about 170. Lions have been wiped out in northern Africa, and in southern Africa, outside the Kruger Park.

The total length of a lion may be up to 9 ft of which 3 ft is tail, the height at the shoulder is 3½ ft and the weight up to 550 lb. The lioness is smaller. The coat is tawny; the mane of the male is tawny to black, dense or thin, and maneless lions occur in some districts. The mane grows on the head, neck and shoulders and may extend to the belly.

▷Shady business: lioness evades the heat.
▷▷An aspiring lion claims a higher position.
▽Pride of the bush: lionesses with their cubs.

Prides and the hunting urge

Lions live in open country with scrub, spreading trees or reedbeds. The only sociable member of the cat family, they live in groups known as prides of up to 20, exceptionally 30, made up of one or more mature lions and a number of lionesses with juveniles or cubs. Members of a pride will co-operate in hunting, to stalk or ambush prey, and they combine for defence. The roar is usually not used when hunting although lions have been heard to roar and to give a grunting roar to keep in touch when stalking. A lion is capable of speeds of up to 40 mph but only in short bursts. It can make standing jumps of up to 12 ft high and leaps of 40 ft. Lions will not normally climb trees but lionesses may jump onto low branches to sun themselves and they as well as lions will sometimes climb trees to reach a kill cached in a fork by a leopard. There is one record of a lioness chasing a leopard, apparently with the intent to kill it, into a tree, but she was foiled by the leopard going into the slender top branches which failed to bear the lioness's weight.

Not wholly carnivorous

Although strongly carnivorous lions take fallen fruit at times. Normally, in addition to the protein, fat, carbohydrate and mineral salts, lions get their vitamins from the entrails of the herbivores they kill. Typically, lions first eat the entrails and hindquarters working forward to the head. In captivity, lions flourish best and breed successfully when vitamins are added to a raw meat diet. Although lionesses often make the kill the lions eat first (hence, 'the lion's share') the lionesses coming next and the cubs last. In general, antelopes and zebra form the bulk of lions' kills but almost anything animal will be taken, from cane rats to elephant, hippopotamus, giraffe, buffalo and even ostrich.

A survey in the Kruger Park showed that in order of numbers killed the prey-species were: wildebeest, impala, zebra, waterbuck, kudu, giraffe, buffalo. A later survey showed a preference descending through waterbuck, wildebeest, kudu, giraffe, sable, tsessebe, zebra, buffalo, reedbuck, impala. When age or injury prevents a lion catching agile prey it may turn to porcupines and smaller rodents, to sheep

▽ *Violence afoot: hampered by the water around them, a pair of paddling lions make the opening moves of a soggy trial of strength.*

and goats, or turn man-killer, taking children and women more particularly. Man-eating can become a habit, however; once a small group of lions at Tsavo held up the building of the Uganda railway through their attacks on the labourers. Dogs may be killed but not eaten.

Exaggerated story of strength

A favourite story is of a lion entering a compound, killing a cow and jumping with it over the stockade. R Hewitt Ivy argues in *African Wild Life* for June 1960 that this is impossible. His explanation is that lions visiting a cattle compound do not all go inside. Possibly one leaps the fence, makes a kill and drags it under the fence to those waiting outside. Should the cattle panic and one leap the fence it will be pulled down by the rest of the pride outside and there eaten.

The lion hunts in silence and it is the lioness that most often kills the prey. The usual method of killing is to leap at the prey and break the neck with the front paws. Alternatively a lion may seize it by the throat with its teeth or throttle it with the forepaws, on the throat or nostrils. Another method is to leap at the hindquarters and pull the prey down. A lion will kill a hippopotamus by scoring its flesh with the claws in a running battle. Lions will kill and eat a crocodile and will also eat carrion, especially if it is fresh, and lion will eat dead lion. An old story tells of the lion's habit of lashing itself into a fury with a spur on the end of its tail, in order to drive itself to attack. Some lions do have what appears to be a claw at the tip of the tail. But this is only the last one or two vertebrae in the tail out of place, due to injury.

Natural control of populations

Lions begin to breed at 2 years but reach their prime at 5 years. The males are polygamous. There is a good deal of roaring before and during mating, and fights with intruding males may take place. Gestation is 105–112 days, the number of cubs in a litter is 2–5, born blind and with a spotted coat. The eyes open at 6 days, weaning is at 3 months after which the lioness teaches the cubs to hunt, which they can do for themselves at a year old. There is a high death rate among cubs because they feed last, so suffering from a diet deficiency, especially of vitamins. This serves as a natural check

▽ *On firmer ground. The skirmish begins as one lion lumbers up onto his rear legs and lunges at his equally cumbersome opponent.*

191

on numbers. Should numbers fall unduly in a district—as when lions are hunted by man or culled in national parks—prey is more easily killed and there is more food to spare. Lionesses will then kill for their cubs and then the cubs eat first. This richer diet makes for a high survival rate among the cubs, so restoring the balance in the population number.

Dangers for the King of Beasts

There are no natural enemies as such, apart from man, but lions are prone to casualties, especially the young and inexperienced. A zebra stallion may lash out and kick a lion in the teeth, after which the lion may have to hunt small game. The sable antelope is more than a match for a single lion and other antelopes have sometimes impaled lions on their horns. A herd of buffalo may trample a lion or toss it from one set of horns to another until it is dead, although two lions will overcome one large buffalo. One female giraffe attacked a lioness trying to kill her calf. Using hoofs of fore and hindlegs, as well as beating the lioness with her neck, she severely mauled her—and chased the lioness away over a distance of 100 yards. This is a better performance than a rhinoceros can manage. A lion will kill rhino up to three-quarters grown.

class	**Mammalia**
order	**Carnivora**
family	**Felidae**
genus & species	***Panthera leo*** *lion*

△▷ Plan of campaign: lion's strategy observed in Kruger Park. Detecting wildbeest, 16 lions deliberated and split into three parties.
▷ Drink up! One lioness remains on watch.
▽▷ Lioness casually accepts a mother's duty.
▽ An affectionate nudge from mother.

Walrus

Although hunted since the time of the Vikings, almost to the point of extinction, the walrus has survived and today, with strict conservation measures, some herds are very slowly recovering their numbers. The two subspecies, the Pacific walrus and the Atlantic walrus, differ in only minor details. The Pacific bulls average 11 – 11½ ft long and weigh a little over 2 000 lb but they can reach 13¾ ft and weigh up to 3 700 lb when carrying maximum blubber. The Atlantic bulls average 10 ft long and up to 1 650 lb in weight but may reach 12 ft and weigh 2 800 lb. The cows of both subspecies are smaller, 8½ – 9½ ft and 1 250 lb, but large Pacific cows may reach almost 12½ ft and a weight of 1 750 lb.

The walrus is heavily built, adult bulls carrying sometimes 900 lb of blubber in winter. The head and muzzle are broad and the neck short, the muzzle being deeper in the Pacific walrus. The cheek teeth are few and of simple structure but the upper canines are elongated to form large ivory tusks, which may reach 3 ft in length and are even longer in the Pacific subspecies. The nostrils in the Pacific subspecies are placed higher on the head. The moustachial bristles are very conspicuous, especially at the corners of the mouth where they may reach a length of 4 or 5 in. The foreflippers are strong and oar-like, being about a quarter the length of the body. The hindflippers are about 6 in. shorter, very broad, but with little real power in them.

The walrus's skin is tough, wrinkled and covered with short hair, reddish-brown or pink in bulls and brown in the cows. The hair becomes scanty after middle age and old males may be almost hairless, with their hide thrown into deep folds.

The Pacific walrus lives mainly in the waters adjacent to Alaska and the Chukchi Sea in the USSR. The Alaskan herds migrate south in the autumn into the Bering Sea and Bristol Bay to escape the encroaching Arctic ice, moving north-wards again in spring when it breaks up.

The Atlantic walrus is sparsely dis-tributed from northern Arctic Canada eastward to western Greenland, with small isolated groups on the east Greenland coast, Spitzbergen, Franz Josef Land and the Barents and Kara Seas. They migrate southward for the winter.

Walruses also inhabit the Laptev Sea near Russia and do not migrate in the winter. It is thought that this herd may be a race midway between the Atlantic and Pacific subspecies.

◁ *A long-in-the-tooth bull walrus of the Pacific subspecies. The elongated upper canine teeth are put to a variety of uses among them defence and digging for clams.*

ruses but not often, the polar bear particularly being wary of attacking an adult bull even when he is ashore and therefore more vulnerable. Panic when killer whales are near may, however, cause high mortality. In 1936 a large herd was attacked by killer whales and driven ashore on St Lawrence Island. They hauled out onto the beach in such panic that they piled up on each other and 200 of them are said to have been smothered or crushed to death.

Slaughter by man

Walruses have been hunted by man from early times. The Eskimo and Chukchee have always depended on the annual kill to supply all their major needs, including meat, blubber, oil, clothing, boat coverings and sled harnesses. Even today they are largely dependent on it. The annual killings by the local people, however, had no very marked effect on the numbers of the herds. It was the coming of commercially-minded Europeans to the Arctic that started the real extermination. From the 15th century onwards they used the walrus's habit of hauling out on the beaches in massed herds to massacre large numbers in the space of a few hours. After 1861, when whales had become scarce, whalers from New England started harpooning walruses. Then they started using rifles and the Eskimos followed suit. More walruses could be killed but large numbers of carcases fell into the water and could not be recovered. An even greater wastage has been that caused by ivory hunters, who kill for the tusks and discard the rest of the carcase.

By the 1930's the world population of walruses had been reduced to less than 100 000 and strict conservation measures have now been enforced. The Pacific walrus now seems safe from extinction but the Atlantic walrus is still in danger.

Tooth-walking bulls

Walruses associate in family herds of cows, calves and young bulls of up to 100 individuals. Except in the breeding season the adult bulls usually form separate herds. They live mainly in shallow coastal waters, sheltering on isolated rocky coasts and islands or congregating on ice floes. Since their persecution by man, however, walruses have learnt to avoid land as much as possible and to keep to the ice floes, sometimes far out to sea. They are normally timid but are readily aroused to belligerence in the face of danger. There seems to be intense devotion to the young, and the killing of a young one will rouse the mother to a fighting fury, quickly joined by the rest.

Walruses can move overland as fast as a man can run and because of their formidable tusks hunters, having roused a herd, have often been hard put to it to keep them at bay. Walruses have even been known to spear the sides of a boat with their tusks or to hook them over the gunwales.

As well as using them as weapons of offence and defence the walrus makes good use of its large tusks for digging food out of the mud and for keeping breathing holes open in the ice. It also uses them as grapnels for hauling itself out onto the ice, heaving up to bring the foreflippers onto the ice. The horny casing of bare hard skin on the palms of the flippers prevents the walrus from slipping. The walrus also uses its tusks for hauling itself along on the ice—indeed the family name Odobenidae means 'those that walk with their teeth'.

Walruses sunbathe and sleep packed close together on the ice floes with their tusks resting on each other's bodies. If the water is not too rough, adult walruses can also sleep vertically in the water by inflating the airsacs under their throats.

Monstrous swine

The walrus was associated in the Middle Ages with a variety of sea monsters. Named the whale-elephant in the 13th century it also became the model for the original seahorse and sea-cow. In addition it was described as 'a monstrous swine . . . which

by means of its teeth climbs to the top of cliffs as up a ladder and then rolls from the summit down into the sea again.'

Clam grubbers

The walrus's diet consists principally of clams, which it grubs out of the mud with its tusks, and sea snails. It will also take mussels and cockles. The snout bristles help in detecting the shellfish. Clams are swallowed whole and no shells have ever been found in the stomach of a walrus, although it is not known how they are disposed of. A walrus also swallows a quantity of pebbles and stones, possibly for helping to crush the food in its stomach. Walruses usually dive for their food in shallow water of about 180 ft or less but occasionally they go down to 300 ft. Probably they deal with pressure problems at such depths by reducing the rate of blood flow as seals do.

Occasionally a walrus, usually an adult bull, will turn carnivorous and feed on whale carcases or it may kill small ringed or bearded seals. Having sampled flesh it may continue to eat it in preference to shellfish.

Hitch-hiking pup

Most matings take place from late April to early June and after a gestation of just over a year one pup is born, every alternate year. Birth takes place on an ice floe. The new-born pup is 4 ft long with a coat of short silver grey hair and weighs 100 – 150 lb. It is able to swim immediately, although not very expertly, and follows its mother in the water. After a week or two it can swim and dive well. Even so, it usually rides on its mother's back for some time after birth, gripping with its flippers. After a month or two the silver grey hair is replaced by a sparser dark brown coat of stiff hairs. The cow nurses the pup for 18 months to two years but they remain together for several months after weaning. The pups grow quickly, males becoming sexually mature at about 5 – 6 years, the females at about 4 – 5 years.

Killed in the rush

Killer whales and polar bears attack wal-

class	**Mammalia**
order	**Pinnipedia**
family	**Odobenidae**
genus	***Odobenus rosmarus divergens*** *Pacific walrus* ***O. r. rosmarus*** *Atlantic walrus*

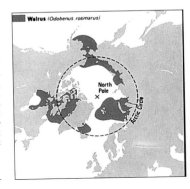

Aardvark

African mammal with a bulky body, 6 ft long including a 2 ft tail, and standing 2 ft high at the shoulder. Its tough grey skin is so sparsely covered with hair that it often appears naked except for areas on the legs and hind quarters. The head is long and narrow, the ears donkey-like; the snout bears a round pig-like muzzle and a small mouth. The tail tapers from a broad root. The feet have very strong claws — four on the front feet and five on the hind feet. The name is the Afrikaans for 'earth-pig'.

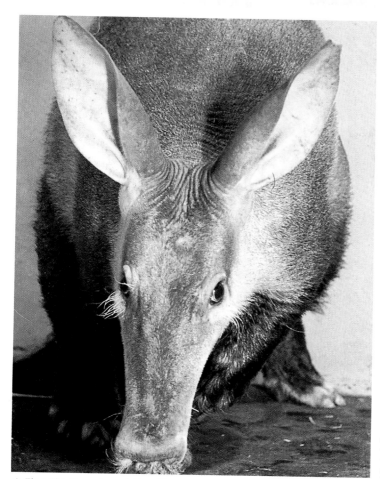

△ *The aardvark's nose is guarded by a fringe of bristles and it can also close its nostrils, as a protection against termites.*

Distribution and habits

The aardvark has powerful limbs and sharp claws so it can burrow into earth at high speed. This it does if disturbed away from its accustomed burrow. There are records of it digging faster than a team of men with spades. When digging, an aardvark rests on its hind legs and tail and pushes the soil back under its body with its powerful fore feet, dispersing it with the hind legs.

The normal burrow, usually occupied by a lone aardvark, is 3–4 yd long, with a sleeping chamber at the end, big enough to allow the animal to turn round. Each animal has several burrows, some of them miles apart. Abandoned ones may be taken over by warthogs and other creatures.

Years can be spent in Africa without seeing an aardvark, although it is found throughout Africa south of the Sahara, except in dense forest. Little is known of its habits as it is nocturnal and secretive, though it may go long distances for food, unlike other burrowing animals.

Termite feeder

The aardvark's principal food is termites. With its powerful claws it can rip through the wall of termite nests that are difficult for a man to break down even with a pick.

Its method is to tear a small hole in the wall with its claws; at this disturbance the termites swarm, and the aardvark then inserts its slender 18 in. tongue into the hole and picks the insects out. It is protected from their attacks by very tough skin and the ability to close its nostrils—further guarded by a palisade of stiff bristles.

As well as tearing open nests, the aardvark will seek out termites in rotten wood or while they are on the march. It also eats other soft-bodied insects and some fruit.

Breeding cycle

The single young (twins happen occasionally) is born in midsummer in its mother's burrow, emerging after two weeks to accompany her on feeding trips. For the next few months it moves with her from burrow to burrow, and at six months is able to dig its own.

◁ *Aardvark at home in African scrub close to a termites' nest where it has been feeding on these soft-bodied insects.*

Digs to escape enemies

The aardvark's main enemies are man, hunting dogs, pythons, lions, cheetahs and leopards, and also the honey badger or ratel, while warthogs will eat the young. When suspicious it sits up kangaroo-like on its hind quarters, supported by its tail, the better to detect danger. If the danger is imminent it runs to its burrow or digs a new one; if cornered, it fights back by striking with the tail or feet, even rolling on its back to strike with all four feet together.

On one occasion, when an aardvark had been killed by a lion, the ground was torn up in all directions, suggesting that the termite-eater had given the carnivore a tough struggle for its meal. However, flight and—above all—superb digging ability are the aardvark's first lines of defence for, as with other animals with acute senses like moles and shrews, even a moderate blow on the head is fatal.

The last of its line

One of the most remarkable things about the aardvark is the difficulty zoologists have had in finding it a place in the scientific classification of animals. At first it was placed in the order Edentata (the toothless ones) along with the armadillos and sloths, simply because of its lack of front teeth (incisors and canines). Now it is placed by itself in the order Tubulidentata (the tube-toothed) so called because of the fine tubes radiating through each tooth. These teeth are in themselves very remarkable, for they have no roots or enamel.

So the aardvark is out on an evolutionary limb, a species all on its own with no close living relatives. Or perhaps we should say rather that it is on an evolutionary dead stump, the last of its line.

What is more, although fossil aardvarks have been found—but very few of them—in North America, Asia, Europe and Africa, they give us no real clue to the aardvark's ancestry or its connections with other animals.

class	**Mammalia**
order	**Tubulidentata** *sole representative*
family	**Orycteropidae**
genus	
& species	***Orycteropus afer***

◁ *The claws of the aardvark are so powerful that it can easily rip through the wall of a termite nest which is so hard it is difficult for a man to break down even with a pick-axe.*

The termites are so disturbed by having their nest opened that they swarm about and the aardvark then puts its pig-like muzzle into the nest to eat them.

It has an 18 in. long, slender, sticky tongue with which it captures and eats the swarming termites that make up the main food of aardvarks.

▷ *A day-old aardvark. It depends on its mother for six months until it can dig its own burrow. The aardvark's snout and round, pig-like muzzle earn it the Afrikaans name for 'earth-pig'.*

Disturbed away from its burrow, the aardvark can escape its enemies by digging at incredible speed. It forces the soil back with its fore feet and kicks it away with its strong hind legs, 'so fast that it can outstrip a team of six men with spades'.

Elephant

The elephant is the largest living land animal and there are two species, the African and the Indian. During fairly recent geological times elephants of many species making up six families ranged over the world except for Australia and Antarctica. The African elephant, the larger of the two surviving species, is up to 11½ ft high and weighs up to 6 tons.

Elephants have a massive body, large head, short neck and stout pillar-like legs. The feet are short and broad with an elastic pad on the sole and hoof-like nails, five on each foot except for the hind foot of the African elephant, which has three. The bones of the skeleton are large, and instead of marrow cavities they are filled with spongy bone. The outstanding feature of elephants is that the snout is remarkably long, forming a flexible trunk with the nostrils at the tip. The trunk is used for carrying food and water to the mouth, for spraying water over the body in bathing or spraying dust in dust-bathing, and for lifting objects, as well as being used for smelling. The single incisor teeth on either side of the upper jaw are elongated and form tusks.

The main differences between the two living species are the larger ears and tusks of the African, its sloping forehead and hollow back, and two 'lips' at the end of the trunk compared with one lip in the Indian elephant.

The African elephant is found in most parts of Africa south of the Sahara, in savannah, bush, forest, river valley or semi-desert. It lives in herds of bulls and cows, each herd being led by an elderly cow, while the older bulls live solitary and join the herd only to mate. The Indian elephant is also native to Sri Lanka, Burma, Thailand, Malaya and Sumatra, living in dense forests. More correctly it should be called Asiatic, not Indian, but the use of 'Indian elephant' is now too deeply rooted for change. The social structure of its herds is much the same as in the African species.

Keeping its skin in condition

Elephants are sometimes grouped with rhinoceroses and hippopotamuses under the loose heading of pachyderms (thick-skins). In all the skin is thick and only sparsely haired, and all need to keep the skin in condition by wallowing. An elephant will bathe in water, almost completely submerging itself and will also spray water over itself with its trunk. It indulges in dust baths, too, and if water is scarce it will wallow in mud. The African elephant at least is adept at finding water in times of drought, boring holes in the ground using one of its tusks as a large awl. The requirements of the two species differ because the Indian elephant keeps mainly to dense shade. This also influences other aspects of their behaviour. The African elephant, for example, must seek what shade it can from the midday sun and cool its body by waving its large ears. The enormous surface these present allows for loss of body heat, which is helped by waving the ears back and forth. The Indian elephant, with much

△ Family group – the youngsters stay with the adults until their teens.

◁ Feeding time. At birth the baby is 3 ft high and weighs some 200 lb. It uses its mouth when suckling from the mother's nipples, situated between the cow's forelegs.

▷ Largest land animals alive today – African elephants feeding and drinking on the river bank. Their vegetarian diet includes grass, foliage and branches of trees and fruit. The mobile trunk is used to gather and carry food to the mouth.

smaller ears, keeps itself to dense shade.

Asleep on their feet

A vexed question of long standing is how elephants sleep. Both species can sleep standing, or lying on one side. To lie down an elephant uses similar movements to a horse, but it does what no horse will do: it will sometimes use a pillow of vegetation pulled together on which to rest its head. When standing asleep an elephant breathes at the normal rate. Lying down it breathes at half this rate. When 17 elephants were kept under observation it was found that they usually slept for 5 hours each night, in two equal periods. Of this 20 minutes were slept standing, the rest lying down.

Dangers of over-population

The diet is entirely vegetarian and includes grass, foliage and branches of trees and fruit. The trunk is used to gather these and convey them to the mouth. African elephants, living where bushes and trees are scattered, will use the forehead to push over small trees to get at the top foliage. When an area becomes over-populated the loss of trees can be serious. In national parks in Africa the populations of elephants, under protection, tend to increase so much that their ranks have to be thinned out by selective shooting, usually spoken of as culling, to prevent destruction of the habitat. Otherwise all the elephants in the area would be in danger from starvation.

Under free conditions elephant herds trek from one area to another, often seasonally in search of particular fruits. Long distances may then be covered, and this relieves the strain on the vegetation, which can regenerate in their absence.

The molars of elephants have broad crushing surfaces for chewing fibrous vegetation. The wear on them is considerable. Every elephant in its lifetime, assuming it dies of old age (70 years in the Indian, 50 years in the African elephant) has 7 teeth in each half of both upper and lower jaws, exclusive of the tusks. The first are 4 milk teeth which are soon shed. After that a succession of 6 teeth moves down each half of both jaws on a conveyor-belt principle. The first is in use alone but as its surface is getting worn down the next tooth behind it is moving forward, to push out the worn stump and take its place. When the last teeth have come forward and been worn down the elephant must die from starvation, if nothing else.

Purring from the stomach

For a long time big-game hunters and naturalists were perplexed by one feature of elephant behaviour: their tummy-rumblings. Nobody was surprised that these abdominal noises should be so loud and persistent, in view of the enormous quantities of food the huge pachyderms must eat. What puzzled people was that the elephants could apparently control the noises, stopping suddenly when someone approached. Within the last few years it has been discovered that these noises have nothing to do with digestion. When elephants are out of sight of each other they keep up this sort of purring. When danger approaches one of them, it becomes silent. The sudden silence alerts the rest of the herd, which also grows silent. Only when danger has passed is the purring resumed, by which the elephants tell each other that all is well.

Trumpet Voluntary

Apart from these sounds elephants will 'trumpet'. The sound is as startling and as loud, if less pure in tone, as that from the brass wind instrument. In paintings of elephants made in the Middle Ages, or even later, the trunk was always given a trumpet-shaped end, the artists being influenced by travellers' stories of the elephants' trumpeting.

Elephant 'midwives'

Mating is preceded by affectionate play, especially with the bull and the cow entwining trunks or caressing each other's head or shoulders with the trunk. The gestation period is 515–760 days, mostly about 22 months. The single baby—twins are rare—is about 3 ft high and weighs about 200 lb. On several occasions hunters or naturalists have seen a cow elephant retire into a thicket accompanied by another cow. Some time later the two come out again accompanied by a baby. Nobody knows whether the second cow acts as midwife or merely

◁ *Woe betide those who ignore this warning notice.*
▷ *Dressed up for a reception at Bahawalpur, West Pakistan, an Indian elephant looks very decorative. It is distinguished from its larger African relative by its smaller ears, arched back, domed forehead and smoother trunk which has only one 'finger' or lobe at its end compared with the African's two (below). In general, the Indian elephant appears to be an animal of jungle or bush country, although it is found in grassland areas.*
▽ *Enjoying a dustbath, an elephant uses its hose-like trunk to snort dirt over its body.*

stands guard while the calf is being born. The baby is able to walk soon after birth and can keep up with the herd in two days.

Hefty train-stoppers

Such large and powerful animals have few enemies. In India a tiger may kill a baby and in Africa the large predators, such as the lion, may do the same. The power of an elephant in defence can be gauged by the several stories told of a bull elephant meeting a train on a railway and charging the engine head on. In all reports it is stated how the engine driver drew the train to a halt and the elephant charged the engine repeatedly, doing itself great injury yet persisting in the attack. Another feature of elephant defence is the close co-operation between members of a herd. Hunters have reported seeing a shot elephant being helped away by two others ranged either side of it, keeping it upright on its feet. On

one occasion the herd combined to drag the carcase of one of their fellows throughout the night, in an abortive attempt at rescue. In 1951, in the Johannesburg *Star*, Major JF Cumming was reported as having seen some elephants dig a grave to bury a dead comrade!

Do they fear mice?

In contrast with the elephant's comparative freedom from large enemies is the longstanding belief that elephants are afraid of mice. Lupton, in his *A Thousand Notable Things*, published in 1595, wrote: 'Elephants of all other beasts do chiefly hate the mouse.' The idea still persists, helped no doubt by such stories as that of the elephant in a zoo found dead from a haemorrhage and with a mouse jammed in its trunk.

In 1938 Francis G Benedict and Robert C Lee, American zoologists, tested zoo elephants with rats and mice in their hay, and

by putting rats and mice in the elephants' house. The pachyderms showed no concern even when the rodents ran over their feet or climbed on their trunks. White mice were also put in the elephants' enclosure, again without result. There was, however, one moment when a rat ran over a piece of paper lying on the ground. The unfamiliar noise of rustling paper set the nearest elephant trumpeting and before long all the others were joining in the chorus.

class	**Mammalia**
order	**Proboscidea**
family	**Elephantidae**
genera & species	***Elephas indicus*** Indian elephant ***Loxodonta africana*** African elephant

△ *Bulls contest for the cow who appears to be rather uninterested in the combat.*
▽ *African elephants were thought to be untameable but the Belgians succeeded at the turn of the century by training immature ones for work using kindness and patience rather than brutality.*

Zebra

Zebras are distinguished from horses and asses by the stripes on their bodies. Their mane is neat and upright. The tail is tufted as in asses, but the hard wart-like knobs known as 'chestnuts', are found on the forelegs only, and not on the hindlegs as in horses. There are differences from both the horse and the ass in the skull and teeth. Three species of zebra live in Africa today. The commonest and best-known is Burchell's zebra, which extends from Zululand in the southeast, and from Etosha Pan in southwest Africa, north as far as southern Somalia and southern Sudan. In this species the stripes reach under the belly, and on the flanks they

broaden and bend backwards towards the rump, forming a Y-shaped 'saddle' pattern. Although the races in the southern and northern parts of the range look quite different, the differences are only clinal. That is, there are gradual changes from south to north, but they all belong to one species. In the southernmost race, the 'true' Burchell's zebra, now extinct but once living in the Orange Free State and neighbouring areas, the ground colour was yellowish rather than white; the legs were white and unstriped; the stripes often did not reach under the belly; and between the broad main stripes of the hindquarters and neck were lighter, smudge-grey alternating stripes commonly known as 'shadow-stripes'.

Further north a race known as Chapman's zebra is still found. It has a lighter ground colour than the true Burchell's, the stripes reach further down the legs—usually to below the knees—and the shadow-stripes are still present. All zebras still living from Zululand north to the Zambezi are referred to as members of this race; but at Etosha Pan there are some zebras that have almost no leg stripes and closely resemble 'true' Burchell's.

North of the Zambezi is the East African race, known as Grant's zebra. Its ground colour is white, the stripes continue all the way down to the hoofs and there are rarely any shadow-stripes. Grant's zebra is smaller than the southern races, about 50 in. high, weighs 500—600 lb, and has a smaller

mane. In the northern districts the mane has disappeared altogether. Maneless zebras occur in southern Sudan, the Karamoja district of Uganda and the Juba valley of Somalia.

South and southwest of the Burchell's zebras' range lives the mountain zebra, about the same size as Burchell's but with a prominent dewlap halfway between the jaw angle and the forelegs. Its stripes always stop short of the white belly. Its ground colour is whitish and, although the stripes on the flanks bend back to the rump, as in Burchell's, the vertical bands continue as well, giving a 'grid iron' effect. The southern race, the stockily built, broad-banded Cape mountain zebra, is nearly extinct, preserved only on a few private properties. The race in southwest Africa, Hartmann's zebra, is still fairly common. It is larger and longer-limbed than the Cape mountain zebra, with narrower stripes and a buff ground colour.

The third species is Grévy's zebra, from Somalia, eastern Ethiopia and northern Kenya, a very striking, tall zebra. The belly is white and unstriped, and there are no stripes on the hindquarters, except the dorsal stripe which bisects it. On the haunches the stripes from the flanks, rump and hindlegs seem to bend towards each other and join up.

▽ At the waterhole: a herd of southeast African Burchell's zebra. This race generally has striped legs and a paler ground colour than the now extinct true Burchell's zebra.

Belligerent stallions

Burchell's zebras are strongly gregarious. Groups of 1–6 mares with their foals keep together under the leadership of a stallion, who protects them and also wards off other stallions. Sometimes, for no apparent reason, the male simply disappears and another one takes his place. The surplus stallions live singly, or in bachelor groups of up to 15 members. Burchell's zebras are rather tame, not showing as much fear of man as the gnu with which they associate. When alarmed they utter their barking alarm call, a hoarse 'kwa-ha, kwa-ha', ending with a whinny. Then the herd wheels off, following the gnu. When cornered, however, the herd stallion puts up a stiff resistance, kicking and biting.

Mountain zebras, said to be more savage than Burchell's, live in herds of up to six, although sometimes they assemble in large numbers where food is plentiful. They seem to have regular paths over the rugged hills and move along them in single file. The call of the mountain zebra has been described as a low, snuffling whinny, quite different from that of the Burchell's.

Although in Grévy's zebra there are family groups as well as bachelor herds, the biggest and strongest stallions, weighing up to1 000 lb, are solitary, each occupying a territory of about a mile in diameter.

Slow breeding rate

A newborn foal has brown stripes and is short-bodied and high-legged like the foal of a domestic horse. It is born after a gestation of 370 days. It weighs 66–77 lb and stands about 33 in. high. The mares come into season again a few days after foaling, but only 15% are fertilised a second time; usually a mare has one foal every three years. They reach sexual maturity at a little over 1 year, but do not seem to be fertile before about 2 years. Young males leave the herd between 1 and 3 years and join the bachelor herd. At 5 or 6 years many of them attempt to kidnap young females and if successful a new one-male herd is formed. The unsuccessful ones remain in the bachelor herd, or become solitary. Zebras live about as long as horses.

Lions beware

Man still hunts the zebra for meat but in protected areas, at least, very little of this continues. The zebra, with the gnu, is the lion's favourite prey. Because zebras are potentially dangerous, the lion must make a swift kill and young lions have been routed by zebra stallions that turned on them. Astley Maberley, the wildlife artist and writer, tells the story of an African poacher who was killed and fearfully mangled by an irate troop of Burchell's zebras after he had killed a foal.

(1) Linear line-up: a row of Grévy's zebra, large, handsomely-marked animals recognised by the huge ears and narrowly-spaced stripes.
(2) Topi antelope and Grant's zebra – a species having stripes that reach below the knees. The odd-looking animal on the left of the picture is a rare melanistic form of Grant's zebra.
(3) Grant's zebra spar in the dust of Ngorongoro crater. Zebra stallions are aggressive not only to males of the same species but also to predators, including man.

1

2

4

3

5

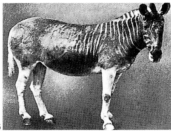

6

The lost quagga

A fourth species of zebra, the quagga, was extremely common in South Africa 150 years ago. It has since been completely exterminated. Most closely resembling Burchell's zebra, the quagga was distinctly striped brown and off-white on the head and neck only. Along the flanks the stripes gradually faded out to a plain brown, sometimes extending to just behind the shoulders, sometimes reaching the haunches. The legs and belly were white. Its barking, high-pitched cry, after which it was named, was rather like that of the Burchell's zebra.

The early explorers, around 1750–1800, met quaggas as far southwest as the Swellendam and Ceres districts, a short way inland from Cape Town. The Boer farmers did not appreciate quaggas except as food for their Hottentot servants. Their method of hunting was to take a train of wagons out onto the veldt and blaze away at everything within sight. Then large numbers of carcases would be loaded onto the wagons, and the rest of the dead and dying animals were simply left to rot. It is no wonder that today Cape Province is virtually denuded of wild game. When Cape Province was emptied, the trekkers to the Orange Free State repeated the process there. By 1820 the quaggas' range was already severely curtailed; they were almost gone even from the broad plains of the Great Fish River, which had been named 'Quagga's Flats' from the vast numbers of them roaming there. A few lingered for another 20 years or so in the far east of Cape Province and in the Orange Free State, the last wild ones being shot near Aberdeen, CP, in 1858, and near Kingwilliamstown in 1861. Strange to say, no one realised that they were even endangered. Zoos looking for replacements for their quaggas that had died were quite shocked to be told, 'But there aren't any more'.

The quagga (Equus quagga)

- ▨ Original known distribution (ca 1800)
- ▦ Range ca 1820
- ▦ Range ca 1840
- ● Last two records ca 1860

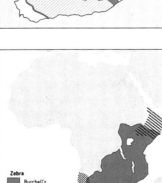

Zebra

- ■ Burchell's (Equus burchelli)
- ⊠ Grévy's (E grevyi)
- ⧄ Hartmann's mountain (E zebra hartmannae)
- * Cape mountain (E.z zebra)

class	**Mammalia**
order	**Perissodactyla**
family	**Equidae**
genus & species	***Equus burchelli burchelli*** *true Burchell's zebra or bontequagga*
	E. b. antiquorum *Chapman's or southeast African Burchell's*
	E. b. boehmi *Grant's or East African Burchell's*
	E. b. borensis *maneless zebra*
	E. grevyi *Grévy's zebra*
	E. quagga *quagga*
	E. zebra zebra *Cape mountain zebra*
	E. z. hartmannae *Hartmann's mountain zebra*

(4) '. . . along a mountain track' – Hartmann's mountain zebra, a race of the Cape mountain zebra described in 1898, has a large dewlap between chin and forelegs and stripes that end short of the belly. The stripes form a 'gridiron' effect on the rump.
(5) Nearly extinct: less than 200 Cape mountain zebra live in specially protected areas of high tableland in western Cape province.
(6) Extinct: the quagga was hunted in large numbers by early white settlers to South Africa.

Hippopotamus

Distantly related to the pigs, the hippopotamus rivals the great Indian rhinoceros as the second largest living land animal. Up to 14 ft long and 4 ft 10 in. at the shoulder it weighs up to 4 tons. The enormous body is supported on short pillar-like legs, each with four toes ending in hoof-like nails, placed well apart. A hippo trail in swamps shows as two deep ruts made by the feet with a dip in the middle made by the belly. The eyes are raised on top of the large flattish head, the ears are small and the nostrils slit-like and high up on the muzzle. The body is hairless except for sparse bristles on the muzzle, inside the ears and on the tip of the short tail. There is a thick layer of fat under the skin and there are pores in the skin which give out an oily pink fluid, known as pink sweat. This lubricates the skin. The mouth is armed with large canine tusks; these average 2½ ft long but may be over 5 ft long including the long root embedded in the gums.

Once numerous in rivers throughout Africa, the hippopotamus is now extinct north of Khartoum and south of the Zambezi river, except for some that are found in a few protected areas such as the Kruger National Park.

The pygmy hippopotamus, a separate species, lives in Liberia, Sierra Leone and parts of southern Nigeria in forest streams. It is 5 ft long, 2 ft 8 in. at the shoulder and weighs up to 600 lb. Its head is smaller in proportion to the body, and it lives singly or in pairs.

Rulebook of the river-horse

The name means literally river-horse and the hippopotamus spends most of its time in water, but comes on land to feed, mainly at night. It can remain submerged for up to 4½ minutes and spends the day basking lethargically on a sandbar, or lazing in the water with little more than ears, eyes and nostrils showing above water, at most with its back and upper part of the head exposed. Where heavily persecuted, hippopotamuses keep to reed beds. Each group, sometimes spoken of as a school, numbers around 20—100 and its territory is made up of a central crèche occupied by females and juveniles with separate areas, known as refuges, around its perimeter each occupied by an adult male. The crèche is on a sandbar in midstream or on a raised bank of the river or lake. Special paths lead from the males' refuges to the feeding grounds, each male marking his own path with his dung. The females have their own paths but are less exclusive.

The organisation of the territories is preserved by rules of behaviour which, in some of their aspects, resemble rules of committees. Outside the breeding season a female may pay a social call on a male and he may return this, but on the female's terms. He must enter the crèche with no sign of aggression and should one of the females rise on her feet he must lie down. Only when she lies down again may he rise. A male failing to observe these rules will be driven out by the adult females attacking him *en masse*.

Matriarch hippos

It was long thought that a hippopotamus school was led by the oldest male. It is in fact a matriarchy. For example, young males, on leaving the crèche, are forced to take up a refuge beyond the ring of refuges lying on the perimeter of the crèche. From there each must win his way to an inner refuge, which entitles him to mate with one of the females, by fighting. Should a young male be over-persecuted by the senior males he can re-enter the crèche for sanctuary, protected by the combined weight of the females.

The characteristic yawning has nothing to do with sleep. It is an aggressive gesture, a preliminary challenge to fight. Combats are vigorous, the two contestants rearing up out of the water, enormous mouths wide open, seeking to deliver slashing cuts with the long tusks. Frightful gashes are inflicted and a wounded hippo falling back into water screams with pain, but the wounds quickly heal. The aim of the fighting is for one hippo to break a foreleg of his opponent. This is fatal because the animal can no longer walk on land to feed.

Nightly wanderings

Hippos feed mostly at night, coming on land to eat mainly grass. During one night an individual may wander anything up to 20 miles but usually does not venture far from water. Hippos have been known to wander through the outskirts of large towns at times, and two surprised just before dawn by a motorist entering Nairobi showed him they could run at 30 mph.

Babies in nursery school

When in season the female goes out to choose her mate and he must treat her with deference as she enters his refuge. The baby is born 210—255 days later. It is 3 ft long, 1½ ft high and 60 lb weight. Birth may take place in water but normally it is on land, the mother preparing a bed of trampled reeds. The baby can walk, run or swim 5 minutes after birth. Outside the crèche

A trio of hippos in single file moves ponderously through a mixed throng of cormorants, pelicans and gulls, with a hippo youngster in the lead.

A mournful-looking pygmy hippo **Choeropsis liberiensis**, *from West Africa. Its well-oiled look is due to the secretion of a clear, viscous material through its skin pores. When frightened, the pygmy hippo prefers to head for the undergrowth, whereas the big hippos invariably seek safety in water.*

the organisation of the school is dependent on fighting and the females educate the young accordingly. This is one of the few instances of deliberate teaching in the animal kingdom. In a short while after its birth the baby hippo is taken on land for walks, not along the usual paths used when going to pasture but in a random promenade. The youngster must walk level with the mother's neck presumably so she can keep an eye on it. If the mother quickens her pace, the baby must do the same. If she stops, it must stop. In water the baby must swim level with her shoulder. On land the lighter female is more agile than the male, so she can defend her baby without difficulty. In the water the larger male, with his longer tusks, has the advantage, so the baby must be where the mother can quickly interpose her own body to protect her offspring from an aggressive male. Later, when she takes it to pasture, the baby must walk at heel, and if she has more than one youngster with her, which can happen because her offspring stay with her for several years, they walk behind her in order of precedence, the elder bringing up the rear.

Obedience, or else . . .

The youngsters must show strict obedience, and the penalty for failing to do so is punishment, the mother lashing the erring youngster with her head, often rolling it over and over. She may even slash it with her tusks. The punishment continues until the youngster cowers in submission, when the mother licks and caresses it.

Babysitting was not invented by the human race: hippos brought it to a fine art long ago. If a female leaves the crèche for feeding or mating she places her youngster in charge of another female, who may already have several others under her supervision. The way for this is made easy, for hippo mothers with young of similar age tend to keep together in the crèche.

The young hippos play with others of similar age, the young females together playing a form of hide-and-seek or rolling over in the water with stiff legs. The young males play together but they indulge in mock fights in addition to the other games.

Few enemies for the hippo

Hippos have few enemies apart from man, the most important being the lion which may occasionally spring on the back of a hippo on land, raking its hide with its claws. But even this is rare.

The wanderlust hippo

Many animals sometimes wander well inland for no obvious reason. Huberta was a famous hippopotamus that wandered a thousand miles. She left St Lucia Bay, in Zululand, in 1928 and wandered on and on until in 1931 she reached Cape Province. Each day she stopped to wallow in a river or lake, and her passage was noted in the local newspapers all along her route, so her journey is fully documented. Throughout that time she never came into contact with another hippo. Huberta became almost a pet of the people of South Africa and a law was passed to protect her. She was finally shot, however, by a trigger-happy person in April 1931, and was then found to be a male. So, it will never be known how much farther Hubert might have wandered.

class	**Mammalia**
order	**Artiodactyla**
family	**Hippopotamidae**
genera & species	*Hippopotamus amphibius* *Choeropsis liberiensis* pygmy hippo

Camel

There are two species of camel: the Arabian or one-humped and the Bactrian or two-humped. The first is not known as a wild animal, though the second survives in the wild in the Gobi desert. A dromedary is a special breed of the one-humped camel, used for riding, although the name is commonly but wrongly used to denote the Arabian camel as a whole.

Camels have long legs and a long neck, coarse hair and tufted tails. Their feet have two toes united by a tough web, with nails and tough padded soles. The length of head, neck and body is up to 10 ft, the tail is 1½ ft long, height at the shoulder is up to 6 ft, and the weight is up to 1100 lb.

Habits

The wild camels of the Gobi desert are active by day, associating in groups of half-a-dozen, made up of one male and the rest females. They are extremely shy and make off at first sight of an intruder, moving with a characteristic swaying stride, due to the

One-humped camels drinking at a water-hole in the desert. Having taken their fill of water, camels can survive for several days in the desert without drinking, or for several weeks if they have access to succulent desert plants. Water is drawn from the body tissues to maintain the fluid in the blood.

fore and hind legs on each side moving together. Their shyness may be partly due to persecution in former times.

It is often said that a camel cannot swim. Reports suggest they do not readily take to water, but they have been seen swimming.

Adaptations to desert life

Everything about a camel, both its external features and its physiology, show it to be adapted to life in deserts. Its eyes have long lashes which protect them from wind-blown sand. The nostrils are muscular so they can be readily closed, or partly closed to keep out sand. The form of the body, with the long neck and long legs, provides a large surface area relative to the volume of the body, which allows for easy loss of heat.

The camel's physiology shows other adaptations which provide protection from overheating, and help it to withstand desiccation and to indulge in physical exertion with a minimum of feeding and drinking. These characteristics are often seen in stories of journeys made across waterless deserts. Many of these are exaggerated, but even those that are true are remarkable enough. There is one instance of a march through Somalia of 8 days without water and in Northern Australia a journey of 537 miles was made, using camels which were without a drink for 34 days. Most of the camels in this second journey died, but a few that were able to graze dew-wetted vegetation survived.

Most desert journeys are made in winter, however, and during that season even a man

can go without drinking if he feeds largely on juicy fruits and vegetables. Knut Schmidt-Nielsen tested camels in the desert winter and found that even on a completely dry diet, camels could go several weeks without drinking, although they lost water steadily through their skin and their breath as well as in the urine and faeces. Normally, however, a camel feeds on desert plants with a high water content.

Do camels store water?

There are many stories of travellers in the desert killing a camel and drinking the water contained in its stomach. From these arose the myth, which has not yet been completely killed, that a camel stores water in its stomach. Pliny (AD 23-79), the Roman naturalist, first set it on record. Buffon (1707-1788) and Cuvier (1769-1832), celebrated French scientists, accepted it. Owen (1804-1892) and Lyddeker (1849-1915), British anatomists and zoologists, supported it.

In 1801 George Shaw, British zoologist, wrote of a camel having four stomachs with a fifth bag which serves as a reservoir for water. Everard Home, the Scottish surgeon, dissected a camel and in 1806 published his celebrated drawing of alleged water pockets in the first two compartments of the stomach, a drawing which has many times been reproduced in books, and which has served to bolster the story. It was not until the researches of Schmidt-Nielsen and his team, working in the Sahara in 1953-4, that the full story emerged. In the living camel, these pockets are filled with an evil-smelling soup,

the liquefied masticated food, which might be drunk, so saving his life, by a man crazy for water – but not otherwise.

Another of the camel's achievements which served to support the story is its ability to drink 27 gallons of water, or more, in 10 minutes. It will do so only to replenish the body supply after intense desiccation. In those 10 minutes a camel will pass from an emaciated animal, showing its ribs, to a normal condition. This is something few other animals can do. But the water does not stay in the stomach; it passes into the tissues, and a camel after a long drink looks swollen.

A camel can lose water equal to 25% of its body weight and show no signs of distress. A man losing 12% of his body water is in dire distress because this water is drawn from his tissues and his blood. The blood becomes thick and sticky, so that the heart has greater difficulty in pumping. A camel loses water from its tissues but not from the blood, so there is no strain on the heart, and an emaciated camel is capable of the same physical exertion as normal. The mechanism for this is not known. The only obvious difference between the blood of a camel and any other mammal is that its red corpuscles are oval instead of being discoid.

The camel's hump

The hump contains a store of fat and it has often been argued that this can be converted to water, and therefore the hump is a water reserve. The hump of the Arabian camel may contain as much as 100 lb of fat, each pound of which can yield 1·1 lb of water, or over 13 gallons for a 100 lb hump, To convert this, however, extra oxygen is needed, and it has been calculated that the breathing needed to get this extra oxygen would itself lead to the loss of more than 13 gallons of water as vapour in the breath. The fat stored in the hump is broken down to supply energy, releasing water which is lost. The hump is thus really a reserve of energy.

Other physiological advantages possessed by a camel are that in summer it excretes less urine and, more important, it sweats little. The highest daytime temperature is 40°C/105°F but during the night it drops to 34°C/93°F. A man's temperature remains constant at just under 39°C/100°F and as soon as the day starts to warm up he begins to feel the heat. A camel starts with a temperature of 34°C/93°F at dawn and does not heat up to 40°C/105°F until nearly midday. A camel's coat provides insulation against the heat of the day and it keeps the animal warm during the cold desert nights.

With all these advantages, camels should be even-tempered, but everyone agrees that they are bad-tempered to a degree. One writer has described them as stupid, unwilling, recalcitrant, obnoxious, untrustworthy and openly vicious, with an ability to bite destructively. There is a traditional joke that there are no wild camels, nor any tame ones.

The power of the bite is linked with the camel's unusual dentition. At birth it has six incisors in both upper and lower jaws, a canine on each side, then a premolar followed by a gap before the cheek teeth are reached. As the young camel grows, it quickly loses all but the outside incisors of the six in the upper jaw and these take on a similar shape to the canines. So in making a slashing bite a camel has, in effect, double the fang capacity of a dog.

Breeding

A baby camel is a miniature of its parents, apart from its incisors, its soft fleece, lack of knee pads and hump. There is a single calf, exceptionally two, born 370–440 days after conception. Its only call is a soft *baa*. It can walk freely at the end of the first day but is not fully independent until 4 years old, and becomes sexually mature at 5 years. Maximum recorded life is 50 years.

Origins of the camel

Camels originated in North America, where many fossils have been found of camels, small and large, with short necks or long, as in the giraffe-like camels. The smallest was the size of a hare, the largest stood 15 ft at the shoulder. As the species multiplied there was one migration southwards into South America and another northwestwards, and then across the land-bridge where the Bering Straits now are, into Asia. As the numerous species died out, over the last 45 million years, the survivors remained as the S. American llamas and Asiatic camels.

A few species reached eastern Europe and died out. None reached Africa. Until 6 000 years or more ago there was only the one species in Asia, the two-humped Bactrian camel. The date is impossible to fix with

In a sandstorm the long lashes protect the camel's eyes, and its nostrils can readily be closed to keep the sand out.

Camels have been used as pack animals since early times, and can carry a load of about 400 lb for long distances.

certainty, as is the date when the one-humped camel came into existence, but the evidence suggests that it is a domesticated form derived from the Bactrian camel. Both readily interbreed, and the offspring usually have two humps, the hind hump smaller than that in front.

Surprisingly, the first record of a one-humped camel is on pottery from the sixth dynasty of Ancient Egypt (about 3500 BC) for the camel was not known in the Nile Valley until 3 000 years later. Its representation on the pottery may have been inspired by a wandering camel train from Asia Minor. Meanwhile, on Assyrian monuments

dated 1115–1102 BC, and from then onwards, the camel appears quite often, and when the Queen of Sheba visited King Solomon in Jerusalem, in 955 BC, she brought with her draught camels. The name seems to be from the Semitic *gamal* or *hamal*, meaning 'carrying a burden'.

The one-humped camel was presumably selectively bred from domesticated two-humped camels, in Central Asia, by peoples who left no records. It is also suggested that the nickname 'ship of the desert' is derived from 'animal brought in a ship from the desert'—a reference to the Assyrian habit of naming an animal

according to the place from which it came. Presumably this would mean camels were brought by ship across the Persian Gulf.

Feral camels

Today the Bactrian camel is confined to Asia but most of the 3 million Arabian camels are on African soil. Some have, however, been introduced into countries far from Africa or Asia. In 1622 some were taken to Tuscany where a herd still lives on the sandy plains near Pisa. On the plains of the Guadalquivir are feral camels taken to Spain by the Moors earlier still. Camels were taken to South America in the 16th century

◁ Camel herd of an Arabian caravan. A miniature from a manuscript of about the 12th century illustrates the work of the poet Harari. (Cairo)

▷ Camels develop leathery callosities on their knees and other joints through kneeling down for loading.

210

by the Spanish conquistadors but these have died out. Others were taken to Virginia in 1701, and there was a second importation into the United States in 1856. The survivors from these were still running wild in the deserts of Arizona and Nevada in 1915. Camels were taken to Northern Australia, and there also they have reverted to the wild.

For a long time text books reiterated that no camels are now known in the wild state, although they had been mentioned in Chinese literature since the 5th century, and Marco Polo wrote about them. Then, in 1879, Nikolai Przewalski reported wild two-humped camels still living around Lake Lob, southeast of the Gobi desert. The local people told him they had been numerous a few decades prior to his visit but that they hunted them for their hides and flesh. There were reports also of camels in the Gobi, but nobody was prepared to say whether these were truly wild or merely feral camels. In 1945, the Soviet zoologist AG Bannikov rediscovered them and in 1955 a Mongolian film unit secured several shots of them.

These Gobi camels are two-humped but the humps are small. They are swift, with long slender legs, small feet and no knee pads. Their coat is short, the ears smaller than in the domesticated camels, and the coat is a brownish-red.

The Mongolian film shows the Gobi camel to be different from the typical Bactrian and Arabian camels, and it would be not unreasonable to conclude that it represents the ancestral stock from which the other two were domesticated.

class	**Mammalia**
order	**Artiodactyla**
suborder	**Tylopoda**
family	**Camelidae**
genus & species	***Camelus dromedarius*** *1-humped camel*
	Camelus bactrianus *2-humped camel*

△ *The camel draws water from the well while his keeper sleeps peacefully.*

▽ *Dromedaries are the riding strain of the one-humped camel, and can travel 100 miles in a day*

Giraffe

Tallest animal in the world, the giraffe is remarkable for its long legs and long neck. An old bull may be 18 ft to the top of his head. Females are smaller. The head tapers to mobile hairy lips, the tongue is extensile and the eyes are large. There are 2–5 horns, bony knobs covered with skin, including one pair on the forehead, a boss in front, and, in some races, a small pair farther back. The shoulders are high and the back slopes down to a long tufted tail. The coat is boldly spotted and irregularly blotched chestnut, dark brown or liver-coloured on a pale buff ground, giving the effect of a network of light-coloured lines. A number of species and races have been recognised in the past, differing mainly in details of colour and number of horns, but the current view is that all belong to one species. The number of races recognised, however, varies between 8 and 13 species depending on the authority.

The present-day range of the giraffe is the dry savannah and semi-desert of Africa south of the Sahara although it was formerly more widespread. Its range today is from Sudan and Somalia south to South Africa and westwards to northern Nigeria. In many parts of its former range it has been wiped out for its hide.

A leisurely anarchy

Giraffes live in herds with a fairly casual social structure. It seems that males live in groups in forested zones, the old males often solitary, and the females and young live apart from them in more open country. Males visit these herds mainly for mating.

Giraffes do not move about much, and tend to walk at a leisurely pace unless disturbed. When walking slowly the legs move in much the same way as those of a horse. That is, the right hindleg touches the ground just after the right foreleg leaves it, and a little later the left legs make the same movement. The body is therefore supported on three legs most of the time while walking. As the pace quickens to a gallop the giraffe's leg movements change to the legs on each side moving forward together, the two right hoofs hitting the ground together followed by the two left legs moving together.

The long neck not only allows a giraffe to browse high foliage, the eyes set on top of the high head form a sort of watch-tower to look out for enemies. In addition, the long neck and heavy head assist movement by acting as a counterpoise. When resting crouched, with legs folded under the body the neck may be held erect or, if sleeping, the giraffe lays its neck along its back. To rise, the forelegs are half-unfolded, the neck being swung back to take the weight off the forequarters. Then it is swung forwards to take the weight off the hindlegs, for them to be unfolded. By repeated movements of this kind the animal finally gets to its feet.

Necking parties

The habit of 'necking' has been something of a puzzle. Two giraffes stand side-by-side

and belabour each other with their heads, swinging their long necks slowly and forcibly. Only rarely does any injury result, and the necking seems to be a ritualised fighting, to establish dominance, and confined exclusively, or nearly so, to the male herds.

Not so dumb

One long-standing puzzle concerns the voice. For a long time everyone accepted the idea that giraffes are mute—yet they have an unusually large voice-box. During the last 25 years it has been found that a young giraffe will bleat like the calf of domestic cattle, that the adult female makes a sound like 'wa-ray' and that adult bulls, and sometimes cows, will make a husky grunt or cough. Nevertheless, there are many zoo-keepers who have never heard a giraffe utter a call and there is still the puzzle why there should be such a large voice-box when so little use is made of it. Some zoologists have suggested the giraffe may use ultra-sonics.

Controlled blood pressure

In feeding, leaves are grasped with the long tongue and mobile lips. Trees and bushes tend to become hourglass-shaped from giraffes browsing all round at a particular level. Acacia is the main source of food but many giraffes are browsed, giraffes showing definite preferences for some species of trees or bushes over others.

Giraffes drink regularly when water is available but can go long periods without drinking. They straddle the front legs widely to bring the head down to water, or else straddle them slightly and then bend them at the knees. Another long-standing puzzle concerns the blood pressure in the head, some zoologists maintaining a giraffe must lower and raise its head slowly to prevent a rush of blood to the head. In fact, the blood vessels have valves, reservoirs of blood in the head and alternative routes for the blood, and so there is no upset from changes in the level of the head, no matter how quickly the giraffe moves.

Casual mothers

Mating and calving appear to take place all the year, with peak periods which may vary from one region to another. The gestation period is 420–468 days, the single calf being able to walk within an hour of birth, when it is 6 ft to the top of the head and weighs 117 lb. Reports vary about the suckling which is said to continue for 9 months, but in one study the calves were browsing at the age of one week and were not seen suckling after that. The bond between mother and infant is, in any case, a loose one. Giraffe milk has a high fat content and the young grow fast. Captive giraffes often live for over 20 years.

Defensive hoofs

Giraffes have few enemies. A lion may take a young calf or several lions may combine to kill an adult. Even these events are rare because the long legs and heavy hoofs can be used to deadly effect, striking down at an attacker.

Symbol of friendliness

Rock engravings of giraffes have been

found over the whole of Africa and some of the most imposing are at Fezzan in the middle of what is now the Sahara desert. The animal must have lingered on in North Africa until 500 B.C. Some of the engravings are life size, or even larger, and many depict the trap used to capture giraffes, while others show typical features of its behaviour, including the necking. The engravings also show ostriches, dibatag, and gerenuk. Giraffes were also figured on the slate palettes, used for grinding malachite and haematite for eye-shadows, the cosmetics used by ladies of rank in Ancient Egypt. The last giraffe depicted in Egyptian antiquities is on the tomb of Rameses the Great, 1225 BC.

There are references to the animal in Greek and Roman writings and a few pictures survive from the Roman era, but from then until the 7th or 8th century AD the principal records are in Arabic literature. The description given by Zakariya al-Qaswini in his 13th-century *Marvels of Creation* reflects the accepted view, that 'the giraffe is produced by the camel mare, the male hyaena and the wild cow'. The giraffe was taken to India by the Arabs, and from there to China, the first arriving in 1414 in the Imperial Zoological Garden in Peking. To the Chinese it symbolised gentleness and peace and the Arabs adopted this symbolism, so a gift of a giraffe became a sign of peace and friendliness between rulers.

In medieval Europe, and until the end of the 18th century, knowledge of the giraffe was based on descriptions in Greek and Roman writings and on hearsay accounts. It was at best a legendary beast.

class	**Mammalia**
order	**Artiodactyla**
family	**Giraffidae**
genus & species	***Giraffa camelopardalis***

▷ *Dappled freaks of the African veld: a group of giraffes rear their extraordinary necks against the skyline of a pale sunset. Wiped out for its hide in many parts of its range, the present day distribution of the giraffe is much reduced. A number of races are recognised within the single species.*

Giraffe *(Giraffa camelopardalis)*

212

Bottlenose dolphin

Also often known as the common porpoise, this is the animal that in the last 20 years has become a star performer in the seaquaria of the United States. It is up to 12 ft long, weighs as much as 440 lb and is black above and white underneath, with a bulbous head and a marked snout. The forehead of the male is more protruding than that of the female. The moderate-sized flippers taper to a point and the fin in the middle of the back has a sharply-pointed apex directed backwards, making the hinder margin concave. It has 20−22 conical teeth in each half of both upper and lower jaw. Although as well suited to life in the water as any fish it is in fact a mammal like whales or, for that matter, man, giving birth to fully-developed young which are suckled on milk. The bottlenose is the commonest cetacean (family name of the whales) off the Atlantic coast of North America, from Florida to Maine. It occurs in the Bay of Biscay and Mediterranean also. It occasionally ranges to Britain, and is also found off West Africa, south to Dakar.

Cooperative schools

Bottlenose dolphins live in schools containing individuals of both sexes and all ages. Apparently there is no leader, but males in the school observe a 'peck order' based on size. When food is plentiful the schools may be large, breaking into smaller schools when it is scarce. The dolphins pack together at times of danger. They also assist an injured member of the school by one ranging either side of it and, pushing their heads under its flippers, raising it to the surface to breathe. In schools they keep in touch by sounds.

They sleep by night and are active by day, although each feeding session is followed by an hour's doze. Females sleep at the surface with only the blowhole exposed and this periodically opens and closes, as it does in stranded dolphins, by reflex action. The males sleep a foot below the surface, periodically rising to breathe.

The main swimming action is in the tail, with its horizontal flukes. This, the flexible part of the animal, is used with an up-and-down movement in swimming, quite unlike that of fishes, with only an occasional sideways movement. The flippers help in steering and balance. The dorsal fin also aids stability, but it is the lungs placed high up in the body that are chiefly responsible for keeping a dolphin balanced.

The depths to which bottle-nosed dolphins can dive has to be deduced from the remains of fishes in their stomachs. These show they go down for food to at least 70 ft, and they can stay submerged for up to 15 minutes. Their lung capacity is half as much again as that of a land animal and in addition they fill their lungs to capacity. Land animals, including ourselves, use only about half the lung capacity and change only 10−15% of the air in the lungs with each breath. A dolphin changes up to 90%.

Tame dolphin leaping some 30 ft into the air to take fish accurately, which proves that its small eyes are still quite useful out of water.

Well equipped for marine life

Since a dolphin's lungs are compressed when diving, air would be squeezed into the bronchial tubes, where no gaseous exchange would take place, unless this were prevented by valves. There are 25−40 of these in the bronchial tubes of the bottlenose dolphin and they act as a series of taps controlling the pressure in the lungs according to whether the animal is diving, swimming on the level or rising to the surface.

At the surface the pulse of the bottlenose dolphin is 110 a minute. When submerged it drops to 50 a minute and starts to increase as the animal nears the surface. The drop is related to the way the blood circulation is shut off so that the oxygen supply goes mainly to essential organs, notably the heart and brain. This extends the time of submergence by reducing the frequency with which visits need be made to the surface to breathe.

Whales and dolphins have an insulating layer of blubber, but they have no sweat glands and they cannot pant, so other means are needed to lose excess body heat. The tail flukes and the flippers are always warmer to the touch than the rest of the body and their temperature is not only higher than that of other parts of the body but varies through a greater range. They also have a much thinner layer of blubber. It is assumed therefore that these parts lose heat to the surrounding water. In brief, whales and dolphins keep cool through their flukes and flippers.

A dolphin's eyesight is not particularly good. Yet the animal can move its eyelids, shut its eyes, even wink. At one time it was thought the eyes were of little value and were quite useless out of water. This last seems proved wrong by the way dolphins in seaquaria will leap out of water and accurately snatch fish from the attendant's hand. Moreover, the visual fields of left and right eyes overlap, so presumably they have partially stereoscopic vision. The sense of smell is, however, either non-existent or almost wholly so.

Hearing is the main sense, apart from taste and touch. This is acute and is especially sensitive to high tones. It is probably second only to the hearing of bats. A dolphin is sensitive to the pulses of an echo-sounder or asdic and will respond to frequencies as high as 120 kilocycles or beyond, whereas we can hear 30 kilocycles at the most. At sea it has been noticed that bottlenose dolphins will avoid a boat that has been used for hunting them but will not be disturbed by other boats. The assumption is that they can recognize individual boats by the sounds they make.

Feeding

Fish form one of the main items in the diet but a fair amount of cuttlefish is eaten, the dolphin spitting out the chalky cuttlebone and swallowing only the soft parts. Shrimps also are eaten. In captivity a bottlenose will eat 22 lb of fish a day, yielding 237 calories per pound of its body weight, compared with the 116 calories/lb taken by man.

Life history

Bottlenose dolphins become sexually mature

at 5–6 years. The breeding season extends from spring to summer. The gestation period is 11–12 months, births taking place mainly from March to May. The baby is born tail-first and as soon as free it rises to the surface to take a breath, often assisted by the mother usually using her snout to lift it gently up. Just prior to the birth the cow slows down and at the moment of birth she is accompanied by two other cows. These swim one either side of her, their role being protective, especially against sharks, who may be attracted to the spot by the smell of blood lost during the birth process. Weaning may take place between 6–18 months; reports vary considerably.

For the first 2 weeks the calf stays close beside the mother, being able to swim rapidly soon after birth. Then it begins to move away, even to chase fish, although quite ineffectively. However, it readily dashes back to its mother's side or to its 'aunt', the latter being another female that attaches herself to the mother and shares in the care of the calf. The aunt is the only one the mother allows near her offspring.

The calf is born with the teeth still embedded in the gums. These begin to erupt in the first weeks of life but the calf makes little attempt to chew until 5 months old and some take much longer before they attempt to swallow solid food. Even then there may be difficulties and in captivity a calf at about this time has been seen to bring up its first meal, the mother then massaging its belly with her snout.

Suckling is under water. The mother's nipples are small and each lies in a groove on the abdomen. The mother slows down to feed her calf which comes in behind her and lies slightly to one side, taking a nipple between its tongue and the palate. The mother then, by muscular pressure on the mammary glands, squirts the milk into its mouth. Should the calf let go the nipple the milk continues to squirt out. The baby bottlenose must come to the surface to breathe every half minute, so suckling must be rapid. In this species it consists of one to nine sucks, each lasting a few seconds. For the first 2 weeks the calf is suckled about twice an hour, night and day, but by 6 months it is down to six feeds a day.

Can dolphins talk?

It is not all that time ago that it was generally believed that whales, porpoises and dolphins were more or less mute, although the whalers themselves held very definite views to the contrary. It was not until after World War II, when bottlenose dolphins were being first kept in captivity in the large seaquaria, first in Florida and later in California and elsewhere, that it began to be realized fully that they have a wide vocabulary of sounds. Then, a few years ago, came the startling suggestion that these cetaceans might be capable of imitating human speech, even perhaps of being able to talk to people, in a sort of Donald Duck language in which words are 'gabbled' in a very high pitch. These high hopes do not seem to have been realised, but apart from this much has been learned about the noises they make.

One thing that has long been known is that air can be released from the blowhole

△△ Bottlenose dolphin jaws are well armed with teeth that help it catch its mainly cuttlefish food.
△ Baby dolphin with its mother. As with most mammals it stays with its mother for some time and is suckled on milk, being weaned after 5 months or more. Note the blowhole or nostril on top of the head.

215

while the animal is still submerged. This can be seen, by direct observation, emerging as a stream of bubbles. It can be used to produce sounds, and part of the mechanism for it is the many small pouches around the exit from the blowhole which act as safety valves, preventing any inrush of water.

It has been known for some time that some cetaceans are attracted over long distances by the cries of their fellows in distress. Conversely, people have been calling the animals to them by using whistles emitting sounds similar to their calls. Pliny, the Roman naturalist of the first century AD, knew of this, and in modern times the people on the Black Sea coasts have continued to do this. Sir Arthur Grimble also left us an account of what he called porpoise calling in South Pacific Islands. He described how local peoples in this area would call the porpoises from a distance to the shore. These items indicate an acute sense of hearing in dolphins and porpoises and a potentiality for communication by sounds on their part.

Underwater microphones as well as more direct observations in the various seaquaria have established that these cetaceans use a wide range of sounds. These have been variously described as whistles, squawks, clicks, creaks, quacks and blats, singing notes and wailings. It has been found that two dolphins which have been companions will, if separated, call to each other, and that a calf separated from its mother will call to her. Dolphins trained to leap out of water for food have been heard to make sounds at their attendants.

These are, however, only the sounds audible to our ears, which can deal only with the lower frequencies. Much of dolphin language is in the ultrasonic range, and if they are able to understand what we are saying, as one investigator has somewhat unconvincingly suggested, they could be using their own vocalizations to call us by rude names without our knowing it!

It has often been said that if whales cried out in pain we might be less ready to slaughter them. Scattered reports suggest that in fact they do precisely this. Freshly captured bottlenose dolphins placed in the tanks in Florida's Marineland have been heard through the thick plate glass windows to cry with shrill notes of discomfort and alarm. At sea similar distress calls have been heard from injured or wounded whales, porpoises and dolphins.

class	**Mammalia**
order	**Cetacea**
family	**Delphinidae**
genus & species	**_Tursiops truncatus_**

Bottlenose dolphins leaping out of the water in formation. This demonstrates the powerful swimming action of the tail with its horizontal fluke unlike a fish's tailfin which is vertical. It also shows their sociability.

Dolphins try to find each other by echo-locating 'clicks'. Then they talk in 'whistles' with a few 'grunts' and 'cracks'. Their sounds were analysed in 1965 when TG Lang and HAP Smith of the US Naval Ordnance Test Station put two newly captured bottlenose dolphins, Doris and Dash, in separate tanks linked by a two-way hydrophone system so the experimenters could tap their conversations. The first 4 of a total of 16 two-minute periods shown here indicate how the animals conversed when they were linked by phone and how sporadic noises were made when the line was 'dead'.

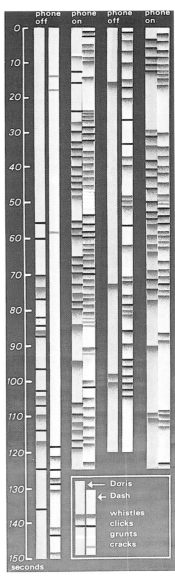

Killer whale

The killer whale is closely related to the false killer whale and also the pilot whale. It has a very bad reputation for ferocity which is probably unjustified. Killer whales are small for whales, the females growing up to a maximum of about 15 ft, but an old male may be as long as 30 ft. They are one of the few whales in which there is a marked difference in size between the sexes, the sperm whale being another example. The colour is very striking and distinctive, both sexes having similar markings, which are black on the back and white on the underside. Occasionally the white is somewhat yellowish. The chin is white and there is a characteristic white oval patch just above and behind the eye. There is a small whitish patch just behind the dorsal fin which varies quite considerably in shape and hue in different animals. The white on the underside sweeps up towards the tail and the flanks are white between the dorsal fin and the tail. The flippers, which are broad and rounded, are black all over, but the underside of the tail flukes are white. The dorsal fin is very conspicuous, usually about 2 ft high, but in the old males it may be 6 ft. The oldest males also have very long flippers, up to ⅕ the animal's total length, the average length of the flipper in juvenile males and adult females being ⅛ only.

Killer whales are found in all seas but are particularly numerous in the Arctic and Antarctic where there is abundant food to satisfy their voracious appetite. They are not uncommon around the British Isles, where a number have been stranded, mainly on the north and east coasts. These strandings take place in most months of the year. A larger number than usual were stranded on British coasts during the last war, mostly on the North Sea coast, probably due in part at least to anti-submarine activities

Killer whale showing off its strength and beauty. Despite their reputation for ferocity, killer whale kept in oceanaria have been unaggressive and many are hand-tame.

Living in packs

Killer whales hunt together in packs made up of both sexes. They are inquisitive and appear to take a close interest in anything likely to be edible. Nothing is known about their movements in the oceans or how much, if at all, the populations in different oceans mix. In the Antarctic they are often seen around whaling factory ships and probably they tend to follow the ships around as they offer an easy source of food. Otherwise very little is known about their habits.

Ruthless hunters

The killer whale is a voracious feeder and will take anything that swims in the sea. Included in its diet are whales, dolphins, seals, penguins, fish and squid. It will attack even the larger blue whales and quite often killers will hunt in packs numbering from two or three up to as many as 40 or more. When attacking a large whale they are said to work as a team. First one or two will seize the tail flukes to stop the whale thrashing about and slow it down, then others will attack the head and try to bite the lips. Gradually the whale becomes exhausted and its tongue lolls from its mouth—to be immediately seized by the killers. At this point all is over for the whale: the tongue is rapidly removed and the killers take their fill, seeming to favour a meal from around the head of their monster victim.

Apart from attacking fully-grown and healthy whales, killers have earned the hate of whalers because they often take the tongues from whales that have been harpooned and are lying alongside the factory ship waiting to be processed. They will even take the tongue from whales being towed by the catcher boat, and in an effort to stop this looting a man may be posted with a rifle to deter the killers. If he should injure a killer all the others in the pack turn on it and it very soon becomes their next meal.

Killer whales also eat seals and porpoises, and there are a number of records of complete seals found in a killer's stomach. The greatest number recorded is the remains of 13 porpoises and 14 seals that were taken from the stomach of one killer whale, while another contained remains of 32 seals. Off the Pribilof Islands in the Bering Sea, killer whales are often seen lying in wait for the young fur seal pups swimming out into the open sea for the first time. The number of seals actually taken by killers is not certain but it is likely that large numbers of pups must meet their end in this way before they reach the age of one year.

In the Antarctic, penguins form an important part of the killer whale diet. On many occasions killer whales have been seen swimming underneath ice floes, either singly or sometimes several at a time, and then coming up quickly under the floe either to tip it or break it up, thereby causing the penguins to fall into the water and into the waiting jaws of the killers.

Once killer whales were seen cruising close to an island where there was a colony of grey seals. As the killers came close in the seals hurried ashore in spite of a couple of people standing nearby. The certain danger from killer whales was more important to the seals than possible danger from man. It is said that when killer whales

△ Running at the surface with blowhole open, a killer whale in relaxed mood.

▽ Affectionate play between a pair of killers. Sensory pits can be seen on the head.

attack grey whales, these become so terrified that they just float on their backs unable to make any effort to escape.

Seven-footer calves

Very little is known about the breeding habits of the whale. They are thought to produce their young towards the end of the year, in November and December after a 16-month gestation. This is supported by examination of some of the stranded whales washed up on the beach and found to be pregnant. The calf at birth is about 7 ft long. The females suckle the young in the same way as other whales, but how long this lasts is not known.

No enemies

The killer whale probably has no real enemies. A few are killed by man, usually irate whalers. They are not a very valuable catch to a whaler although some Russian whaling fleets do catch a few, usually if there is nothing else worth shooting.

Chased by killers

The most famous story of killer whales is that told by Herbert Ponting who was the official photographer to the British *Terra Nova* Antarctic expedition led by Captain Scott in 1911. While the ship's cargo was being unloaded onto the ice some killer whales appeared nearby. Ponting went to take some photographs carrying the bulky photographic apparatus of those days over the floes. As he went across the ice the killers thrust up alongside and then followed him as he crossed the floes, tipping them from beneath. Ponting just managed to get to the safety of the fast ice in front of the killers – a lucky escape.

Ponting's experience must have been terrifying, yet it is often found that a reputation for ferocity is unfounded. Divers who have met killer whales have not been molested and several killer whales have been kept in oceanaria. All have been un-aggressive or even hand-tame. One story tells of a fisherman of Long Island, New York, who threw a harpoon at a killer whale. The whale pulled free and followed the boat and its terrified occupants to shallow water, but it made no attempt to harm them despite such severe provocation.

class	Mammalia
order	Cetacea
family	Delphinidae
genus & species	*Orcinus orca* *killer whale*

◁ *Flukes aloft, a killer sounds with a minimum of splash – a tribute to its streamlining.*

△ *A killer pack surges round the edges of encroaching ice.* ▽ *Killer curiosity.*

*Grey whale **Eschrichtius glaucus**.*

Grey whale

At one time the Californian grey whale lived in the Atlantic Ocean, for its remains have been found in reclaimed land in the Zuider Zee. Now it is confined to the North Pacific where there are populations on both sides of that ocean.

It is a rather unusual whale, having points in common with both the rorqual (family Balaenopteridae) and right whales (family Balaenidae). It is about the size of the right whales, reaching 45 ft long and 20 tons in weight. The flukes of the tail are proportionally longer and more delicate than those of right whales, but more stubby than those of rorquals. The dorsal fin is replaced by 8 – 10 small humps along the tail just in front of the flukes. On the throat the grey whale has 2 – 3, rarely 4, grooves extending a short distance as compared with the 40 – 100 grooves extending to the belly in rorquals and the complete absence of grooves in right whales.

As the name implies, the grey whale is usually dark slate-grey but it may sometimes be blackish. It is lighter on the belly than on the back, as is usual in marine animals. Many grey whales have crescent-shaped marks or patches on the skin, especially on the back. These are caused either by lampreys or by barnacles.

Sluggish swimmers
Grey whales are very slow, usually swimming at 2 – 3 knots with bursts of 6 – 7 knots when alarmed, compared with 20 knots of a fin whale. As they also come very close inshore this makes them very vulnerable to hunters. In early spring the grey whales migrate down the west coast of North America. In 1840 there were estimated to be around 25 000 grey whales but soon after this there was very intense hunting all along the coast. By 1875 it was unusual to see more than 50 migrating whales at a time, although they used to be seen by the thousand. While the whales were in the Arctic Ocean they

were hunted by Eskimos; in the Bay of Vancouver and around the Queen Charlotte Islands they were attacked by Indians from canoes, and farther south the Yankee whalers chased them in sailing boats.

Dog food or tourist bait?
By 1936 the world population was thought to be as low as 100 – 200. Then the governments of America, Japan and Russia came to an agreement on the future of the grey whale and declared it a protected species. This protection, together with the animal's fairly high rate of reproduction, has resulted in a gradual build-up of the population and it is now thought that they number between 5 and 10 thousand. But the grey whale's future is still dubious: it has recently been reported that the Mexican government is planning to kill grey whales when they migrate south to Mexican water, the idea being to use the carcases as dog food. This is a short-sighted plan: far more could be made out of tourism, for each year thousands of tourists gather on the west coast to watch the grey whales come down from the Bering Sea to give birth to their calves in the shallow and sheltered coastal waters of California and Mexico.

Straining out their food
Like the rarer blue whale the grey whales collect their food by means of rows of baleen plates in their mouths. Various crustaceans and molluscs floating in the sea are eaten in this manner.

Swimming south to breed
The migration of the grey whale is one of the better known aspects of its behaviour. They spend the summer months in the far north, principally in the Bering Sea, where they live in mixed herds. As summer draws to a close they swim slowly southwards and come in close to the coast, particularly so when they approach California where they can be seen swimming only a mile or so off-shore. Here the herds segregate; the females stay together and led by an older cow come really close into the bays and lagoons where they get shelter from the weather to give birth to the calves. These are usually born at about the end of January, measuring

about 15 ft in length and weighing around 1 500 lb. Normally only a single calf is produced but twin births have been recorded, the calves suckling for about 9 – 10 months. As spring approaches the migration is reversed. The males, who have been waiting in deeper water, join the females with their newborn calves and the herds make their way back to the northern oceans to feed again in the colder waters where food is more abundant.

Chivalrous males
It has sometimes been noticed that grey whales show a one-sided faithfulness. If a female is injured or gets into difficulties one or more males may go to her aid, either to keep her at the surface where she can breathe, or to defend her from the attacks of killer whales. But if a male gets into similar difficulties, the females have been seen swimming away from the scene of trouble!

After man, killer whales are the greatest danger to grey whales. It is said that when a small school of grey whales are attacked by a large group of killers they may become so terrified by the attacks that they just float at the surface, belly uppermost, paralysed by fear and making themselves extremely vulnerable to further attack. The grey whales' habit of coming close inshore during the breeding season probably keeps them fairly clear of the attacks of killer whales who prefer deeper water. Sometimes grey whales have come so close inshore that they have practically run aground, and on one occasion a grey whale was seen playing about in the surf like a seal. They have also been found stranded at low tide, apparently without ill effect as they just floated off again at the next high water. This is most unusual since, for almost every other species of whale, stranding means death.

class	**Mammalia**
order	**Cetacea**
family	**Eschrichtidae**
genus	***Eschrichtius glaucus***
& species	*grey whale*

Index